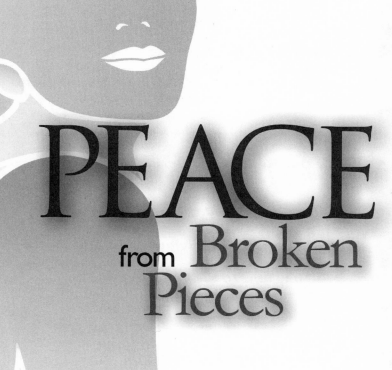

PEACE
from Broken
Pieces

ALSO BY IYANLA VANZANT

Tapping the Power Within: *A Path to Self-Empowerment for Women—20th Anniversary Edition*

Acts of Faith

Faith in the Valley: *Lessons for Women on the Journey to Peace*

Every Day I Pray: *Prayers for Awakening to the Grace of Inner Communion*

In the Meantime

One Day My Soul Just Opened Up: *40 Days and 40 Nights Toward Spiritual Strength and Personal Growth*

Until Today Cards: *A 50-Card Deck*

Tips for Daily Living Cards: *A 50-Card Deck*

The Value in the Valley: *A Black Woman's Guide Through Life's Dilemmas*

‡✢‡

Please visit the distributor of SmileyBooks:

Hay House USA: **www.hayhouse.com**®
Hay House Australia: **www.hayhouse.com.au**
Hay House UK: **www.hayhouse.co.uk**
Hay House South Africa: **www.hayhouse.co.za**
Hay House India: **www.hayhouse.co.in**

PEACE
from Broken
Pieces

HOW TO GET THROUGH
WHAT YOU'RE GOING THROUGH

Iyanla Vanzant

SMILEYBOOKS

DISTRIBUTED BY HAY HOUSE, INC.

Carlsbad, California • New York City
London • Sydney • Johannesburg
Vancouver • Hong Kong • New Delhi

Published in the United States by: SmileyBooks

Distributed in the United States by: Hay House, Inc.: www.hayhouse .com • *Published and distributed in Australia by:* Hay House Australia Pty. Ltd.: www.hayhouse.com.au • *Published and distributed in the United Kingdom by:* Hay House UK, Ltd.: www.hayhouse. co.uk • *Published and distributed in the Republic of South Africa by:* Hay House SA (Pty), Ltd.: www.hayhouse.co.za • *Distributed in Canada by: Raincoast:* www.raincoast.com • *Published and Distributed in India by:* Hay House Publishers India: www.hayhouse.com

Send inquiries to: SmileyBooks, 250 Park Avenue South, Suite 201, New York, NY 10003

Design: Nick C. Welch

Library of Congress Control Number: 2010933582

ISBN: 978-1-4019-2822-3
Digital ISBN: 978-1-4019-2859-9

14 13 12 11   6 5 4 3
1st edition, November 2010
3rd edition, January 2011

Printed in the United States of America

This book is dedicated to

Gemmia Lynnette Vanzant,

Omo Obatala,

OrisaSami,

*and Niamoja Adilah Afi for her contribution
to the next seventeen generations
of a healing love*

CONTENTS

AUTHOR'S NOTE

This is a work of nonfiction.
Conversations have been reconstructed
to the best of my recollection.

I found Jesus.
He was behind the sofa.
He said; "Come near;
    get down and stay down.
    I'll take care of everything."
So, I did.
And then, He did.

PROLOGUE

CHRISTMAS DAY

1:00 A.M.

I had just nodded off when they arrived: My dearest friends from New York, Tulani and her husband Stan, had come to spend Christmas Day with us at Gemmia's house. I was exhausted but excited about having guests for the holiday. After the last few days with Gemmia, I needed some comfort and support. My husband was sprawled across the living room sofa, fully dressed, with his shoes on. I wasn't sure where he had come from or when he had arrived. Like me, he was ecstatic to see our friends, our extended family. Tulani was like a sister who had helped me raise Gemmia. There are few things more comforting than having good, close friends with you when you are going through a difficult time.

After our greeting, with a lot of jumping up and down, kissing and hugging, we all went upstairs to Gemmia's bedroom. Gemmia was down to 91 pounds now, but if Tulani was at all shocked at her appearance, she never let on. She and Gemmia stared into each other's eyes like long-lost lovers. It was beautiful to see the love pass from one to the other. I was holding on to Stan because I knew he loved me as much as Tulani loved Gemmia. My husband just watched. I felt a twinge of sadness that he didn't love me like that, like Tulani loved Gemmia, but when I felt my heart sinking, I shook off that thought and squeezed Stan's hand.

2:20 A.M.

We sat around chatting, remembering the good ol' days in Brooklyn, reminding each other who had married whom, left whom, and was now with whom. Gemmia was alert and very talkative between naps. When she was awake, the men excused themselves while Tulani helped me get her on and off the Porta-Potty. She really wanted to use the toilet, but in her condition, the bathroom door on the other side of her bedroom was just too far to go.

I really did understand. My exhaustion from the past week made it feel like I had lead bricks in my feet. My head, although it had not grown in size, felt as if it weighed 20, no, 50 pounds. It was only sheer determination holding it upright. I could not crumble! If I did, Gemmia would also. That was not acceptable! Not now. She seemed to be getting weak again. Perhaps she was hungry. No, she just wanted to lie down.

3:40 A.M.

When I woke up, everyone else was still asleep. Tulani was curled up in Gemmia's favorite chair in front of the window. My husband and Tulani's husband were curled up in opposite corners on the floor. I sat up on the corner of the bed where I too had been tightly curled. Gemmia was lying behind me. I checked to see if she was breathing. *Don't be stupid! Of course she's breathing!* This was Christmas Day. I told myself that she would be breathing all day long.

I wondered if my younger daughter Nisa had finished wrapping the children's gifts. I tried to lift myself from the bed slowly so that I would not wake Gemmia. But as soon as I stood up she asked, "Where you goin'?"

"To see if the gifts are wrapped."

"Okay," she said. Then, "Don't go."

"Don't go where? Don't go home?" I tried not to sound alarmed, but everything she said set off bells and whistles in my mind. "I'm not going home, sweetie. I'm going downstairs."

She was silent. Asleep again, perhaps. Then I heard a small sigh. "Don't go." As gently as I could, I sat back on the bed. I waited to see if she would say anything else. She didn't.

6:17 A.M.

When my son, Damon, came into the room, I realized that I had been asleep in a sitting position. "What time are you opening the gifts?" he asked.

"As soon as the kids wake up. We don't have much because I never got to go shopping."

"Ma, they don't care about that. They just want to be here, and they want their Auntie Gemmia to get better."

I knew he was right. But Christmas in our family had always been such a big deal, not so much for the presents as for the folks and the food. It was Gemmia's favorite holiday, and she went all out to make sure the children and everyone else had a really good time. We stayed up all night wrapping gifts, drinking virgin piña coladas, and wishing we didn't have to cook. This year it was very different. There were a host of nieces, nephews, grandchildren, and the children of friends spread throughout the house, Gemmia's daughter Niamoja among them. This was as it had always been. The difference was that we were not in my home as usual. We were at Gemmia's house because we needed to be. I really tried to believe that everything and everyone was going to be okay.

6:30 A.M.

The house and everyone in it was still, except me. I could hear Gemmia's soft sighs as she slept, in counterpoint to my husband's light snoring. I decided to go downstairs to make a pot of coffee and call my prayer partner, because I knew she would understand the vision I had had the evening before. My friend had been through every step of this journey with me and always made herself available to my Mother Bear ravings. She had the perfect spiritual understanding of my vision. We had been talking for a while when my husband came into the kitchen. He said, "You'd better come upstairs. Something is happening."

7:12 A.M.

Gemmia was staring off into space, laughing to herself. "They're doing it again."

"Who?" I asked her. "Who is doing what?" She turned her face toward me, peering as if she could not see me.

"They are doing that open-eyed meditation," she said with a soft smile. I knew she was talking about my dear friend who had been with me day and night for the past month. Gemmia was in the room. The friend was not.

"Where are you, honey? Gemmia, tell me where you are!" She seemed to listen for a moment.

"I'm at Damon's house . . . I think. Yes, this is Damon's house."

I am not sure why my knees didn't buckle, but they didn't. I covered my mouth to stifle a scream. Oh my God! She's traveling. It is said that before a person makes the transition from life to the afterlife, they travel to say goodbye to those they love.

As I looked around the room, I realized that it was full of people and everyone was staring at me. They wanted to know what I was going to do next. They wanted to know what I knew. Where had they come from? Who let them in? My entire staff, 14 people, had come into the house with me noticing them.

"Somebody give me the phone, please." I wanted to call Gemmia's godmother. I needed to talk to her. She needed to talk to Gemmia. Suddenly, I had a telephone in my hand. At the sound of her godmother's voice, I felt the tears welling up in my eyes. I took a deep breath, trying to find the words to speak what I did not want to say. Somehow she knew.

"Is she still here?"

As if she could see me through the telephone, I shook my head.

"Let me speak to her."

I held the telephone to Gemmia's ear, refusing to give my tears permission to fall on her. From that moment forward, everything happened quickly; but not really.

7:30 A.M.

I am not sure when it started to happen, but my body had become rigid. I was not cold, but it felt like there was a cool breeze blowing through me. When I looked around the room, I could see people, but I could not feel my body. When I tried to move, my feet would not cooperate. I closed my eyes, placed my hand on Gemmia's head, and started to pray.

After a while, I asked where Gemmia's daughter was. "She's downstairs with her father," Nisa said. He had come to pick her up for the day; this was to be the Christmas they would spend together, away from her mother for the first time. I gathered enough of my senses to walk down to the kitchen. They were in there, fixing toast.

"Come here, sweetie." I reached out to my granddaughter. Her eyes were brimming with tears.

"I guess you're pretty scared, huh?" As she nodded yes, the tears began to fall. "Yeah, me too! I'm scared too, my love."

"Is Mommy going to die?"

"I don't know, sweetie, but I sure hope not. Do you want to go with Daddy or do you want to stay here?" She glanced over at her father. He motioned to her to respond.

"I'll go."

"Do you want to go?" She glanced at him again. *Why does she need his permission to speak to me?*

"Yeah, I guess."

"Okay, I'll tell you what. You take my cell phone and I will call you if anything happens. You put it in your pocket, and I promise I will call you." We hugged and I ran back upstairs.

8:12 A.M.

People continued to gather in Gemmia's bedroom. Somebody must have gotten the word out to come and come quickly. They all seemed to know what I could not, would not acknowledge. It was unthinkable, unspeakable, and they all seemed to know as I continued to hope against hope.

Gemmia was going in and out of consciousness. I kept talking to her and she answered as she could. With one hand I stroked her head, and with the other I held the telephone so that I could talk to her godmother, who was keeping me from losing it. Periodically I would put the telephone to Gemmia's ear so she could hear her soft, soothing voice also. Although I hated to admit it, her godmother's voice seemed to keep her alert in a way I could not. How could I? I could barely keep myself from banging my head against the wall and tearing at my flesh with my teeth. In a room filled with words of prayer, with all of my family and friends watching me, I'm not sure anyone one could comprehend what I was experiencing. For that matter, I didn't know what I was experiencing.

Then without warning, I felt it start to happen. That cold breeze again, around and throughout my body. A strange heaviness in my legs, and at the same time, a lightness—almost numbness—in my feet. The sensations became so intense I had to sit down on the edge of the bed. *Oh my God! My child is dying! Help me God! Please help me!* Those were the words I was thinking but I couldn't get my mouth open to speak them aloud. Without anyone prompting it, everyone in the room started praying aloud. Somebody put music on. One by one, people came over to the bed, bent down and prayed into Gemmia's ear. Some she acknowledged, others she did not. When I prayed for her, tears began to roll down her face. She was trying to speak but she could not. I asked someone to call my granddaughter at my cell phone number. She needed to come back home.

9:30 A.M.

Everyone had fallen into silence. For one instant, I closed my eyes and I could see her: Gemmia, strong and healthy. She was standing in the same place I had seen her in my vision the night before. It was the place where I had encountered Jesus. He was standing there also. She was midway between the two of us. I wanted to open my eyes, as if that would make what I was feeling less real, but it seemed as if my eyes had been glued shut.

Then I couldn't see Gemmia any more. Instead, I saw what appeared to be a black curtain dangling in front of me. I was focused on the curtain when I felt the jolt in my head. *How can this be?* Intuitively, I knew that Gemmia's brain was about to shut down. My entire head felt numb. I also felt a strange sensation in my lower back. No pain, just intense pressure. As suddenly as it had begun, it was gone. One by one her organs shut down. I could feel it in my body. Pieces and parts of me were dying. The kidney, the liver, the pancreas. It felt like sludge was being pushed through my veins as the flow of blood through her body slowed to a halt.

Nisa let me know that my granddaughter had come home. I turned my head to see her standing in the doorway of the bedroom with her father. She looked terrified. I told them both to say goodbye. Everyone in the room did the same. Professing their love, praying and saying goodbye to our angel, our beloved angel Gemmia.

I sensed that I was near her, even though I could not quite figure out where I had gone in my mind. Reaching out, I felt her body. It was still warm. I kissed her face all over like I had done when she was a baby and told her I loved her. I heard her sigh. Then her heart stopped. When it did, my eyes flew open. Gemmia was sitting propped up on a pillow. Her head was dangling slightly to one side. Someone was lifting me up, from where I did not know. It was 10:18 A.M. Christmas morning.

My daughter Gemmia was not the only one who died that morning. My family of origin died. My marriage, already in its coffin, died for good. My ministry, which had been the foundation of my relationship to God, was counted among the fatalities, too. My career, my personal vision, my life's purpose as I had come to know it came to an abrupt end. Most important of all, when my best friend, my middle child, took her last breath, my sense of self died along with her. I was a woman whose dance card was suddenly filled with death and whose heart had shattered into a million pieces.

What is it that would make a creature as fierce, majestic and powerful as a lion is, subject itself to the intimidation of a man, a whip and a chair? The lion has been taught to forget what it is.

CHAPTER 1

HERE IS ALSO THERE

It is often difficult to identify the exact moment that your life falls apart. In most cases, it is not a one-shot deal. If you ask most people who have had the experience of losing everything they love or believe in, they will probably say it was not one telephone call or one letter, one revelation or realization that caused the collapse of life as they knew it. I now understand that my life fell apart one piece at a time. Piece by piece; one experience, one situation, and one circumstance at a time, until I found myself standing in the midst of a heap of broken promises, splintered relationships, and shattered dreams. It is not a place I ever imagined I would find myself again, after I had gotten through it the first and second times.

The breaking down into pieces of a life is a painful thing to watch and even more painful to endure. Even more devastating is that as your life begins to unravel, day by day, piece by piece, there is absolutely nothing you can do to stop it. You see what is happening. You know what is happening. And you want anything other than what is happening to happen. You see, somewhere deep inside, we all know that lives are not built to fall apart. That is just not what lives are meant to do. The lives we are given by God are meant by God to grow, to blossom and flourish. The reality is, however, lives do crumble.

I now realize that lives fall apart when they need to be rebuilt. Lives fall apart when the foundation upon which they were built needs to be relaid. Lives fall apart, not because God is punishing us for what we have or have not done. Lives fall apart because they need to. They need to because they weren't built the right way in the first place. I came to this realization one day, after many days, weeks, months, and years of trying to fix the cracks in my foundation. One day, one moment of time, as I sat helplessly surveying the broken pieces of my mind, heart, and life, I recognized that a broken life is a test of faith of the highest order.

In that testing moment, I thought I had only a few choices. I could take the handful of pills I was holding in my left hand, or I could take the gun in my right hand, raise it to my temple, and pull the trigger. I just wanted the pain of the brokenness to stop. I had another choice, but it was the last thing I thought I could do. The other choice was to give myself permission to feel the pain, fear, and devastation of all that confronted me, hoping that something miraculous would occur.

Obviously, I didn't take the pills or pull the trigger. And somewhere amid my broken mental and emotional pieces, I knew that any attempt to manage my misery would be futile. That moment of helplessness led me into a moment of surrender. I buried my face in my pillow and cried for hours. It was a single act of human surrender, one instant of being willing to trust myself and my Creator, that was as close as I could get to *lifting my eyes toward the hills*, from where I *hoped* my help would come. My help did come and it only took five and a half years to reach me.

When I come face to face with the truth, my heart races and my ears get hot. There was a time when I thought that this physical response was fear. I now know that it is not fear at all. When I come face to face with the truth, my bloated humanness falls away, and I experience the energetic surge of my soul as it stands up within me. The truth is that I knew for a long time, five years to be exact, that I needed to share the story of my most recent life experiences. The experiences I had after I had become famous. The truth is that I was being disobedient to my own inner guidance. Friends and family had told me to write about all that I had learned as a result of leaving *The Oprah Winfrey Show*, falling flat on my face doing my own show, ending my marriage to my lifelong love, losing my daughter—my best friend—to colon cancer, and seeing my life fall apart over the two years that followed. The truth is, I flat out refused to do it!

In my refusal process, I started three other books, completing only one. I started several other writing and recording projects, only to lose interest and drop out. Rather than doing what my own inner guidance directed me to do, I allowed myself to become engrossed in more pleasurable activities, like making scrapbooks, watching reruns of *Law & Order*, and anything else I could think of to keep me busy. The good news is that when you have something to do, life will not allow you to move forward until you do it. The bad news is the same. I told myself and anyone who asked that I had already shared enough of my life, my heart, my wisdom with the world. There are some things people do not need to know; certain things I had a right to keep private. The truth is, *I was scared*. I wasn't scared to tell the story. I was afraid of walking through the pain of the story. I was afraid of facing head-on what I had discovered about myself and my life as it crumbled around my feet. Most of all, I was deathly afraid of the responsibility of standing up straight in the power and majesty of what my life was becoming. You see, when you experience some of the things that I have experienced, something happens to you. First, you are humbled. Then, you get clear. Once you get clear about who you are, what you do, and what you are being called to do, you become powerful. As you sort through the pieces of your life story, as you sift through the rubble of what is left, your character becomes stronger. You are propelled into a higher level of responsibility for yourself, into a deeper appreciation for all of the pieces of your life, and into a deeper level of accountability to God. I was afraid of what that much responsibility would require of me. Fear will make you resistant, rebellious, defiant, and disobedient.

There were some other things that I was afraid of, too. I was afraid of telling a story that involved other people. I care about these people. I care about what they think of me. I was afraid they would be hurt by what I had learned about them, as I learned so much more about myself. The fear I experienced, I had to admit, was my attempt to *fight evidence about reality*. The truth is, we all have our own personal reality. My experience leads to my reality, and their experience would lead them to theirs. My story has nothing to do with anyone except me, and the same is true for everyone else. Anyone who has raised children can attest to the reality that each child will have a different perception of the same experience. This results in the telling of different stories, by different people about the same occurrence. The truth is, I was making a valiant search for an excuse to be disobedient to the voice of my own Spirit. As a good friend of mine would say, *I am better now!*

I am going to tell you a story about how a *New York Times* best-selling author ends up flat broke, looking for a place to live. I am going to show you how a 37-year relationship ends in divorce by e-mail. I am going to share with you the intimate details of how an internationally recognized spiritual teacher ends up on the edge of the bed in a million-dollar home slated for foreclosure, contemplating suicide. I am also going to tell you about the power of friends, faith, and prayer.

I am going to tell you about betrayal and the devastation it causes for everyone involved. I want to share with you what I have learned about having and not having a vision, and the cost of holding on to a vision that is not yours. I want you to know what I have learned about personality flaws, human weaknesses, a corrupted mind, a broken heart, and a depleted spirit. These are the pieces of my life that led to its total and complete collapse, pieces of a puzzle I didn't even know existed until my life fell into pieces.

The puzzle and all of its pieces came from my family of origin; some people I knew, others I had never met. What held the puzzle pieces in place was their blood running through my veins. The puzzle was in my genes. By virtue of my life, their lives and lies remained alive, in me, and as me. I have come to believe that my story is very much like the story of many women, particularly African American women. Many of us marinated in wombs that did not support the development of a solid foundation, a clearly defined puzzle picture, a strong sense of who we are. This is not to blame our mothers. They too most probably did not have a clear picture of who they were or from what and whom they originated.

Sure, our parents and grandparents may tell us family stories and reminisce about the good old days. However, it's rare that we get the low-down, dirty, all-the-news-that's-fit-to-print truth about who did what to whom and what was really going on when we came into being.

I believe that my story, like so many other stories, is a demonstration of the generational karma visited upon women as a result of the families we are born into. Some people believe in karma. Others do not. I am not advocating for it one way or the other. What I am offering is that there is this thing—something—that moves through generation after generation of women, affecting how we see ourselves and how that identity often works against our own best interest. It is an energy that many of us are born into, live through, and struggle valiantly to live beyond. Whether or not you believe there is such a thing as karma—the lessons and deeds of past lives unfolding as the experiences and affairs of this life—you do know that there is a law of cause and effect. It is a universal law of nature: For every action, there is an equal and opposite reaction. In my life, I experienced many *reactions* for which I could find no action, no first cause. From this I concluded that there was something else going on. I came to recognize that there was this piece of me, one I did not understand, that controlled how I moved in the world. This *thing* meant I had a propensity to think a certain way, to nurse certain emotions and beliefs, and to hold on to certain expectations and limitations. This thing, I came to believe, was a generational karmic energy passed on to me through my bloodline.

My story is also what I call a story of *pathology*. Pathology is the study of the nature and origin of dis-ease, and disease is readily carried in the blood. The disease I discovered in my life experience was cancer. Not just the breast cancer that killed my mother or the colon cancer that stole my daughter's life. I am not just talking about physical cancer. I am addressing pathology of mental, emotional, and behavioral disease, patterns that had infected the foundation of my life. I found it interesting, puzzling, and quite disturbing that although my mother had died when I was two years old, I had repeated many of her mistakes in relationships and parenting. Equally astounding was that while I had no conscious memory of her and little knowledge of her life experiences, I was like her in many respects. How I came to be like my mother was a missing piece of my puzzle. I sense that many women live a pathology like this, of beliefs and behaviors passed down from one generation to the next, causing them to live lives plagued by low self-value and a diminished sense of worth.

My story describes a pathology of abandonment and shame; abuse and self-abuse; betrayal and guilt; unworthiness and loss. My story is very much like my mother's story. Her story was very much like her mother's, who died when she was 13. And my story is very much like that of my daughter, whose mental and emotional pieces were shaped by my pathology, though I did not know it at the time.

My story is a story of distorted pictures and patterns: mental, emotional, and behavioral patterns. Some I recognized as they were playing out, others I did not. When I did recognize the pattern, the puzzle piece, I felt powerless to change it into something else. When I could not or did not change them, the patterns dominated my life. When I was unaware of the pattern, I felt like a victim. Many women I have worked with over the years live lives of victimhood (*this is happening to me*) and victimization (*they are doing this to me*), just as their mothers and grandmothers did. I came to discover that I was not a victim. Instead, I learned that I was making both conscious and unconscious choices that were grounded in a pathology that I in part inherited and in part created. My greatest lesson was the discovery that I held the key to my freedom in the center of my being. The key was my Spirit. No pathology is stronger than your Spirit, and there is no puzzle that your Spirit cannot put together.

As you read my story, I want to offer you some encouragement. I want to encourage you to remember that this is my story; how I see it and how I remember it. It has nothing to do with how anyone else sees it or remembers it. I want to encourage you *not* to read my story at the level of personality: yours, mine, or that of anyone involved. If you look only at the personality, you will be confused, angry, and heartbroken. Instead, I encourage you to read my story with the awareness that we each come into this life with—a spiritual curriculum. Our spiritual curriculum is *chosen* by our souls to facilitate growth, learning, and healing. It frames the lesson we must master through the experiences we encounter. The spiritual curriculum of each life has one aim: to get us back to God. If we judge our spiritual curriculum as good or bad, right or wrong, fair or unfair, we will miss the point of the lesson, and we will repeat the class over and over until we understand that what we go through in life is the road map back to God.

In this journey we are about to take together, I also want you to know about the value of a daily spiritual practice—the painful and necessary process of surrendering your life into God's hands and the slow, revealing process of personal redemption, leading to that moment when you are redeemed in your own eyes. I want to tell you what I have learned about joy and pain, fear and courage, anger and passion, and most of all, peace. I want you to know how I found peace among the broken pieces of my life. One powerful tool that I use to sustain my peace is EFT or the Emotional Freedom Technique, also called Tapping.

What I want you to know now, before you read any of these stories, is that none of us is immune to the challenges of life. No matter how famous you are, how much money you make, or how "big" you become in the eyes of the world, none of us is immune to the challenges, difficulties, and pain of life and being human. Although I would have never said it aloud, I thought I *should be* immune. I was quite horrified to discover I was not.

Finally, I want to share with you what I have learned about the power of family patterns and the permanent marks they leave on your life. It is the presence and power of these patterns that live in our blood that make it absolutely necessary to have a solid spiritual foundation, an intimate and viable relationship with God. If I have learned nothing else in the last five years of my life, I have learned that I can depend on God. I now know, without a shadow of doubt, that God can and always will hold me up, sit me down, push me forward, pull me back, turn me around, keep me in line, move me along, teach me what I need to know, and remind me of what I already know. In the stories I will share with you in this book, I pray that you too will come to understand that God can and will do in you, through you, and for you everything that is required, at just the right time, in the perfect way. This is what I have learned and what I have been asked to share with you. I do it with the prayerful hope that my story and your story will converge at some point with such power and love that we will all become beacons of peace on the earth. Toward that end, I am in peace, not pieces.

Let It Be So!
Iyanla

When you have no positive pictures and, are unable to access the feelings those pictures would evoke, you have a tendency to make up what you want the pictures to be. More often than not, the pictures you create are not fully developed, causing you to live your life in the blur of false images.

CHAPTER 2

THE WALKING WOUNDED

It is hard for me to imagine that after loving someone for more than forty years of my life, I would arrive at a day when the mere thought of being in the same room with him would be distasteful. Now, don't get me wrong; I wish him no harm. In fact, there is still a part of me that actually loves him. Fortunately, I am proud to say, today I love me more.

Oh, but there was a time! A time when I was blinded and crippled by what I thought was loving him. Suffice it to say that we wanted to love each other. We really tried to love each other, and on a good day, we were convinced that we did love each other. I wish I could say that it was a real love, but today I choose to no longer deceive myself in that way. Today, I understand that I was hooked on my own denigration. I was hooked on my own dysfunction. There was a hook inside of me that got caught on proving to myself that I could never and would never have what I wanted. He just happened to be passing by when I threw my hook into the sea of life.

My first husband was a Vietnam veteran who struggled with the demons of drugs and re-entry when he came home. The second was a functional illiterate and recovering heroin addict. My third husband was the embodiment of everything I needed to live out my lifelong fantasy. The fantasy that my father would love, accept, and rescue me. By then, I could afford the kind of wedding that I always wanted my father to provide for me: large and extravagant. Because I wanted everyone to know that I was worth it. Worth every extravagant dime.

My third husband was my forbidden fruit—the thing I could not have and did not need, which made me want him even more. He was the prize that would prove to me and everyone else that I was worthy of my father's love. The truth of the matter is, everything about him was really about my father. I had a tremendous amount of unfinished business with my daddy. The men I married were the souls who volunteered to spend time in my life so that I could work through that business.

When I married Eden, I was at the beginning of being a success in my life, while emotionally, there was a place in me that still felt like a failure. The spiritual bones of my life were ill-formed and far from solid. I loved God but I didn't really know God, not then, not yet. I was transforming from who I had been into who I was becoming; but I still wasn't quite sure of who I was, what I wanted, or where my life was heading. To the naked eye, I looked fine. I could walk and talk and tie my shoes while spelling my name. I was earning more money than I ever thought was possible. I was traveling the world and doing things that I never imagined I could or would be able to do. My children were grown and making it on their own with the broken pieces of myself that I had given to them. And then there was this one other thing I forgot. In the process of planning and having a wedding, I forgot there would actually be a marriage, a union of minds, bodies, souls, and issues that would come together as soon as the ceremony was over.

Finally, I had a home and a husband. However, just beneath the surface, the bones of my soul were aching; some were smashed and others were held together by small fragile pins. My relationship with the man I thought would make everything all right was not doing what I demanded that it should do: make me feel whole. He was not happy and I was miserable. We tried as best as we could to fix it. If you were to ask him, he would probably say the demise of our marriage was about me: what I did and didn't do. Or perhaps, he would say it was about him: what he could not and would not do.

If you were to ask me, I would tell you unequivocally that it was all about him: loving, wanting, needing him. Being afraid to love and know him; trying to figure out how to please him. And feeling that I had failed him miserably.

It started as puppy love. I met Eden when I was a 14-year-old youth worker. He was a 17-year-old senior youth counselor. He was tall and thin. I was short and sort of round. I was nervous and chatty. He was very calm and collected. He walked with me through a several-day process of trying to get the New York City Summer Youth Program to find my records and issue my check. Each day, for seven long days, he made all of the telephone calls, talked to all of the people, and helped me fill out all of the forms required to remedy an administrative blunder. He never got upset with the ridiculous questions we were asked. He never, not even once, got upset when a person in this office sent us over to a person in that office, only to have that person send us back to the first office. Each day he would ask me if I had bus fare. He would also ask me if I had lunch money. When I did not, he would buy lunch for me. Each day that we were together, I grew more in love with him.

Maybe it was his gentle nature or the way he spoke firmly but softly. Maybe it was the way he smiled or the way he smelled. I don't remember exactly what it was, but I do know that for the first time in my life, I felt I mattered. He was the first man who ever seemed willing to stand up for me. At least that is what I told myself. Then again, remember, I was only 14 at the time. Eight months earlier, I had given birth to a child. Two months earlier, I had buried her. To say I was an emotionally vulnerable mess would be an understatement. And still, there was something about him. He seemed so willing to protect me, to make sure that I had what I needed when I needed it. That was a new experience for me. That was the hook. Maybe he was all the things I thought he was. Maybe not. Could be. Who knows? There was, however, one slight challenge: He was involved with one of my closest friends, and he had another lover, an older woman, on the side. Or perhaps my friend was his side dish. It was hard to know back then.

The winter after our summer "together," he broke up with my friend and married the other woman. They stayed together for 15 years and had five children together, while I watched and loved him from a distance. I never forgot—could never forget—the way I felt when I was with him. I wanted to feel like that again, forever. I made up that it would only be possible with him. That was not the truth.

Back then, in the beginning, I loved him and everything about him even after he was married. I loved the way he looked; the way he walked; the way he smelled—like sandalwood—behind his ears, in his beard, and on his wrists. I loved the scent of him that lingered in the room long after he was gone. He was the first man who held my hand. When he looked at me, I thought he could see me. In my mind, that meant he accepted me, and I fell in love with that idea about him. I am told that you could see my love for him in my eyes. That love grew from a puppy into a pit bull that would rip pieces from the fibers of my soul for 37 years.

True love is powerful, though not always in the way you think. Even when your experiences with love have nothing to do with the truth that love is, your desire to know love will have a powerful impact on your life. It will dredge up everything that is unloving within you and around you. The more I loved him, the more unlovable I felt. The more unlovable I felt, the uglier I believed I was. The uglier I believed I was, the more unworthy I thought I was in my own mind. The more unworthy I thought I was, the harder I held on to what I thought I did not deserve. It was painful; loving him and believing I didn't deserve to be loved. Back then, pain was my drug of choice. It was a vicious cycle that had very little to do with him. A friend said it was almost like I was possessed. And I was. I was so possessed by him that I forgot, on many occasions, to possess myself; to honor me and love me. I was possessed enough to stay with him, knowing, as I did, that there were pieces of me that were badly broken or missing altogether.

In our close-knit Brooklyn circle, Eden was The Man; someone well known and admired in the cultural nationalist, social activist community. He was the "go-to" man, well connected, who knew how to get things done. If what you needed or wanted had anything to do with culture, politics, or community affairs, he was involved. Although he didn't own a car and had never worn a suit, he was the one people called upon when there was something of importance going on in the community. I wanted to put on a benefit concert for the refugees of war-torn Biafra. At the time, I was a 30-year-old college student making a name for myself as President of the Student Government Association of Medgar Evers College. I needed connections and contacts, so I went to him. He was more than willing to help and knew exactly who I needed to speak to. We made a plan and walked through it together. In the process, those familiar feelings resurfaced and I was hooked again.

Before I knew what was happening, Eden and I were talking every day, first about the concert and then about other things too. We were meeting and eating lunch together. We were laughing together. On the day of the concert, he made sure that everyone and everything was in place. He managed the stage and served as master of ceremonies. It was a beautiful event, and we raised over $1,000. We were so proud of what we had done together, and of each other.

The first few days after the event, we had to make excuses to call each other. Then it just became natural. One day as we were sitting in my car, he told me about the breakup with his wife. He was sad and, I think, very angry. He was living with his mother in Queens, so I would drop him off at the subway station. It was hard for him to get out of the car that day. It was even harder for me to watch him go. For the next few weeks, I became his sounding board. He talked about his wife and children. He talked about how wrong she was and how bad it hurt. He talked about his hopes and dreams and wishes for his future. He also talked about how difficult it was for him to make the transition from being a married man to being single. I listened and tried to help him see things another way, a better way. I think his sense of pride was hurt because his sense of value and worth was rooted in his family but I also knew his heart was broken.

Back then, I didn't know anything about rebound relationships. I didn't know that it takes a respectable amount of time for one person to get over another person and come to a place of completion. Back then, I only knew how he made me feel. I was really sorry, with him and for him, that his marriage had fallen apart. I was also really happy and really scared for me. It felt like I was about to have something that I really wanted, something that made me feel good about myself. I was happy because, hey, what woman wouldn't be happy to have a fine-looking, intelligent man in her life? I was scared because I thought I was unlovable, ugly, and unworthy. I didn't tell him that I felt that way, but I did.

Then, one evening while we were sitting at the subway station, he asked me if he could kiss me. Can you believe it? He asked me! We had spent so much time talking about his wife, his children, and his plans, I felt like his therapist, not a potential lover. Even back then, I knew I could not be both, so I asked him a question. "Do you want to be in my head or in my bed? You cannot have both." My response to his response was, I took him home with me that night. The rest is now our history.

When you want and need something as bad as I wanted and needed to be loved, you will allow yourself to believe anything at all. I made up that the universe had put the stars in just the right place, at just the right time, to bring us together. It all seemed to make sense to me—that's why he had taken such tender care of me when I was 14 years old. That's why we were never too far from each other's reach. That's why I continued to drool over him for the 15 years that he was with someone else. God and the universe knew that the day would come when he would leave his wife and five children to be with me. It makes absolutely no sense to me now, but at age 30, it is what I told myself.

I needed and wanted to be accepted. I needed and wanted to matter. I existed on the fringes of the cultural community as a dancer. I was always involved in community activities, but I was not a member of the in-crowd. Most of the people who knew him only knew me in passing. In his crowd, I was just "the next one." I did not know I was expected to be friends with his ex-wives and ex-girlfriends. I did not know that an angry, hurt man who was not accountable to anyone in his life was a dangerous person.

I never thought of myself as being involved with a married man, but the truth is, he was only separated from his wife. They still owned the house she lived in, and they still co-parented their children. They still spoke almost every day, and the truth is, he still wanted her. He was mad as hell at her, but he wanted to be with his family.

My mother was also the "other woman" in someone's marriage. She loved my father enough to have two children with him while he was married to someone else. My father left my mother every night to go home to his wife, who lived within walking distance of the place where my parents conceived my brother and me. Undoubtedly, that was when my mother drank. I am told that my father and mother had a tumultuous and sometimes violent relationship. I am told that, in spite of the pleading of her sisters, my mother would not leave my father. I am told that she really loved him. Without even knowing it or me, my mother taught me how to love a man. It was a self-denying, self-debasing kind of love. It became something that I despised about myself.

My mother was an alcoholic who discovered she had breast cancer when she was pregnant with me. My father wanted her to have an abortion, which back then would have meant a coat hanger and a kitchen table. She refused. As I was being formed in my mother's womb, my being was being filled with guilt, fear, and suffering, programmed at a cellular level with her pathology of worthlessness and pain. I eventually figured out that this explained why, for more than half of my life, I felt so bad about myself; why I thought I was such a bad person. Eventually, I discovered that my badness was a story that I inherited.

I think my cultural warrior thought he loved me, and I know he needed me at that time. I was his escape, "a temporary distraction," as one of his ex-girlfriends called me. I knew I loved him, or perhaps I loved what he represented for me: stability, protection, and acceptance. I was determined to make it work for us; for me. I stayed with him that first time for five years, despite the fact that I spent most of my time wondering when he was going to leave. Eden had several affairs that I knew about, and a host of ex-lovers who were now just friends. He was the father of five. You might ask how I could stay with him in the face of his failure to commit to me or our relationship fully. My first answer would be, I was addicted to pain; debilitating and devastating emotional pain.

My second answer is that I felt profoundly connected to this man. I thought we were good friends and that we talked about everything. I thought he was a great listener and that his feedback was being offered with care, concern, and compassion simply because he didn't yell at me. One powerful lesson I learned from him was that just because a man is a good man, it does not mean that he knows how to be a good partner. Then again, it could be that some people, even people who love each other, are simply not cut out to be together. When two broken people bring their broken pieces together, chances are they will never become a whole anything.

✣✣✣

There were so many signs along the way that he and I were not going to work. I chose to ignore the signs. Like the time I went to visit a friend in the Bronx and left my keys at home. When I returned at 2 A.M., my children were dead-to-the-world asleep. I walked the five blocks from my apartment to his, hoping to sleep for a few hours until they woke up. I rang his bell for several minutes before he came down. To my surprise, he looked wide awake. After a few seconds of silence, he told me "This is not a good time." I didn't catch his meaning until I realized he wasn't moving out of the doorway.

"What does that mean, this is not a good time?"

"It means it's not."

"Why not?"

"I have a friend over. She's sleeping."

"So I guess you are telling me to sleep in the street."

"No. But this is not a good time."

"Well, I guess it's not."

I took a cab to my girlfriend's house on the other side of town. She stayed up with me for the rest of the night as I cried my heart out. By the time I got home, he had called several times. I waited until he called at least ten more times before I called him back. He was sorry. He was so very sorry. I wanted to end the suffering, so I accepted his apology. I never asked him anything about that night.

Shortly after that, he went back to school to get his graduate degree, and I went to law school. I helped him type his papers. There was little he could do to help with my studies. We enjoyed being together and being good friends, talking and laughing together, sharing money and child care. What we did not do was talk about a future. We never talked about him getting a divorce or us getting married. We never talked about getting a house where all of the children could be together. We never talked about my plans after law school or his plans after graduate school. In fact, we avoided talking about anything that would give our relationship permanency.

One day, something shifted. We never talked about it, but I could feel it. Before I could figure out what to say or do about it, he started disappearing. If I called him to say good-night, he wouldn't answer. If I called to tell him to have a good day, he was already gone. I was in such deep denial, I refused to believe that a married man having a relationship with the "other woman" would dare to have another other woman. I was wrong and I was right.

One Friday night when I should have been studying, I went to his apartment and let myself in. Everything was dark and quiet. I have never been a snooper, so I did not look in his closet or his drawers. Instead, I sat on the edge of the bed in the dark, and I waited—just like I had waited for my father many times before.

He arrived as the sun was coming up. He had come home to get dressed for work. He was shocked to see me, but I am sure he knew it was coming sooner or later.

"How long have you been here?"

"All night."

Trying to think of what to say or what to do, I patted on the bed indicating that he should come and sit down next to me. He did. We were silent for several long minutes.

"Tell me what is going on."

"I'm not sure."

"Well, you've got to know something, because you didn't come home last night. Just tell me what you want to do."

"I'm really not sure." More silence. Then the one-two punch. "Carol always said she wondered what it would be like to be the other woman. And now she is."

"You were with Carol?"

"Yes."

"Are you two getting back together?"

"I'm really not sure."

I was getting just a bit tired of "I'm not sure."

"Well, when do you think you might be able to figure it out?" More silence.

"The only thing I know right now is that I don't want to lose you. I love you and I love what we have. But Carol and the children are a part of who I am."

I gathered my purse, my dignity, and the little pieces of my brain that were spilling out of my ears onto the floor, and without another word I walked out of the apartment.

Over the next three weeks, we spoke on the phone just a few times. Many nights when he did not call, I would drive by her house—their house—to see if his car was there. It always was. One night, I left a note on his windshield: *I guess you have figured out what you want to do. It would have been nice of you to let me know.*

After that, I fell apart. I slept all day and cried all night. I quit my job and rarely went to class. For all intents and purposes, I abandoned my children on the other side of the bedroom door. Every morning, I would get up and walk three blocks to the Catholic church that was open 24 hours a day. I prayed to St Jude, the Patron of Impossible Causes. I prayed to the Blessed Mother. Sometimes I just sat in the church and cried, hoping that God would take pity on me. This went on for months. I remember that when summer turned to fall, I was still praying in that church. I stopped going when it got cold.

Between sleeping, praying, and crying, I would call him. I would beg. I would plead. Nothing worked. He said very little. The same way he failed to commit to being with me, he wouldn't commit to leaving me either—he simply wouldn't talk about it. I thought about killing myself, but I would not do that to my children. Instead, I made up two good plan B's. The first was to get evicted from my apartment. I didn't need to plan that consciously—it is sure to happen when you quit your job and stop paying the rent. Surely if I had no place to live, he would come to rescue me. He had moved from his first apartment and was sharing a duplex home with a friend. I thought it was a good sign that he had not moved back "home" yet, and if I needed a place, he would definitely provide one for me. I was right and I was wrong.

He told me he was going to Cuba for two weeks and that I could come and stay at his place. Then he told me that when he came back, he would be moving back home. So I implemented my second plan B: I stopped breathing. I took in just enough air to keep me alive, but not enough to move life's energy through my body; that way, I didn't have to feel my heart exploding into a million pieces. If I just continued to sip in little snatches of air and spaced them far enough apart, I would not lose my mind. *I was right!* I didn't lose my mind, but it went on a long vacation. It took me three years to breathe again.

This is my story, the way it was for me back then, when I thought I was experiencing true love, when what I was actually experiencing was self-abuse and self-denial. This is my story of how I learned to tell myself the truth about myself only when it became too excruciatingly painful to hold on to the lie. This is my story of discovery, about how a broken little girl becomes a broken woman who creates a broken life because she needs broken people to support the fiction she has created to keep herself emotionally safe. These were not bad people. In fact, they were teachers of the highest order because they drove me straight into the arms of God. This is my story of how personal defects can lead you to the edge of your personal power, and how loving and accepting yourself in the midst of all that you discover about yourself will force you to jump head first into your greatness.

*When your life is going downhill,
it doesn't get better just because you
want it to. Nor can you will it to be better.
Your life will only get better when you get better.*

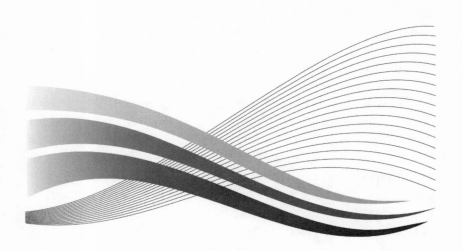

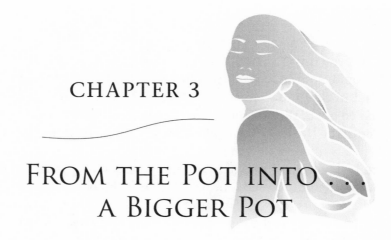

CHAPTER 3

FROM THE POT INTO ... A BIGGER POT

I was about 26 years old, married with three children, when I realized that there was something seriously out of order in my mind and heart. I was in New York City, riding in a taxicab. It was a scorching summer day and the taxi was freezing. I sat in the back seat in my tank top with my teeth chattering. Then I realized that as a paying customer, I could ask the driver to turn the air conditioning down. But I could not get my mouth open. I could not ask this man whom I was going to pay $10 or $12 to take me to my destination to adjust the temperature in his car so I could stop shivering. When I thought about asking him, a huge lump formed in my throat. I decided I had no right to ask because he might get upset with me. Instead, I tucked my arms down inside my tank top and slid into the corner of the back seat.

There was an argument raging in my mind between the rational adult that I was and the wounded, abused child I had been. The child remembered times when I had asked for something I needed or wanted. The child remembered names I had been called and things I had been told about myself. The adult reminded me that I was paying for a service and I had a right to be comfortable. No! I did not! I did not have the right.

After several minutes of the back and forth in my mind, I could feel the tears forming in my eyes. My heart was racing and my throat was closing. I knocked on the partition and motioned the driver to pull over. I am sure he could see that I was distraught.

"Are you okay?"

I couldn't speak; I was struggling to stifle the scream that had formed in my throat. I shoved a $10 bill into the little cup and stumbled out of the taxi, nowhere near my destination. The driver peered at me through the window and then pulled off. I stumbled over to a wall and stood there trying to gather my wits. I realized that I had suffered through many indignities rather than ask for what I needed or wanted, out of fear that if the person got upset, I could get hurt. It was a pattern I learned as a child. It was an ingredient in my pathology. It was, I believe, the reason I stayed for nine years in that physically abusive marriage.

In medicine, pathology is the study of the causes of disease. In human life, pathology is the disease; the stuff going on beneath the surface, handed down or passed on to you, the family stuff that you can see and feel even though no one ever talks about it. From a purely human, non-scientific perspective, it's why so-and-so does such-and-such when so-and-so is or is not around. It's why no one talks to so-and-so or talks about them as soon as they leave the room. We, all in our own way, live out or attempt to avoid living out the pathologies of our lineage; the pathologies of the shameful, dirty family secrets; the secret desires, secret behaviors, secret liaisons, and unconscious motivations. There can be some very good family patterns, but I am not concerned about those right now. For the most part, my story is about the dysfunctional pathology, the self-debasing patterns, the things I heard and saw the adults do that gave rise to the picture I held in my mind and heart about myself specifically, and about life in general.

We all have patterns of thought, belief, and behavior that we inherit from our family of origin. In the same way that our ears, our eyes, our nose, and the texture of our hair are inherited, we inherit certain mental, emotional, and even spiritual proclivities. We call them habits. Habits are hard to break and, despite our most earnest efforts, we usually remain loyal to our family patterns, even when they are dysfunctional. It is a function of the family cloth from which we are cut. In certain cases, like my case, you can awaken enough to decide early in life, *I don't want to be like these people!* Somewhere in your being, you know that something is just not right. Unfortunately, when you are a child, you don't know how to change. You don't know how to not be like the people who feed, clothe, and shelter you. So, you wait, growing more like them each day. You wait until you are old enough to move away, run away, hide from, or flat-out deny that you have anything at all to do with "these people." But sooner or later you realize that whether you are a block away, a state away, or on the other side of the world, you cannot deny the fabric of your being. Somehow, you will discover that you do what they did, or you say what they said, like they said it. Or you find that you act like the one person on earth you would not want to act like. Your mother, perhaps. If not her, your father for sure. And, just in case you're wondering, it doesn't matter if you knew them or not. That's the puzzling part! How is it that you end up with the karmic drainage and inherited damage of people you may not even know? This is the function of the family of origin: The family sets up the pathology and the patterns that you are called to heal in your lifetime.

Understanding the emotional propensities we inherit through our parents DNA is the missing puzzle piece. It was my missing piece. I became aware that there were puzzle pieces that I inherited from my parents that were alive in my emotional DNA. These were tapes playing in my subconscious mind. The enemy was within me. The harder I tried to overcome my internal demons, the harder they fought back. My saving grace was God. My only way out was through the Spirit. Somehow I tapped into a sacred knowledge and wisdom that let me know that prayer and meditation could and would save me.

It was my vigilant prayer life that allowed me to speak brilliantly to thousands while my personal life was crumbling. It was my deep and abiding desire to know and serve God that enabled me to bypass the beliefs of guilt and unworthiness, to listen within for the inspiration to write book after book that changed the lives of many. There were days when, on my way to a speaking engagement, I battled thoughts of suicide. My soul was weary; my heart, shattered.

At a personality level, I couldn't get the man I absolutely adored, even worshipped, to see me for who I really was and treat me accordingly. I felt his support and his criticism, but never his compassion. But at a soul level, God could use me, a deeply flawed vessel, and I could look in the eyes of another human being and speak three words that would pierce their soul, resulting in their personal transformation. No matter how much I did, or how "famous" I became, I never felt good enough. At the time, it made no sense to me at all. Now, I understand the maze of inherited pain. Just knowing that, and recognizing that I could live beyond the pain eventually brought me to a sense of peace. Unfortunately, my journey to peace may have cost my daughter her life.

There was a time when I would think about all the things that the adults in my life did not give me and my soul would weep with sadness. That sadness turned to sorrow when I realized I had done the same exact thing to my own children. There were so many things I needed to know that no one taught me; things that would have changed the way I saw myself and lived my life. No one ever taught me about personhood or womanhood or parenthood; love or sex; vision or purpose. I did learn to keep my body and home clean. I learned to make the best of what I had and not dare dream about having more. I also learned how to avoid, ignore, and dismiss the truth. If only I had been raised by adults, instead of wounded children, maybe—just maybe—my path would have been less traumatic. Then again, I've learned we all get exactly what we need, when we need it, in order to learn what God intends for us to know so we can be who God intends for us to be.

✜✜✜

I don't remember anything about my mother dying. What I do remember is the day of the funeral. I remember my grandmother cooking and people bringing food to our house. I remember because the food was everywhere and I could not touch or eat any of it. I remember that a few days before the food arrived, I got a new dress and a brand-new pair of white patent-leather shoes.

I'm not sure why I remember that. I also remember the day of the funeral because we rode in a big black car. It had buttons that made the windows go up and down. I remember playing with the buttons and getting yelled at for it, then slapped across the face for ignoring the warnings. I remember finally being able to eat the food and being warned not to get dirty—which I did. I remember getting snatched up and dragged into the bathroom, where I was chastised for ruining a brand-new dress. I was told I didn't know how to listen or how to take care of anything. What I was not told was that my mother was dead or that I had just seen her being put into the ground. I was three years old.

My mother's death was like an amputation. She was there. Then she was gone. Her voice was gone; the voice I had come to know in the womb. Her touch was gone; the touch of her hands on my body, her face pressed against my face. Her love was gone; a love I can't even fathom because I have no conscious memory of it. However, I do know that it created a void in my being that I did not discover until 30 years later.

My paternal grandmother was the mother figure I knew, the mother I identified with for the next two years of my life, as my patterns of thought and behavior solidified. My grandmother's home was supposed to be the sanctuary where I would heal after my amputation. Instead, my mind and body were infected by Grandma's anger, resentment, and inability to express love. Through her speech and behavior, she taught me that nothing I did was ever good enough. Because she was my primary caregiver, she created an incontestable picture of who I was and who I would always be—bad, wrong, and never good enough.

I always thought my grandmother was a huge woman. When I was 3 years old and two feet tall, she was 40 years old and stood 5' 9" tall. It seemed to me that no matter how much I grew, she grew taller and bigger. Perhaps she stood as an overwhelming figure in my life because she was so stern, or as some might say, just plain old mean. In the family, she had a reputation of being meaner than a wet cat! And, if you knew what was good for you, you'd better not cross her. But I didn't understand why

I was with Grandma in the first place, and I didn't have a clue about how to navigate the minefield of living with her. I didn't know how to move fast enough or slow enough. I didn't know how to answer questions properly or when not to answer at all. I did learn that everything had to be done the right way, which was *her* way. It had to be done completely to her satisfaction, in her time, to her specifications, and I had better have done it with the proper look on my face. I also learned that no matter what I did or how I did it, it was wrong. It was wrong because I was bad. It was wrong because I didn't listen. It was wrong because I was hardheaded or because I must be stupid. It was wrong because I was a pain in the butt—just like my father. I figured out that it was not a good thing to be like him, because the only person my grandma disliked almost as much as me was my father.

When Grandma was working, my father would stop by the apartment several times a day to check on my brother Ray and me. I never knew when he was coming. I didn't know where he lived. It was strange to me that he didn't sleep at Grandma's house, but I knew better than to ask why. I wanted him to be there to rescue me from Grandma. I also knew better than to mention it to him.

I really loved my daddy, even though he rarely said more to me than "Hey, baby." I loved his mustache and the way he smelled. He was the most handsome man I had ever seen. He always wore a crisply starched shirt and a hat tipped to the side of his head. I knew the sound of his footsteps coming up the stairs. I would jump up from whatever I was doing and run to the door because Daddy was home, and it could mean a popsicle, a piece of Bazooka bubble gum, or a stick of Wrigley's. The truth is, it didn't matter whether he brought me anything or not; he was *my* daddy and he was the only my anything that I had.

My daddy was a numbers runner. He always had Wrigley's because that's where he wrote the numbers that the people in the neighborhood bet on. Even that made him clever in my mind.

Over time, I learned to stop expecting my daddy to save me from Grandma's wrath. When he did try to speak up on my behalf, she would shift the focus of her name-calling from me to him. If he raised his voice, she would throw something, not at him but in his direction. I remember the few times he did attempt to stand up for me. That would really set her off. I don't remember much of what she said, but I do remember how her venomous barrage usually ended. He would beg her to stop, telling her it was enough, she was right. Then he would find a reason to take me with him wherever he was going, to give us both a few minutes of peace. I'm not sure if he knew that when he took me back home and left me there, Grandma would continue the barrage against me.

I loved those rare occasions when my daddy took me for a ride in his car. I thought it was our special time together. Sometimes, we would go to the candy store his best friend owned. On most occasions, Daddy would take me to a lady's house to get my hair braided. Rarely did I go to the same lady more than twice. There were many. Some pretty, some not. Some nice, most not. When I got a new hairdo, Daddy didn't walk me all the way upstairs at Grandma's house. He would kiss me on the third floor and wait as I walked the last two landings to our fourth-floor apartment, instructing me to tell Grandma he would see her later. She always wanted to know who had done my hair. What was her name? Where did she live? And did she give me any money? Then she would retreat to the kitchen to mutter and cuss to herself. I would find Ray and sit really close to him, just in case the muttering to herself turned into slapping of me. I sometimes got slapped for not knowing the answers to her questions. If I was sitting close to Ray, the slap was often reduced to a pinch or a push; those usually didn't upset him and only hurt me a little.

Unlike me, Ray had the map to the minefield. Even though he was a year older than me, he always seemed much more fragile and, as a result, more acceptable to Grandma. His melancholy disposition, a sharp contrast to my incessant chattering, helped him avoid Grandma's wrath in a way I never learned to do. Because Ray was asthmatic, Grandma was very tender and gentle with him. He got to do special things with her, like sit in her lap and sleep in her bed, while I slept on the floor alongside. He also had fewer chores than I did. Because I only knew Grandma's harsh and brutal side, I often watched with curiosity and amazement as she transformed into a tender, nurturing mother figure with my brother. It was painful because I made up that it meant there was something about me that made her angry and mean. I couldn't figure out what I needed to do or how I needed to be to experience her softness, to experience the Grandma that Ray knew and loved. It taught me that boys were somehow entitled to more than me and that there was a standard for being loved that I did not meet.

It is one thing to get beat down. It's another thing when your beat-down is known to someone else—someone you love. Someone you think cares about you. When someone you care about watches your beat-down and doesn't help you, it feels like a betrayal, and the memory of it stays with you. Perhaps sitting close to my brother was a way to avoid the full wrath of Grandma is what led me to conclude that the most I could hope for from the men in my life was presence in body, if not in mind and heart. It taught me that gentle male souls can offer some small measure of hope. Perhaps that is why I found my first love so appealing. He too was quiet and gentle like my brother. Perhaps. Who knows? I also recall, however, the betrayal of my brother moving out of the way when Grandma did decide to slap or shake me.

Just because you are defective does not mean you cannot see the defects in others. I must have been slightly more than four years old when I figured out that Grandma was just plain crazy. In modern-day terms, she would be considered emotionally unstable or perhaps depressed. I now know that there is a form of depression, particularly among black women, that leads to sudden, erratic, and violent behavior. It is caused by stress, and it is deemed to be a mental illness. When I was growing up, you didn't talk about mental illness. You just didn't. No one dared challenge or confront the pattern of abuse. Instead, the dysfunction was denied, avoided, and hidden. I was simply collateral damage.

In my story, Grandma's mental instability was about me. I was so wrong and so bad, I made her angry. As a result of just being me, I was snatched, shaken, beaten, or pushed out of the way. In most cases, it happened so that Grandma could demonstrate to me the right way to do a thing. That thing could be ironing a pillowcase or a shirt sleeve. Or it could be cleaning the toilet or sink with a torn-up undershirt. Or it could be tucking my undershirt down in my panties so that the bottom of the shirt lay flat on my butt through the leg holes. That was the only way to keep my undershirt from rolling up and exposing my fat belly to everyone who cared to notice it. In most instances, I simply couldn't do what Grandma demonstrated, because by the time she finished showing me the right way to do it, I was terrified. I could hardly hear her instructions through the barrage of cuss words. I couldn't see what she was doing because my eyes were filled with tears that *dared* not fall down my cheeks. If you cried in Grandma's presence, one of those huge hands of hers would give you something to really cry about.

Living with Grandma broke the innocence and curiosity of my little-girl spirit into a million pieces that I did not know how to pick up—at least, not in the right way. In Grandma's house, it was best not to ask anything and to surrender totally the need to know anything. When I did make the mistake of asking, the response was more often than not about me; my physical characteristics or the wrongness of me. It is a wonder that I learned anything at all during my tenancy with Grandma, but I did learn some things that it has taken most of my adult life to unlearn. Grandma taught me that no matter how bad something hurt, it was best to not ask anyone for help. In Grandma's house, I learned the silent, crushing pain of not being wanted and feeling I was unloved.

Grandma taught me how to suck up to people who had something I needed or wanted, and she taught me that I was powerless to influence how it would be doled out. When I wanted something from Grandma, I would sit quietly in her line of sight, without a toy, without saying a word. If I sat there long enough, she would ask what was wrong with me. Her tone of voice would let me know if I should ask for a sandwich or a cookie or if I could watch something on television—or if it was safer to lie and say that nothing was wrong. When I did ask, her granting permission was usually preceded by complaints about me. I learned to tolerate the put-downs in order to get what I wanted. One of the more important lessons Grandma taught me was that if someone told you she loved you, or if you thought she was supposed to love you, it was okay for her to treat you badly. In fact, you should expect the people you loved and needed to treat you badly. It was a sign of how much they loved you.

Despite all that she did not do for me and did not give to me, Grandma did teach me how to cook. Or perhaps I should say I learned to do the dirty work so that she could cook. Oh my God, could the woman cook! In fact, that's what she did for a living. Being an uneducated mix of Native American and African, she had to do what she was good at, and that was cleaning and cooking. She was what they called a "domestic," cooking for wealthy people who lived in White Plains and Yonkers, New York. There were times when she worked as far away as Connecticut, riding the Harlem-Hudson line as early as 5 A.M. She would cook for her "madam," then come home and cook for my brother and me.

Grandma taught me that I had to earn my keep to stay in her house. I was too short to reach on top of the stove, but I could stand on a wooden milk crate at the sink. She taught me how to clean the gook out of the back of the chicken and pull the slimy stuff from under the skin. She taught me how to dip the feet into a bowl of hot water and peel off the crusty outer layer. I was deathly afraid of chicken feet, but I learned to keep my mouth shut and hold those nasty feet with a napkin. She showed me how to mix the yeast in hot water when making homemade rolls and how to sprinkle salt and pepper evenly on both sides of the pork chops before I patted them down with flour. All of these were things little girls of my generation needed to know; the problem was, she barked her instructions and never complimented me for doing a good job. Learning and cooking with Grandma was not fun, it was work. It taught me that I should always expect to work hard for everything I needed or wanted, and that work was not supposed to be fun. Surprisingly, I love to cook, but I must admit, it is serious business in my house.

On my father's side my great-grandfather was a second-generation share-cropper married to a Native American. Together they had 16 children; thirteen survived. My grandmother, the ninth of the 13, was married to a mulatto at 14 and widowed at 15. Some in the family say that she was sold to pay a debt. Others say she was won in a bet. She would never talk about it. My grandmother had one child, my father, whom she left behind when he was just five years old so she could travel to New York and work as a cook. He followed her when he was 12 so that he could go to school in the city and work as a houseboy for my grandmother's employer. On my mother's side, my grandmother was in the second generation born of Dahomian ancestry in this country, the baby of six children. She died when my mother was six years old, and my mother was raised by her older sisters. At age 15, she left home to work for the railroad as a car cleaner. She was working there when she first met my father. She was 29 years old and he was 22, on his way to serve in the United States Army. Somehow, four years later, after he was dishonorably discharged, they got together. I'm not sure if he forgot to tell her that he was married or if she knew and didn't care. I now understand that our life experiences come forth from our souls and that nothing really happens to us; it all happens for our benefit. If it is true that we choose the conditions of our birth and the families we are born into, I wonder why I would choose a family grouping that needed so much and had so little to offer. This is a huge piece of the puzzle. Even now, I wonder what my soul was seeking as I lived through the bad behavior, irresponsibility, and rage of the adults in my life who were supposed to be guiding me.

A little girl needs a nurturing, feminine figure—or a reasonable facsimile thereof—who can usher her into womanhood. I had neither, not that I consciously remember. My mother lost her mother, and my father had the facsimile. What I did have in my life was a collection of women who gave me conflicting messages about who they were as women, and who provided a distorted view of what would be expected of me when I became one. There were a host of other strange and distorted messages I received from both the women and the men in my family, each one an ill-fitting piece of the puzzle. When I was in the room with these people all at once—trying to figure out who had the power and what I needed to do to be safe in their presence—the pressure of it all did severe damage to my sense of self in the world.

The relationship with my grandmother, a woman I loved and feared at the same time, taught me that women must be hard, loud, and mean in order to survive. My childhood relationship with my father led me to believe that men could come and go in your life without rhyme or reason, and that when they showed up, you needed to be on your best behavior to hold their attention. After my mother's death, my father abandoned me. He was "around," but he was not really present with me or for me, his only daughter. I never figured out if he didn't want to be or if he just didn't know how. I needed emotional support from my father. I needed to know that I was loved, protected, and valued by him in my mother's absence. More important, I needed to know the truth; his truth, mine, and my mother's. My father was either unwilling or unable to stand in the truth, much less tell it to me.

I think my grandmother was a huge piece of that puzzle. Just like me, my father knew that if he said the wrong thing, in the wrong way, at the wrong time, Grandma would have a screaming hissy fit. If he spoke too soon or too loud, she would go after him with her mouth as though he were a cheap cut of tough meat. When she did, he would sit in a kitchen chair with his legs crossed while she paced back and forth in front of him. The foot of whichever leg was crossed would be shaking back and forth at the same pace as Grandma's speaking. When she pressed him for a response, he would grab his head saying, "Please, Ma, please." Or, "I don't know, Ma, please." The only time I ever heard my daddy raise his voice with Grandma was the day my brother and I moved out. Not only did he raise his voice, he pushed her away from the door so that we could get out.

I know I was five years old because I was excited about going to school like my brother Ray. I also know that it was summertime because Ray and I were home alone; Grandma was at work when Mr. Fletcher came to the door. Mr. Fletcher was the insurance man. He came around every two weeks or so to collect money from Grandma. He was very tall, and he always gave me and Ray a lollipop. On most of his visits, he would meet Grandma on the front steps of our building. On this particular day, when Ray and I were home alone, Mr. Fletcher walked right up to our apartment door and knocked.

Grandma always left us with strict instructions not to open the door for anyone. But this was Mr. Fletcher. I knew because he knocked and announced himself. When I heard his name, I must have had visions of sucking on a red, orange, or even a green lollipop. Ray didn't move. So, without guidance from my older brother, I went to the door. I said that Grandma wasn't home. Sweet old Mr. Fletcher told me he had some papers for her. In an effort to be helpful, I dragged a kitchen chair over to the door, turned the lock, got down, and welcomed Mr. Lollipop like I had good home training.

Mr. Fletcher didn't come in. He handed me the papers, instructed me to give them to Grandma, and then said, "Now lock the door. I'll stand here to make sure."

I wanted to ask him for a lollipop, but since he didn't offer me one, I knew better than to ask. When he heard the lock click, he said again to make sure I gave the papers to Grandma, and then he was gone.

When Grandma came home, I was so proud of myself, she was hardly in the door before I jumped up and shoved the papers into her hands. It took her a moment to catch on.

"Did your daddy come here today?"

Ray was mum. I told her no.

"How did you get the papers from Mr. Fletcher?"

I remember that was the exact moment that Ray left the kitchen.

"I opened the door but I didn't let him in." I explained everything just as it happened, but it didn't help. As soon as I spoke the last word, a hand went up and came down right across my face. Everything that followed was an out-of-body experience. I remember that I went to bed that night without dinner. I know because Ray managed to hide a piece of his dinner roll under his shirt. He gave it to me when he was sure that Grandma would not discover him leaning over my bed.

Maybe a week or so later, a pretty lady came to pick me up. Her name was Nett, which was short for Lynnette. I had met her on several occasions when Daddy took me and Ray for a ride in his car. She was one of the many ladies he took riding with us. She was always nice to me, and she smelled really good. Nett was my father's wife, my stepmother, and my relationship with her became my saving grace. Nett accepted, nurtured, and encouraged me. What she could not and did not do was stand up for me. We loved each other deeply, but she taught me to love in secret in order to keep the power of our love alive.

On this day, Nett had come to take me school shopping. When we talked about the experience many years later, she told me that she wanted to give me a bath because I had a slight odor. To her surprise, when she removed my undershirt, she also removed most of the skin from my back. She was horrified, and I was petrified because it meant that I would have to tell what happened. I told her about the Mr. Fletcher incident and how Grandma beat me with the ironing cord until my back was raw. I begged her not to tell my daddy because Grandma said if I did, she would throw me out of the kitchen window, down into the alley with the dogs. I did not want to be eaten by the dogs.

But Nett did tell my daddy what had happened. Within hours, I, my brother, and all of our clothing and toys were packed. We were about to leave when Grandma came home from work. There was yelling and screaming. I saw something I had never in my life seen before: Grandma crying. As Daddy pushed her away from the door so that we could get out, she fell to her knees crying and begging: "Please, please, take her but don't take Ray! Leave him with me, please!"

Daddy yelling! Grandma crying! These were new and totally confusing experiences. So was moving into a one-bedroom apartment where my daddy came home every night and where Ray and I slept on a pull-out couch. I had never seen one of those before.

‡‡‡

Once he moved us into the one-bedroom apartment, Daddy gave us all strict orders that we were not to let Grandma in—ever! On most days, I could look out of the living room window and see her standing outside, watching the house. Sometimes she would wait by the school playground for me and Ray to get out of school. She never spoke to us, and we acted like we didn't see her. Ray would grab my hand, and we would skip by her as if she were a light post. Grandma would follow us, walking a half block behind us until we got home. Nett worked, so Ray had a key and would let us into the house. We knew to do our homework and watch television until one of the adults came home. I must admit, it felt kind of good to know that somebody was watching us when we were home alone, even if it was Grandma.

We only lived in the small apartment for a few weeks. After that, we moved into a two-bedroom apartment where Ray and I shared a room. We each had a twin bed, a nightstand, a dresser, and a lamp. We had to share the closet, which I didn't mind because there was enough room under the clothes for us to hide from each other.

Ray was my hero whom I absolutely loved and admired. When he wasn't preoccupied by his asthma—a real and ever-present threat to his life—he was a sweet, gentle spirit who could always make me laugh. He felt things very deeply, but because he was a boy who was supposed to be tough, he rarely showed his gentle side. Instead, he seemed to steel himself against the world, against everyone and everything in it. He rarely smiled and he never cried; his eyes told the story.

When he was frightened, his eyes would become glazed and fixed. It would look as if the fluid in his eyeballs was frozen because his eyes were so shiny and still. When he was upset or angry, he would squint as if trying to find his way out of a dark room.

He did this a lot when Daddy lectured him about being tough and not acting like a sissy. After one of those lectures, Ray would push me away and tell me to leave him alone, as if I had done something wrong. No matter what I offered or how much I begged him to tell me what was wrong, he would refuse to speak. This would go on for days until something, I'm not sure what, softened his heart again. When his heart was open, Ray was the only place I could find comfort. The thing I remember most about my brother Ray is his compassion. After I got slapped or snatched for doing or saying something out of line at Grandma's house, I would go sit by Ray. If no one was looking, he would let me rest my head on his shoulder and cry. A few times, he even put his arms around me and kissed my cheek. If, however, we heard Grandma's footsteps coming, he would disentangle himself from me and act like I wasn't even there.

I remember one Halloween—I must have been six or seven years old—we had not seen or heard from my father for several days. To keep us occupied, Nett dressed us in Halloween costumes she created from old clothes. Ray had on a suit that was six times too big for him, one of my father's old hats and a pair of his shoes. I had on one of my stepmom's old dresses, accessorized by some old jewelry, high-heeled shoes, and a purse. The thing that excited me the most was the lipstick. My stepmom covered my cheeks and my lips with red lipstick. I looked fabulous. Absolutely so! We were allowed to go trick-or-treating through the four floors of the apartment building we lived in. We each had a brown shopping bag, and by the time we visited every door on every floor of our building, the bags were filled to capacity.

We were sitting in the middle of the living-room floor, still dressed in our homemade costumes, sifting through our goodies when Daddy came home. He took one look at us and said to my stepmother, "What the f—— is going on? Why does she look like that?"

She was explaining to him that it was Halloween and she had let us go out for trick-or-treating in the building. He looked me dead in the eyes and said, "Come here!" He didn't say a word to

Ray. I walked over to him proud as punch in my dressed-up-like-a-lady costume. I may have even been smiling until he grabbed my cheeks with his hands.

"Why do you have all of that crap on your face?"

I wasn't sure what crap he meant. Surely he wasn't referring to my lipstick! Before I could say a word, which probably would have been the wrong word, he released my face with a quick snap of his wrist, jerking my head to the side.

"Wash that shit off your face."

I looked at my stepmom for support. Scurrying, she took me by the hand and we rushed off to the bathroom where I was stripped back down to my normal self. Daddy told Ray to get that mess out of the middle of the floor and go to bed. By the time Ray came into our room, I had my pajamas on. Before turning off the lights, my stepmom whispered, "Don't worry, I'll save the candy for you. I'm really sorry."

I could hear them talking on the other side of the closed door. It would all have blown over silently, like everything else in our house, if I had just stayed in the bed like Ray and gone to sleep. But I had another brilliant idea.

On my first trip to the bathroom, I saw the lipstick lying on the side of the sink. I wanted that lipstick! I wanted to look pretty again. I couldn't figure out what to do with it, so I went back to bed. On my second trip to the bathroom, I found exactly what I needed to activate my plan—a flashlight. It was hanging on a hook behind the bathroom door. I'm not sure how I got it down, but I did. I took it and the lipstick back into the bedroom with me. I figured that if I got under the covers, I could use the flashlight to help me put the lipstick on, and I could sleep in my beautiful Halloween face. *Brilliant!* When I got back in bed, however, I realized I could not see my lips. A mirror! I needed my stepmom's small hand-held mirror. That necessitated a third trip to the bathroom—one trip too many. Just as I snagged the mirror, one sudden move sent the half-full bottle of Listerine crashing to the hard, cold tile floor.

"What are you doing?"

I didn't answer. I heard the kitchen chair screech across the linoleum floor. I fled the bathroom, jumping across the shattered glass, made it into my room and jumped back in my bed, knowing full well that all hell was about to break loose.

"What the hell are you doing?"

Even before he saw the broken Listerine bottle, I am sure he smelled it. I don't think he even stopped in the bathroom. He came straight into our room and turned on the light.

"What the f——! Look at you! You've got lipstick all over the goddamn sheets!"

He didn't even mention the Listerine. Instead, he yanked me by my shoulder so that I almost flew out of the bed. He held on to me with one hand while he undid his belt with the other. He was talking, saying something, perhaps reminding me of how disobedient and destructive I was. I couldn't hear him, though; my heart was pounding too loudly in my ears. When the first blow landed, my heart stopped pounding—I needed all my energy to scream.

Now, I have been beaten by the best. Grandma was the best beater in the world. In most cases, she prepared you for her beatings by telling you what she was going to do. She would always describe how she was going to take the ironing cord or the extension cord or the switch and beat you until this or that happened. Daddy's beatings did not come with any descriptive warnings.

The first swing of my daddy's belt was nothing compared to the second, third, fourth, and onward. My daddy beat me for what seemed like hours. He swung his belt with every fiber of his being. It landed on the skin of my young body with the force one would imagine he'd use in fighting a man his age and his size. The only time I got any reprieve was when I slipped out of the clutch of his hand. Trying to get away from him, I would head straight for the corner of my bedroom where the radiator sat. Inevitably, I would run into it, burn my leg or arm, and head back in the other direction, giving my daddy the opportunity he needed to grab hold of me again. My daddy beat me until he started sweating. Swinging wildly so that he missed me as often as his belt connected with my flesh, he beat me until all the furniture, except the beds, was scattered throughout the room. He beat me above the pleas of my stepmother to stop before he killed me. When one of his wild swings missed me, it hit her. My daddy beat me until his pants fell off. And then he stopped, not because I was barely conscious, but because someone was knocking—no—banging on the door.

The neighbors had called the police. Somehow, my stepmother got them to go away without coming in. I don't remember where she found me. I do remember waking up in the bathtub with her crying over my bruised and battered body. I don't remember if I was still crying. I do remember that my entire body was throbbing and one of my eyes was swollen shut. I remember because there was a cool washcloth lying across that side of my face. I also remember the exact words Nett spoke when I was conscious enough to hear:

"Why do you have to make him so mad? Why can't you ever do what you are told?"

If I live to be 100, I will never forget those words. I will never forget lying in that bathtub, with the scent of Listerine lingering, beaten to within what felt like an inch of my life by a stark raving lunatic and believing it was my fault. And I did believe it.

After all, I did get lipstick on the sheets.

The beating was only one aspect of the devastation I experienced that Halloween night. At some point, I must have sought refuge under my bed or Ray's bed. What I saw when I looked up is etched into my mind even now: my older brother, my hero, crouched down in the closet, with most of his body hidden by the clothing hanging above his head. His head was resting on his knees. At one point, our eyes locked. If my eyes were communicating anything, it was, *help me!* Which of course he did not—he could not. Like I said, it is one thing to get a beat-down. It's a whole other thing when the beat-down is silently witnessed by your hero. That turns the beat-down into a slaughter.

Pathology. What causes a grown, unemployed man who hasn't been home in four or five days to come home and violently, viciously beat his baby girl? Perhaps he wasn't grown up all the way. Perhaps my childhood was a shadow of his own, in which he was stuck. Perhaps it was the pressure of being a man who didn't have a job, couldn't get a job, and had two kids and a wife to feed. Perhaps it was just a diversion to avoid my stepmother's questions about where he had been and why. Maybe. Maybe not. Could be. Who knows?

Puzzle. What causes a grown, employed woman who has accepted a child born during and outside of her marriage to the child's father, who has agreed to rescue that child from being battered, to hold that child responsible for her battering? Perhaps it was the pressure of working for very little and stretching it a long way to care for children who were not her own. Perhaps she had just been glad that *her man* was home and my shenanigans had ruined her plans for the evening. Or perhaps they were both crazy—just so plumb crazy with their own grief and guilt and anger and sadness and woundedness that they had to inflict pain on somebody. What I do know is that the depth and breadth of physical, psychological, and emotional wounding I experienced could have only been inflicted by people who, if not insane, had definitely run *out of sanity*.

Pieces. Fifty-something years later, I can still feel and hear and smell and taste the bloodiness of that beating. It wounded me in places that were too deep to bleed, places that allowed parts of my self to leak out. That Halloween fright night taught me lessons I would spend half of my life trying to unlearn. Each time my father drew back his belted hand and violently, vengefully brought it forward to make contact with my body, he taught me that love will hurt you, and men will beat you, and somehow it's your fault. This was a lesson that I could not, would not escape for a long time, but my brother did. He escaped and he watched; probably grateful that it wasn't him being brutalized; probably convinced that he never wanted to have anything at all to do with my father. Maybe he really wanted to help me and didn't know how. I married two men who were just like that—men who wanted to be men but just didn't know how. That Halloween beating defined an aspect of my sense of self that I took into every relationship, with every man and every woman for the better part of my adult life. Like so many children who are brutalized, abandoned, and neglected, I came to believe that who I was and what happened to me didn't matter. It didn't matter to the people who hurt me, and it didn't matter to God.

I made certain other decisions about myself and life that night. I decided that I was unlovable. No one who was loved would be treated in that way, and no one who loved me would do that to me. Or would they? I also decided that men could do whatever they wanted and get away with it. That's why the police left without a real investigation of the facts. In fact, my father got away with what he had done because my stepmother made an excuse for it. So I learned that I too had to make excuses for men who treated me badly. I learned that it was best not to expect a man to help me, defend me, or stand up for me. If my brother couldn't do it, wouldn't do it, *who would?* Another big lesson I learned from my stepmother that night was to do whatever was required to keep the peace.

After the police left, she didn't take me into her bed so she could nurse my wounds and rock me to sleep. It would have been soothing for me to sleep with Nett on the pullout sofa in the living room, like we did some Friday nights when we watched movies. But we didn't. Nor did she tell me to "move over," like she sometimes did, and curl up next to me, pulling me close so that I would feel safe in my own bed. Instead, she went into the bedroom with my father and shut the door. My brother told me what it meant when we heard the rhythmic thump-thump, thump-thump on the wall of our bedroom that was connected to theirs. I listened to those thumps and then to the silence because I was afraid to go to sleep. Somewhere between the time the police left and the time the sun came up the next morning, I must have decided that even when a man treats you badly, you still have to sleep with him.

A lot of things changed after we moved into the bigger apartment. Daddy was still writing numbers, but he started to get arrested. Once, the police surrounded him when he was getting out of his car. Ray and I were sitting on the fire escape; we saw the whole sordid affair. They threw Daddy against the car and searched his pockets. I guess they found what they were looking for, because they shoved him head first into the police car and drove away. Another time, Daddy was leaving a neighbor's apartment after collecting a bet when the police stopped him in the hallway and carted him off to jail. Nett told us that all the people in the building pitched in to pay Daddy's bail. When he came home later that hot summer night, people sitting around outside applauded. That was the first and only time I was proud to be his daughter.

That pride didn't last long. One day shortly thereafter, Ray and I were in our room watching television when we heard knocking—no—banging at the door to our apartment. The door came crashing in and Daddy came running down the hallway with several white police officers in pursuit. Ray headed for his favorite place, the closet. In a short time a whole lot happened: The front door was lying on the floor, Nett had been slammed into a wall and had a huge bruise rising up on her forehead, most of the rooms in the house had been deconstructed, and Daddy had been taken away. Miss Brooks, our neighbor from down the hall, grabbed me as I was biting the police officer who was swinging Nett around by her hair. As Miss Brooks carried me out into the hallway, I noticed that Ray was already there. She took us to her apartment down the hall and made us tea.

Mr. Rootman, Daddy's friend who owned the candy store down the street from Grandma's house, came by Miss Brooks's apartment. He brought treats for me and Ray and a huge wad of money for Nett. Then he dropped a bomb. The word on the street was that Grandma had turned Daddy in to the police. I'm not sure I understood what "turned him in" meant, but from the names Nett called her on the telephone, I knew that what Grandma did *could not* have been a good thing. I also knew that no one would ever do anything about it. Adult mistakes never bore any consequences in my family.

Shortly after Daddy went to jail, my brother and I went to live with Nancy and Lee. We knew them as our aunt and uncle, although I found out much later that they were not related to us by blood. Nancy was my birth mother's best friend. I was told they were like sisters. Although Nett told us it would only be for a few weeks, two months at most, we ended up living with Nancy and Lee just short of six years. In that home, my new home on a nice quiet street in Brooklyn, I learned how to physically and emotionally fight for my life. I learned how to fight the quiet, dirty fight that many women fight to stay in painful relationships. Unfortunately, my young mind became confused about the messages I received, and I ended up creating the exact same negative scenarios in my life that the adults modeled for me. In fact, one day I realized that the apartment I lived in with my physically abusive husband had the same exact floor plan as the apartment where I experienced the Halloween horror. The pathology had manifested in a very concrete way.

To be a good fighter,
you have to be stripped down to nothing.
A fighter is trained to forget what they
know and who they are outside of the ring.
Once a fighter is stripped down,
they can be built up by one voice;
The trainer's voice.
And it is assumed that the trainer
has the fighter's best interest in mind.

CHAPTER 4

BLIND IN ONE EYE . . . CAN'T SEE OUT OF THE OTHER

Secure the children first! It is the responsibility of every parent and every adult to ensure that the children in their care are safe and secure. What I am referring to goes way beyond feeding, clothing, and washing behind a child's ears. What I mean is that adults, I believe, have a God-given responsibility to make sure that all children over whom they exercise authority are guided, nurtured, and protected from harm—all types of harm. Unfortunately, in far too many instances this never happens.

Aunt Nancy and Uncle Lee were pillars in our family. Unlike my parents, they had been married forever. They had one child, a girl, my older cousin Bunny. She became my make-believe sister. Aunt Nancy was short and very round with a sweet round face. She looked like a walking, talking pumpkin. She was a stay-at-home mom who took in and cared for other people's children during the day. Today she would be called an entrepreneur with a home-based day care. She wasn't a stranger to me, because I had spent many afternoons at her home before I started going to school. Uncle Lee was a mystery. He was tall and very thin. He barely looked at me when he spoke, and when he did, I could hardly hear him. In all the time I had been in his company, I'm not sure he had ever spoken ten words to me, or to anyone else for that matter.

Aunt Nancy and Uncle Lee owned their own home with a finished basement and a backyard in a multi-ethnic, working-class neighborhood in Crown Heights. Their home was the place where most relatives wound up when they were going through difficult times. No one ever explained their family ties. Yet I was expected to give all of these people access to my head and heart; to treat them like intimates although I didn't know who they were, where they came from, or why they were a part of my life. I also had to do what they told me to do and trust that their intentions toward me were honorable.

Uncle Lee was a school-bus driver, a functioning alcoholic, and a creature of habit. He went to work at 4 A.M. every school day to drive wealthy children in the Flatbush section of Brooklyn to their small private school. While the children were in class, Uncle Lee doubled as a cook. At 3 P.M., he drove the children home. He was home every evening at 6:20 P.M. to flop down into his old recliner in front of the television set. He ate his dinner in that chair, watching television as if his life depended on it, until he fell asleep. Day in, day out, that was his routine, until Friday. Friday night was a totally different story. On most Fridays when Uncle Lee came home, he was rip-roaring drunk. He would stagger in the house, singing loud and off key. If he made it to his chair, he would sit there cracking corny jokes and trying to tickle everybody who passed by him. If he didn't make it to the chair, he would plop down wherever he fell to sing his songs and tell his jokes. Aunt Nancy would push him away when he grabbed at her while they exchanged affectionate hugs and kisses, and she always laughed at his jokes.

At some point, Friday nights changed and everything else followed suit. Uncle Lee stopped coming home after work on Fridays. When it first started happening, Aunt Nancy would sit in the window, waiting for Uncle Lee's car to appear. Sometimes she would cry. Other than that time Grandma was pleading with my daddy not to take Ray away, I had never seen an adult cry. I knew that my own tears were usually attached to some sort of physical pain; I had learned long ago not to cry when I was sad or disappointed or when someone hurt my feelings. So watching Aunt Nancy cry made me very uncomfortable. It gave me a funny feeling in my chest that sometimes made it hard for me to breathe.

One Friday, after several hours of sitting in the window, Aunt Nancy called a taxicab. This was huge! We never took a taxi anywhere unless it was an emergency; besides, we had a car. Well, actually, Uncle Lee had a car. The only thing she said to me was "Come on!" I scurried to follow her out of the door. Without a word to me, Aunt Nancy told the driver where to go. It was an area I didn't know. When we arrived, she told him to slow down so we could cruise along the block. I saw the car first. I had no clue about what we were doing, so with great enthusiasm and as loud as I could, I shared my discovery:

"There's Uncle Lee's car!"

The cab screeched to a halt. Aunt Nancy peered out the window. The driver asked, "Is this it?"

Aunt Nancy was silent. Finally, she said, "Take me back to Schenectady Avenue."

I was totally confused. I thought we had come to get Uncle Lee. So, I asked, "Why are we leaving? We're leaving the car? Is Uncle Lee coming home?"

Aunt Nancy shot me an icy shut-the-hell-up glance. And I did.

Aunt Nancy had discovered, through "wifely investigation," that Uncle Lee was seeing another woman. Although I only heard bits and pieces of their whispered conversations, I am sure he denied that he was having an affair. I suspect that Aunt Nancy knew the truth, but it must have taken her a while to get the information and inspiration she needed to address the problem head-on. Unfortunately, she was not mindful of what she was teaching me in the process of her own learning.

When we got home after the taxi ride, Aunt Nancy went back to her perch at the window and told me to go to bed. It was hard for me to figure out what was really going on or how to feel about it. I knew there was trouble brewing but I could not tell who it was that was in trouble, crying Aunt Nancy or absent Uncle Lee. Like most children caught between two troubled adults, I made it all about me. Somehow, in my mind, I felt it was my responsibility to make things better.

At some point in the wee hours of Saturday morning, Uncle Lee finally came home. Drunk. I heard glass shattering in the kitchen, my cousin Bunny's voice, then my brother's voice. My curiosity and fear brought me to the kitchen door. There was a human minefield on the floor. Aunt Nancy was on top of Uncle Lee. Uncle Lee was entangled with Bunny, my brother had a foot— not sure whose—in his hand. My first instinct was to laugh, until I saw the blood. Aunt Nancy was cussing and clutching something in her teeth. It was a hand; Uncle Lee's hand. This was a knock-down, drag-out fight between two people who supposedly loved each other. This was a mess! A confusing mess! And because I was the one who saw Aunt Nancy crying, the one who rode in the taxi and saw Uncle Lee's car, somehow this was all my fault.

Children are often required to clean up the mess that adults make, even when the adults show no concern at all for how their messes infect children's lives. After everyone was separated, Ray and Bunny and I set about administering first aid. I focused on Aunt Nancy because she had the least blood flowing. I rescued her wig from the doorknob and attempted to apply a wet facecloth to her swollen, bloody lip. I handed her the wig and she promptly threw it across the room at Uncle Lee, calling him a string of filthy names that told the whole story for us children. Bunny was crying and dabbing blood from her daddy's head where the glass or *whatever* had made contact with his skull. One of Uncle Lee's eyes was hugely swollen and both his lips were bleeding. He was so drunk he could hardly speak, though he kept trying.

Not a word was spoken about the events of that night, but they became the weekend pattern. Uncle Lee would not come home on Friday. Aunt Nancy and I would take a cab ride to locate his car. When Uncle Lee did come home, drunk, Aunt Nancy would attack him, beat the mess out of him, and then patch him up. After the first two or three fights, we children stopped interfering. Instead, we would wait until they were both asleep, curled up against each other, and then clean up the mess. On Monday, it was back to work, to school, to childcare, to preparing dinner, as if the weekend had never happened.

I'm not sure when Aunt Nancy became "my mother" or when Uncle Lee became "my father" or when my cousin became "my sister." I do know it was a gradual transition that made me feel somewhat more secure, yet sad at the same time. I knew that my brother and I had come to the family refuge because my father had gone to jail, not because he didn't love or want us. But when I realized that my father had been released from jail several months after we'd been adopted into Aunt Nancy and Uncle Lee's family, I wondered why he or my stepmother didn't come to take us back home. I discovered he had been released from jail the day he drove by my aunt and uncle's house without stopping. I ran down the street screaming like a lunatic, assuming he had not seen and couldn't hear me. By the fifth or sixth time it happened, I resigned myself to believing that it wasn't him; it was just a car that looked like his. I knew that was a lie, but anything else would have been too crushing to consider.

Sometimes Daddy would call and say he was coming to pick us up to take us out. Aunt Nancy would scrub us down and dress us up, and then we would wait. Several times we waited for him and he never showed. After a while, my brother refused to wait, and on the rare occasions that Daddy did show up, Ray refused to go with him. I wasn't so easily angered. I kept waiting. Usually, around 9 or 10 P.M., my aunt would make me a sandwich and tell me to take off my clothes and go to bed. In that house, bed seemed to be the place you went to avoid talking about anything.

Although I am sure that my stepmother thought leaving me at Aunt Nancy and Uncle Lee's house would provide a stable and secure environment while she ironed out the difficulties of her own household, my tenancy there was anything but stable. I had already learned from Grandma that home was a violent place where unexpected outbursts of rage were to be expected. Now, in my new temporary home, with my *make-believe* parents and my *make-believe* sister, I was learning how to live a lie. I am not referring here to the "open your mouth and don't tell the truth" kind of lying. I am referring to the "see what is going on and act like you don't see it, lie-to-yourself" kind of lie; the silently brutal kind of lying that distorts your sense of self and worth. What I learned from the pillars of stability in my family was the "act like you are okay and everything is fine" kind of lie that is the foundation of emotional dishonesty and self-deception. It became a pattern that stuck with me.

Living with my aunt and uncle, I needed attention, affection, and affirmation. I needed to know that I was safe from harm both inside and outside of the house. But the adults were too busy mismanaging their own lives to realize how they were dismantling mine. I was a good student in school; I did my work with little or no help, and I always got a glowing report card. What I did not get was any type of reward or acknowledgment. While everything "bad" I did was noticed at Grandma's house, nothing "good" I did was noticed in this place. This only served to reinforce the message that nothing about me was good enough.

Beside the snide remarks about who was or was not my mother or father, the other thing I remember was the "earning your keep" remarks that reminded me to be grateful and that I needed to earn my stay in the household.

My stay with Aunt Nancy and Uncle Lee extended into years. It no longer had anything to do with the issues my parents were working through. Instead, it had everything to do with how useful I made myself. I had to cook, not because I was a girl and it would one day be a necessary skill to have, but because people who were not my parents were spending their money to buy food for me. I had to get on my knees and scrub the bathroom floor with a brush because nobody owed me anything. The only way I could secure *my place* in the place I found myself was to say very little, ask for very little, need very little, and do a lot to make sure that others were satisfied with the way I met their needs. Another pattern.

One good thing about living with Aunt Nancy and Uncle Lee was that I made friends. There were other kids on our block whose home life gave me a glimpse of what was considered "normal." From my childlike vantage point, they had everything I needed and wanted. They lived with their parents. They were kissed and hugged daily, helped with their homework and their problems.

They had siblings who spoke to them regularly and looked out for the younger ones. Becoming involved in the day-to-day home life of my friends not only awakened a deep and desperate yearning in my soul; it gave me a vision of what was possible. Without the model of my friends and their parents, I wonder if I would have ever known what to do with my own children.

No one else was teaching me the things I needed to know. No one explained why Aunt Nancy and Uncle Lee fought on Saturday night, why my father didn't reclaim me, how I was related to these people, or what anything in life really meant to me as a budding young woman. Beyond "work hard, don't ask for anything," "lie about what you see," and "be on the lookout for something crazy to happen at any moment," I received no guidance at all about how to live this thing called life. I wasn't taught anything about money except there was never enough. I wasn't taught about making choices or taking responsibility for myself. I wasn't taught anything at all about giving and receiving love or how to distinguish between love and anything else that showed up bearing the name of love. In the absence of guidance I made up my own explanation about almost everything, including myself.

I remember confiding my pain and devastation to a friend the first time I broke up with the man who would become my third husband. She tried her best to help me pull myself together. In the midst of our conversation she asked me, "What would your mother say to you? What did she tell you about how to make it through a broken heart?"

My brain instantly turned to bacon sizzling on a barbeque. I realized that not one of the women in my life had ever talked to me about anything I would face as a woman. I had learned about my menstrual cycle from a friend the day it started. No one ever talked to me about boyfriends or, for that matter, how to be a friend. I got no instruction at all about my body, my mind, or my heart. I never considered, not even once, that a relationship could end and you would move on. I thought I was supposed to do what I had seen the women in my family do: put up with the crap and fight it out as required. Bunny took me to Woolworth's to buy my first training bra, my first bottle of nail polish, and my first eyeliner, but she never once talked to me about the subtle and not-so-subtle requirements of *being* a woman. *I knew nothing!* Absolutely nothing about how to interact with men or other women, other than what I had made up on my own from watching the dysfunction of the adults who moved in and out of my life. They had failed me miserably and somehow it was my fault.

Bunny, my make-believe sister, was the divine exception to our dysfunctional household rules. She introduced me to worlds that I could have never imagined. Bunny was a dancer with a very diverse group of friends who all adored me, and she took me almost everywhere with her. When they were dancing, I followed along in the back of the room. One of the group would always come back and help me get the steps right. From them, I learned classical ballet, modern dance, and my first love, traditional African dance. Through them, I met Katherine Dunham, Alvin Ailey, Arthur Mitchell, and Chuck Davis. These were Bunny's friends and colleagues. They were my aunties and uncles. They were the bright lights of my life.

Bunny danced with Michael Babatunde Olatunji at the New York World's Fair in the African pavilion, and whatever she learned there, she taught me. In addition to the dance and art of this powerful culture, specifically Yoruba culture, I learned their spiritual philosophy. I learned that African people did not see or worship God the same way American people did. For Africans, God was everywhere, in all things, at all times present, alive in everyone. God had many names, because God took on many forms in order for people to know, worship, and honor God. Bunny explained to me that there really was only one God and that when you took culture into consideration, God had to resemble the people who were worshipping. That's why, she said, Buddha was Asian and Jesus was portrayed as white. This meant there was a God that looked like me: brown and female.

It all seemed to make sense to me back then. Grandma's God wanted to smite me like she did. Bunny's God wanted to dance, sing, and make me happy like Bunny and her friends did. What didn't make sense to me was why God didn't stop the madness in my life. Why didn't God smite Uncle Lee for drinking too much and fighting with Aunt Nancy? Why didn't Daddy get his eyes plucked out for demeaning Ray and beating me? Why didn't God fix Ray's asthma and stop Grandma from being so mean? Despite what Bunny told me, I not only had a distorted concept of God, I had a dysfunctional relationship with God. I learned to pray to God *for* things, not *about* things, promising to gain God's favor by what I would do or stop doing. I had no real idea about what, who, or where God was. I only knew that when I thought I needed God, I mean really needed God to help me, God was nowhere to be found.

It wasn't until the pathology of my family of origin had become a life-threatening disease in my mind and heart that I realized, if not for a loving, merciful, and omnipresent God, I would never have made it out alive. I spent three-quarters of my life believing that God had abandoned me before I discovered that I had abandoned myself. That was the pathology. It was the pattern that I followed. It was what I had been taught and, like I said, I was a very good student.

‡‡‡

You simply cannot pay the debts that come along with believing you are unworthy. Unworthiness always puts you in debt to anyone and everyone who shows you the slightest degree of attention or love or energy. Eventually, in this form of bankrupt relationship, your benefactors will demand or expect more than you are able or willing to give. This is the precise moment they will choose to call in the loan.

I had just swallowed the last drop of soda when I heard the commotion in the kitchen. I shoved all of my loot under the bed and jumped to my feet. I wasn't as concerned about what was going on in the kitchen as I was about someone finding my loot— my stolen loot. I had taken some money from Uncle Lee. I had done this many times before, but I always limited myself to coins; fifty cents here, thirty-five cents another time. But today, he was so drunk and he had so many dollar bills hanging out of his pocket, I had helped myself to five whole dollars and treated myself to all sorts of goodies that I did not want to be discovered. Ray was holed up in his room. Bunny was off dancing and Aunt Nancy was out playing cards. Hopefully Uncle Lee was still too drunk to notice that the money was gone. Maybe. Maybe not.

Uncle Lee had fallen down in the kitchen. He was trying to pick himself up by the time I got there, and I kept my distance. I had come to hate the smell of the stale liquor as it oozed from his body and hung on his breath. Seeming satisfied just to know that he wasn't home alone, he stumbled back to the basement.

When he called me several minutes later, my heart sank. *He knows! He knows I took his money.* I slid my comic books back under the bed and headed for the stairs leading down to the basement with my heart racing and pounding in my ears. When I saw him sprawled out on the floor at the bottom of the steps, I knew he still had no idea about what I had done.

He wanted me to come down and talk to him. He also wanted me to bring him some of the pickled pig's feet we had in a jar in the refrigerator. I couldn't figure out which was worse—touching a pig's foot or sitting close enough to Uncle Lee to inhale the stench of liquor. *Lucky me!* I was about to have both of those experiences! I thought about telling him the pig's feet were gone and making him a sandwich instead. But stealing and lying in one day was too much even for me, so I fished two big, juicy feet out of the jar and put them on a plate with some potato salad. Throughout my tenancy in that house, like when Aunt Nancy stopped speaking to Uncle Lee but still made me fix him a dinner plate, I had been taught to *be nice to the men no matter what.* So I put the plate, a napkin and silverware, and a nice tall glass of iced water on a tray and carried them down the stairs into the basement to serve my make-believe father, Uncle Lee. All the way down the stairs I prayed that he would not ask me about the money.

He had made it to the sofa. I placed the tray on the coffee table, carefully avoiding his drunken gaze. I would not give him an opportunity to detect any guilt in my eyes.

"Sit down baby. C'mon. Sit down here and talk to me."

He was patting the sofa cushion next to him. Walking around the coffee table, still being careful not to look directly at him, I could see him bite into one of the pig's feet out of the corner of my eye. The vinegar from Uncle Lee's tasty treat; the stench of the liquor hanging in the air; the guilt of being a thief; it was all causing my stomach to flip and me to gag.

"Why don't you eat this one?"

Uncle Lee extended the other pig's foot in my direction. *Does he expect me to take it with my bare hands?* Before I could, he dropped it; right on the sofa, between his legs. Rather than use his hands to retrieve his lunch, he grabbed me by the wrist. Instinctively, I pushed him with my free hand, which gave him the opportunity to grab my other wrist. Something was very, very wrong, but I couldn't figure out what it was. The mixture of scents flowing into my nostrils, the queasiness in my stomach, and the strange smile on Uncle Lee's face had rendered me feeble-minded, drained of all defenses. My face was too close to his. His tongue had no business being in my ear. Why was his foul-smelling, sticky mouth on my mouth? The more I twisted and turned to get away, the tighter his grasp became. I could feel my body become rigid just before it went numb.

"Stop fighting me. Don't fight me. We're gonna have some fun. I'm gonna show you how to have fun."

My blouse was torn. My panties were ripped. His weight was smashing me into the sofa. His breath was foul. His calloused hands were groping at my private parts. He was hurting me; ripping my insides apart. He was punishing me for taking his money, and there was nothing I could do but lie there, numb and guilty, listening to him say that he loved me.

I am not sure where my mind went; I just know that when it left, I was able to escape the stench, the pain, and the guilt. I wondered what my father would do if he knew this was going on. I wondered about the whispers I heard from the adults that Nett was not my real mother. I wondered if Ray was sleeping or if he would come downstairs and discover what was being done to me. I wondered where he would run to, where he would hide. There were no closets in the basement. I wondered how long I had been lying there and if I would be the one who would have to clean the pig's-foot juice off the sofa.

Somehow, I found myself in the upstairs bathroom sitting in a tub of water. I wasn't sure what to do about the blood floating around my body or the excruciating pain in my head. Since there was no one at home that I could ask about these things, I just wondered. I remembered the vomit under the kitchen table. I would need to clean that up. I also needed to stop the bleeding. It had stained two fresh pairs of panties already. A big wad of toilet paper did the trick, and it stayed in place while I cleaned up the kitchen floor. I was sitting on the edge of the bed, holding the cat, half out of my mind when Aunt Nancy came home.

All the fighting I had seen in that household finally paid off. I knew I had to fight for myself. This could not—no—would not happen to me again. *Not ever!* No stench of liquor in my face! No tongues in my ears! No ripping of my insides ever again! I told Aunt Nancy what drunken Uncle Lee had done to me. At first she just stared. After what seemed like forever, she turned on her heels and headed for the basement. I was still clutching the cat to my flat chest when I heard her call my name. I decided not to take the cat with me just in case any violence erupted. The cat had been through enough of that and so had I.

"Tell him what you told me!"

I wasn't sure if it was a request or a command. I did know that it was torture. Alternating between glancing at Aunt Nancy and staring at the empty liquor bottles on the bar, I gave my account of what had taken place. I had the ripped blouse and the bloody panties to prove it, but I hoped it wouldn't come to that. It didn't. Not because Aunt Nancy believed me and took me into her arms to console me. No, I didn't need my evidence because Uncle Lee denied it. He denied that he hurt me. He denied that he penetrated me, whatever that meant. Aunt Nancy just stared at him without indicating whom she believed or what she planned to do. Then, without a single word of anger toward him or the slightest gesture of comfort toward me, she said simply:

"Go to your room. Go on and go to bed."

The house remained silent for the rest of the night. There was no yelling. No crashing of bottles or furniture. There was no music, no television, no running water, nothing. Just silence for as long as I remained awake. The next day the silence continued, and for many days after that it hung in the air. That silence stripped me of my dignity. That silence destroyed my sense of worth. That silence huddled over me and the entire household for the next four years, until a few months after Aunt Nancy died.

My stepmother knew. Somehow she knew. We were sitting in the Horn and Hardart automat when she looked at me and asked:

"Did Lee ever touch you? Did he ever do anything nasty to you?"

The silence had rendered me deaf, dumb, and blind. Suddenly, I could hear again. I could see and smell again. I just couldn't understand why no one had said anything to me until now.

"Did Uncle Lee ever put his hands under your clothes or anything like that?"

I could feel my head starting to move from side to side, indicating no. I didn't want to say no, but my body seemed to be responding automatically. I was shivering and shaking my head from side to side. Nett stared at me. She told me that she was my friend. She told me that I could trust her. She told me that she had seen the way he looked at me and that she didn't like it. I could feel something strange going on inside of me. Finally, I knew that it mattered, that I mattered. I was so relieved. But my head was saying no and my mouth was screaming:

"Stop it! Stop it!"

Who was I talking to? To Nett? To Uncle Lee? To the silence that had followed me like a stench? It wasn't making any sense. I wanted to tell her the truth. I wanted to tell her everything, but the pattern of lies had kicked in, the pathology of *act like everything's all right* had flared up, and both of these were fighting my deep need to trust this woman who I really believed cared about me.

As I wailed and trembled, Nett helped me to my feet and into the ladies' room. Once there, I dropped to my knees and crawled into a corner. Nett crawled with me. She sat with me and rocked me. Several women who came in and saw us offered us tissues. Other women came in, saw us, stared, and left. We sat and rocked for a long time.

The next day Nett sent me back to Uncle Lee's, told me to pack, promising that she would be there to get me before nightfall. She kept her promise. After a brief conversation with Uncle Lee and Bunny, we packed all of my belongings into the trunk of a taxicab and left my temporary home forever. Ray joined us two weeks later.

*You don't throw away a whole life
just because it's banged up a little.*

— Jeff Bridges' character
in *Seabiscuit*

CHAPTER 5

TERRITORIAL INVASION

Many of the families in my neighborhood had television sets in their living rooms or kitchens that did not work. One family I knew sat the working television on top of the broken one. Others used the broken set like an end table to hold knick-knacks or framed pictures. I always thought it was bit odd to hold on to something that was broken rather than throw it out and get a new one. Then I thought about my family. When you inherit a broken family, you can't throw it away and get a new one. What you can do is find people and situations that provide for you what your family cannot. Or if, like me, you are convinced that you are worthless and unimportant, you can seek out people and situations that strengthen the pathology and the patterns that your family set in the first place.

Being back at home with Nett seemed almost normal. My father was still writing numbers and struggling to survive on the streets of New York. Off Track Betting had been established in New York State, which meant that people could now bet on the horse races legally. This cut the street numbers game almost in half, and my father's income along with it. He was home during the day and gone most nights. Grandma had found her way back into my father's good graces, although no one explained how. Now she was in our home several days a week preparing dinner and doing laundry while Nett was at work. Although she was still abrupt and abrasive, she never put her hands on me, or perhaps I never gave her the opportunity; I stayed at least two feet away from her at all times. When she did raise her voice, I braced myself, ready to make an Aunt Nancy or Uncle Lee Friday-night move against her if the need should arise.

I was busy with school, dance classes, and trying to find my sense of self as a budding teenager. In the summer, I had already met, fallen in love with, and become obsessed with the man who would eventually become my third husband. When the summer ended, we went our separate ways, and I met another young man, a grown man. Teddy was 19, almost 20. He lived on the top floor of our apartment building. I was so awestruck when he told me that I was attractive, I let him take me into his bedroom while both of our mothers were at work. At the age of 13 and a half, I discovered that I was pregnant. Of course, by the time I made the discovery, Teddy had disappeared. I lied about who the baby's father was. Didn't matter. I was still a disgrace to the family and fodder for neighborhood gossip mongers. Grandma said she knew it was going to happen sooner or later. My father never said a single word.

Nett was devastated, but she didn't yell or call me names. Instead, she told me that I needed to finish school and that she could not afford to take care of a baby. She told me how hard it was just to keep a roof over our heads and food on the table. She reminded me how small the apartment was and how expensive babysitters were. She asked me why I hadn't talked to her about having sex. I had never talked to any adult in my life about anything. Why should now be any different? I just listened and cried. Nett talked and cried. That was as close as I had ever felt to any member of my family—and we weren't even related by blood.

Nett found a foster home for unwed mothers in Jamaica, Queens. She came to visit almost every Saturday during the six months I lived there. I gave birth to Tracy three weeks after the assassination of Dr. Martin Luther King and immediately turned her over to the foster-care system. Six months later, Tracy died and a piece of my soul died with her. SIDS. The foster-care agency tried to explain it to me so that I would know that no one had harmed her. Back then, they had no real explanation. Like so many other times in my life, I had to suck it up and move on with very little information and virtually no support.

It took almost three years, but I managed to get myself involved with another transient young man, Gary, a 19-year-old athlete. Gary was another forbidden fruit— something I wanted and could not have. He was handsome and aloof and only paid attention to me when no one else was around. It took me a while to figure why he didn't speak to me when he was with his friends. By the time I discovered that he had another girlfriend, I was two months pregnant and just completing the eleventh grade.

Gary saw our son three times: once when Damon was born, again when the child was three months old, and the last time the day before he married another woman. In fact, I only discovered that he was getting married when his soon-to-be-wife called to inform me that my son would always be welcomed in her home. She wanted her Gary to be a good father to his children so that he would be a good father to their children. I wasn't sure if she was being kind or sarcastic. Didn't matter. *Another fantasy destroyed!* I had allowed myself to believe that once I had the baby, Gary would want me, he would choose me, and we would live happily ever after. Instead, it was like waiting for my father all over again. It was the same lesson I'd learned throughout my childhood: Men will hurt you, and when they do, you must make excuses for them. Men will abandon you, but you mustn't say a word about it to anyone. If you do everything that men want, need, and ask of you, and if you submit yourself to them for their pleasure and just act like everything is okay, maybe they will stay—maybe.

As a young child, I knew nothing about the law of karma; living with Grandma, however, taught me a lot about the law of cause and effect. I learned that there was something about me that caused Grandma to be either upset or angry. The effect of her emotional turmoil was usually some act of violence against me. All the while she was disciplining me as she called it—giving me a beat-down as I called it—she would be asking God to fix me, change me or, take the devil out of me. She would tell God how hard she was trying, and how disobedient and hard-headed I was. The beating was one thing; but the mental conditioning about the person I was created a lasting impression. The principle of cause and effect meant, if it was happening to me, I somehow caused it. When people treated me badly, somehow I deserved it.

Over time, I decided that I had to take my verbal or physical punishment without question or complaint, because there was something in me that just made people mad. This, I decided, was the explanation for my disastrous relationships with men. There was something wrong with me that made them all leave. The missing piece of the puzzle was that I didn't know what was so wrong about me or how to fix it.

In today's world, there is a great deal of controversy over the use of the *N-word*. There is a split decision over whether it is a term of endearment or an overt sign of disrespect. In our families there is another N-word that is rarely discussed, although its effect devastates parents and children alike. *Neglect.* Physical, emotional, and psychological neglect cripples more children than any hip-hop liner notes ever written. It is a form of passive abuse when a person responsible for a child's care and upbringing fails to safeguard the child's emotional and physical well-being. And whether caused by poverty, carelessness, or a chaotic home life, child neglect tends to be more common and more chronic than other forms of abuse. Often, because it is so subtle or because there appear to be logical explanations for caregivers' behavior, it goes unrecognized. Often, because harm to the child is not the intended consequence, those who do notice are hesitant to interfere.

My early life was a series of emergencies that, under the strict guidelines of child welfare today, would have landed someone in jail and me in a foster home. Back then, it was considered nobody's business outside of the family. It didn't happen all at once; there was no single trauma that broke my heart, ripped holes in my spirit, or shattered my sense of self. But the repeated instances of neglect, violence, rejection, and deception left a gaping wound in my soul that everyone knew about and no one acknowledged.

The wounds inflicted on children by adults, passively or actively, are so much more than just devastating—they are debilitating. They sap the strength and vitality of the innocent child's heart and mind. They weaken the child's will to live and grow. They distort and deplete the child's God-given right to explore the possibilities of life and experience the joy of living out his or her own divinity. Unable to negotiate the behaviors and hypocrisies of the unavailable and unaccountable adults entrusted with their care, children feel inadequate, ineffective, and victimized as they move through adolescence and into adulthood. I cannot speak to the effect on male children other than what I saw in my brother. Ray died at the age of 49 from a heroin overdose. He was addicted to drugs and alcohol from the age of 16 until he took his last breath. As a female who endured abuse and neglect at the hands of unconscious adults for most of my childhood, I can say without one shred of doubt that it was only the grace of God that saved my sanity.

I can also say that I was almost 30 years old before I realized that I was insane, and 50 years old when I actually became sane. I spent 20 years discovering patterns and solving the puzzles that I inherited. Today, I understand that each of my family members contributed to my soul's purpose. It didn't feel good back then, nor did I know it until much later, but who I am is a function of who they were in my life. I realize that my story, my history, was a *divine setup* to usher me into who I would become.

I was a neglected child. There was a persistent and consistent ignoring of my need for nurturing, encouragement, education, and protection. Other than to correct or punish me for some act of childhood innocence, I was categorically rejected by my father, my grandmother, and even my brother. I'm still not sure if it was active, meaning they meant to do it, or passive, meaning they didn't know how not to do it. I can honestly say that when I was 30 years old and my father took his life, he had never kissed me. I was always fed and clothed, but I was also physically abused and terrorized. For Grandma, I was a problem that needed to be fixed; for Aunt Nancy and Uncle Lee, I was a burden to be endured; and for my father, I was a responsibility that could be ignored, set aside, and ultimately cast off on someone else.

Back then, adults, particularly adults with little economic means and great financial responsibilities, accepted poverty and family discord as normal. Unlike today, children were not expected to tell anyone what went on behind closed doors. You didn't tell, because you were warned not to tell. You didn't tell, because you were ashamed—of yourself and of your family. I was ashamed of not having parents with the same last name, and I was ashamed about whatever it was that was wrong with me that made people treat me so badly. I was ashamed of what I had become and what I was becoming: an ugly, abandoned girl/woman who so desperately wanted to feel loved that I slept with boys and men who treated me badly, who would ultimately leave me for someone prettier, better, more lovable, or for no good reason at all.

One puzzle piece I discovered early on in my spiritual journey was that unconditional love was never a part of my childhood. This absence made me desperate to prove to myself that I was loveable. I did not want to be like the teenage girls from the projects, had been knocked up and abandoned by some teenage projects boy. Oh, no! I was different. Yes, I had been knocked up and abandoned by my first child's father, but it was different. His parents didn't want him to be with me. I was, they said, too dark. It wasn't his fault. Didn't matter. I was desperate to prove that there was somebody, a male somebody, who wanted me and would stay with me. He was a gorgeous black man with a potentially brilliant future and a stable income. His name was Carl. After meeting only once, we had a love-by-mail relationship for two years during his tour in Vietnam.

I hadn't received a letter from him in four months when he suddenly showed up on my doorstep, engagement ring in hand. We courted for the next three months. He seemed to get along well with my son. He was a gentle soul like my brother, and he seemed to genuinely like me as a person. Didn't matter. I simply wanted to know and feel that I was acceptable in someone's eyes. As long as he could spell his name, tie his shoes, and didn't drool in public, he probably would have seemed normal to me. I thought that marrying a military man would propel me into a truly enviable position of respectability.

Three days after my lovely little church-house wedding, I packed up and moved to Georgia with a husband I hardly knew.

He had reenlisted for two more years as an Army engineer and was even thinking about becoming a career military man. By the time I discovered that he was addicted to heroin, I was pregnant and he was in jail. So much for happily-ever-after. We had been married for a brief four months when my new husband was arrested, convicted of burglary, and sentenced to three years in prison. I was evicted from our Army-base housing, and the monthly allotment checks stopped coming. Within six weeks, I found myself alone in Fort Benning, Georgia, with my two-year-old son, racing to get out before the marshal came to sit my furniture on the curb. I had $37 in cash. Nett sent me a bus ticket back to the extra bedroom in her home in the Brooklyn projects. When I stepped off the Greyhound bus, she reached for Damon, taking him from my arms to hug and kiss him. Then she took one look at me and announced, "You're pregnant." I hadn't had a clue.

On my second day back in Brooklyn, I headed straight to the abortion clinic at Kings County Hospital, the free hospital for poor people. I had no job, no money, and no more military-sponsored medical insurance. Terminating the pregnancy seemed like the economically responsible thing to do. I remember being proud when I checked the box for "married" under marital status. *Yeah, that's right! I'm married!* There was no need to mention that my husband was an incarcerated substance abuser. I was happy just to be beyond the judgment and speculation of whichever clerk would process my paperwork. I knew what those people thought about the likes of me: poor, black, teenaged, with one baby and another one on the way. They probably thought I didn't even know who the baby's daddy was. In my case, however, a little "x" in the married box would surely raise an eyebrow or two. And it did.

"Where's your husband?"

No "what is your name?" No "what is your address?" Just: "Where is your husband?"

"He's in the army." I was lost in my own fantasy.

"Oh, so you have medical insurance. Why didn't you go to the base hospital?"

"Well, it's been discontinued."

"Why is that? Is he out?"

"He's been arrested and falsely accused of something he didn't do." I really thought that last part would give me a leg up. It did not.

"Have you applied for welfare? You need to apply before you have the procedure, and you may not have time."

Suddenly, that "x" in the married box had no meaning whatsoever. The clerk asked and answered most of her own questions as if I weren't even there. She reached into a bin next to her desk, handed me a hospital gown, and pointed to where I needed to change before my examination. In one fell swoop, my greatest fears had fallen into my lap. I wasn't any different than the others. I told myself that somehow I was worse.

When a woman contemplates an abortion, all of the traumas in her life ricochet inside of the life growing inside her body. Abort her. This is what I planned to do to my precious jewel, my Gemmia. Though you couldn't tell it from looking at me, my emotional framework was twisted and disjointed from a lack of stability, security, and safety. I went through great pains, and even more spray starch, to make sure I looked crisp and clean and to give the appearance that my head was screwed on right. The truth is, despite the fact that I was a mother and a wife, my spine was weak and my head was haunted with dark thoughts and beliefs. All of the distortions and dysfunctions possible in a human's life had come crashing in on me, and I was ready to impose my devastation on her. This was not a decision that I carefully contemplated. I thought I had to do it to save myself and my son. I had a husband who had thrown away our future for a dime bag of dope. I thought it was my job to find a way to take care of myself and build a home for our family. I wanted to go to nursing school. I wanted to buy a house. I wanted to be different, damn it! I wanted to move beyond the pain I had known all of my life. Another child simply did not fit into the picture.

On my first visit, my blood pressure was too low for the procedure. The doctor sent me home with three prescriptions and instructions to eat breakfast every day. Two weeks later, after ingesting nine different pills a day and eating grits and bacon or Cheerios every single morning, I marched myself right back to the free abortion clinic. This time I wasn't desperate. I was determined.

"You've been here before?"

"Yes, two weeks ago. I had to take medication to stabilize my blood pressure."

"Too high for the procedure, huh? It's good that you caught it in time. Most of us have high blood pressure, but you are so young."

"It wasn't high. It was too low." My God! She was still answering all her own questions.

"No, I have not applied for public assistance. Once I get this taken care of, I am going back to work."

"Well, you should be about 22 weeks now. You may have to wait."

Wait for what? I wasn't waiting for anything except to get out of there as quickly as I could.

Then the next blow landed. The doctor explained that I could not have the simple procedure, the D and C, or dilation and curettage, the surgical abortion procedure used to terminate a pregnancy between 13 and 15 weeks' gestation. I was too far along. I would need to have an induction abortion, in which salt water or potassium chloride is injected into the amniotic sac, causing the fetus to expire. Once this occurred, I would deliver the dead child by a natural vaginal birth. This procedure could not be performed until I was 24 weeks along, since the fetus had to be fully formed. They also told me that I might feel the first flutter or movement before that. Damn!

I think I walked home. Or maybe I took a cab. I do remember picking up my son from the neighbor's apartment and weeping at the kitchen table, holding him on my lap. I remember his sweet voice telling me, "Don't cry, mommy," while he patted me on my back, arm, and head as I had so often done for him.

When my stepmother arrived home from work, my face was swollen and my eyes were bloodshot. "What the hell happened to you?"

I told her what I had learned at the hospital earlier in the day. Without saying a word, she retreated to her room to change out of her work clothes. We ate dinner in silence, except for the few words she said to Damon. I needed someone to talk to, someone who could navigate me through the terrain of my racing mind. But while I washed the dishes, she went into her room and closed the door. I perched myself on the windowsill, staring at the passing cars and people until the wee hours of the morning. I had learned that the window was the place to sit when you had trouble in your life.

In the morning, my stepmother emerged from her bedroom crisply starched and ready for work. She made our morning coffee without a single word to me. No girly chatter that morning. Damon seemed thrown off by the silence, too. He ate his Cheerios and drank his orange juice while talking to himself. Finally, as Nett opened the door to leave, she spoke. These, I thought, would be the words of wisdom, comfort, and support. With her hand on the doorknob, her voice distant and firm, looking me squarely in the eyes, she said quite simply:

"If you do this, I will never speak to you again. Do you hear me? Never!"

Six months later, on the Friday before Mother's Day, I gave birth to a healthy baby girl, Gemmia, which means "my precious jewel." She was 6 pounds, 13 ounces, 19 inches long, born in an inter-uterine position, with her legs bent upward instead of downward. Her feet were resting on her shoulders instead of dangling below her waist. When I unwrapped her blanket, you can't even imagine the horror. I thought that my child was deformed. It was punishment for what I had planned to do to her. Unable to face the reality of having not only another child, but a deformed one to boot, I made up that this was not my child at all. There must have been some mistake! They had confused my child with someone else's, and *I did not want this baby!*

One of the more compassionate nurses told me not to worry about her legs. She said this was quite common and showed me how to bend the legs back into place. She assured me that with two weeks of this exercise, the legs would stay. She was absolutely right! And those strong, sturdy, beautiful legs carried me through most of her life. This little girl, who almost didn't make it into this lifetime, born with legs that bent the wrong way to a mentally and emotionally fractured mother was more than just another human being. She was an angel in disguise. She taught me about life, about myself, and about the power of unconditional love. All that she taught me gave me a life. All that she taught me cost her her life.

‡‡‡

Every Sunday morning, in a place beyond the beyond, the place commonly called heaven, the Creator, known to all as God, hosts a weekly Sunday brunch. The guests are all of the souls becoming. For the souls becoming, the Sunday brunch is a really big thing. Besides the tasty dishes and the live music that God provides, this is where the souls becoming sign up to live human lives on earth.

A soul becoming is the true essence at the center of every human being. It is the spark of divinity that keeps all human beings connected to God. At the divinely appointed time, a soul becoming takes on a life assignment—a life—and agrees to become a living demonstration of the nature of God in human form. Within its life assignment, the soul becoming will encounter one or more learning agreements to help it become a stronger and wiser *being*, more useful and pleasing to God. At the Sunday morning brunch, God provides details on the latest life assignments available. A soul can choose to stay in heaven with God or sign up for a life on earth.

All of the souls becoming know that fulfilling the learning agreements of a life assignment according to God's specifications is a good thing. They also know that the minute a life assignment begins, the soul forgets its learning agreements. The soul must work very hard to maintain its connection to God or risk being overwhelmed by the experiences of the assignment. When that happens, well, let's just say it is not a good thing. Successfully completing a learning agreement requires skill, and building skills requires the right tools. So God provides every soul becoming with the tools it will need, in the form of principles. Using these *principles* in the right way at the right time supports a soul in developing a good human character and a heart that remains connected to God.

The air is filled with anticipation as the souls becoming wait to find out if there are assignments suited to the skills they have and the lessons they still need to learn. Every life assignment provides a soul with the opportunity to shine in the world, and all souls love to shine. It is for this reason that some souls are recycled through many life assignments. These are known as advanced souls, and they get to stand at the front of the brunch line. They also get the best courtyard seats. It's not that God has favorites, oh no! God loves every soul in the same measure. It's just that an advanced soul has learned a lot about life and is eager for the opportunity to learn more. An advanced soul knows that life can be a joyful process. An advanced soul also knows that if it is to experience joy in a life assignment, it must learn and live the truth: God's truth that is buried alive in each and every soul. Once a soul becomes a being, the truth has a way of becoming very elusive.

Since time has no meaning in God's plan, the Sunday morning brunch takes the equivalent of two days. In that period, God details hundreds of thousands of life assignments: the country in which the assignment will begin; the language the soul will need to speak; the race and gender the soul will express; and the challenges the soul will face. When a soul hears the assignment it is called to, a light goes on in its heart center. In that moment, the soul receives a name, and the name is planted in God's heart.

On Sunday evening, in a personal consultation, the soul becoming is imprinted by God with specific instructions about the gifts required to shine brightly in the state of being human. God also whispers in the soul's ear about the particular principles it must master and the skills it must perfect to joyfully navigate through the process ahead. The principles, God cautions, will be revealed in a variety of ways, not always obvious. Recognizing them is absolutely essential to living a fulfilling life, a life that pleases God. Before the consultation ends, each soul is blessed with God's love and instructed to use it in every situation it encounters. Love, the soul is told, is God's healing balm. Love is like super glue! It maintains a soul's connection to God. It overrides every possible error a soul can make. And God's supply of love can never be diminished, no matter how much is used.

One Sunday morning, God read an assignment that involved a man we'll call Festus and a woman we'll call Lullabelle. They were married or in some other kind of intimate relationship. They were also, consciously or unconsciously, willing and ready to bring forth a new human being named *you*. Festus and Lullabelle lived in your hometown. They were your race and nationality. They had everything required for the soul-becoming-human that was you to create a life that was pleasing to God. Festus was a fireman, a police officer, an army lieutenant, an unemployed construction worker, or whatever your earthly father was or is in his life. In God's eyes, Festus was a beautiful, loving soul, becoming a better human being through his relationships and experiences with life and with you. Although he tried very hard, things did not always turn out the way Festus thought they should. This upset him very much. You see, like all souls becoming, Festus forgot his learning agreement. Then he became overwhelmed by the experiences of his life assignment and lost his connection to God. In the process, he also forgot the instructions that God had imprinted on his heart about you and his relationship with you. Lullabelle was not much better off. Although she did things in a very different way, she also forgot much of what God had told her about becoming human. Their loss of memory created the lesson you came to life to learn.

On another bright and sunny Sunday morning, God read another life assignment involving a man named Horace Lester Harris and a woman named Sahara Elizabeth Jefferson. My soul, an advanced soul, was sitting very close to God when this life assignment was offered. God made clear that it would be a very difficult assignment, because there were lessons that needed to be mastered rather than just learned. My soul knew that accepting this particular life assignment would mean some suffering and a great deal of loss. It also knew that the experiences I would have were necessary for the fulfillment of God's plan—that I would teach other souls to learn to trust, have faith in God, and love unconditionally.

My soul joyfully accepted the assignment to be born through Horace and Sahara knowing that Sahara would not live long, leaving me to be raised by a grandmother who would abuse me and a father who would abandon me. My soul was aware that one of God's angels, in the form of a stepmother, would be at my side to help me. My soul was well aware that I would become confused about my identity, lose my connection to God, and forget why I had come to life in the first place. This is how life becomes a puzzle. Thank goodness my soul was also clear about two important things: First, that I would eventually regain the faith and trust I was born with and turn back to my Creator for instructions; and second, that I would live to fulfill God's plan for my life to the best of my ability. My soul also knew that in the process of becoming human, and in response to some of my human experiences, I would believe that I had become what many human beings refer to as a *victim*. My soul knew better.

I did not grow up knowing that I was an abused child. I was well into my adult life when I realized that I had been neglected. In fact, I was 30 years old when someone explained to me that anytime an adult male forces himself onto a child sexually, it is considered rape. I didn't tell Aunt Nancy because I thought it was wrong. I told because I didn't like it, it was painful, and because I simply was not willing to endure the smell of stale liquor forced upon me just to keep a roof over my head. Children are flexible and adaptable. They adapt to their environment with or without the labels. They learn what to accept and what to expect in response to what they see, hear, and are taught. I don't believe that children who have no parents wake up each day bemoaning their fate or calling themselves orphans. Even those who have known the joys and security of a well-established family life will adapt to whatever the next day brings and offers them, even if it means that the family they once knew has disappeared. Children are simply innocent, willing souls.

I believe that God has placed in everyone the desire to live and know life in its fullest and most glorious expression. Children *want* to live and learn and grow. They are excited and intrigued about the wonders and mysteries of life. It takes children quite a while to realize when the people around them are not behaving in their best interest. How can they know? Children will love the most imbalanced people and adapt to the most dysfunctional situations. I think it is because children hold on to some memory of what they heard God whisper into their souls.

In many cases, children aspire to be just like the people who raise them. In other cases, like mine, they want to be anything and anyone other than the people who raised them. They get lost in the process of trying to be themselves while trying not to be like someone else. For a great deal of my life, I did not know who I was, but I knew who I would not be: Grandma, my father, Aunt Nancy, or Uncle Lee. I also knew that my children would never have to experience what I had experienced. That, I decided, was *unacceptable!* I had no idea that their souls had assignments and lessons just like mine.

Gemmia spent the first six months of her life crying. She cried all day and most of the night. She cried if I held her, she cried if I laid her down. Most days she cried until she was hoarse and fell asleep, I think to rest her throat. As soon as she woke up, she would eat and begin her cry-fest again. For a long time, I actually believed that she was crying because her father was absent. I thought that this young, innocent soul was crying about that loss because I refused to cry about it. Or perhaps she was communicating how I had felt during the entire nine months I carried her. Grandma said that she was probably going to be mean. I knew better than to listen to her. On most days, once I knew that Gemmia was dry and fed, I had no choice but to let her cry. I never yelled or became annoyed, although there were days I would turn the television up to its maximum volume to drown her out. My son had a better idea.

I always let Damon help me hold, change, and feed his baby sister. He was amazed by her little feet, and it didn't bother him at all that she was screaming her head off most of the time. I also gave him very clear instructions that he was never to touch the baby unless Nett or I was around. One day, I was doing laundry in the kitchen, Gemmia was crying as usual, and I thought Damon was watching *Sesame Street*. Suddenly I realized that it had been several minutes since I heard Gemmia. I figured she had fallen off to sleep, but I also thought I needed to check on her just to make sure. As I left the kitchen on my way into the bedroom, I noticed that Damon was not sitting in front of the television. S——! My walk became a trot up the short hallway. At the bedroom door, I saw Damon standing on his tippy-toes peering into Gemmia's bassinet. He turned with a burst of excitement, saying, "Baby no cry. Baby no cry, Mommy." He was right, but the reason why was horrifying!

Over the edge of the bassinet I could see Gemmia's little hands and feet flailing. I also heard a slight gurgling sound. Upon closer inspection, I saw that she had a mouthful of pennies. Damon had taken pennies from the dish I kept on the nightstand and dropped them into his baby sister's open mouth. The child was choking! As quickly as I could, I flipped her over onto her stomach and patted her back. One by one, the pennies fell out until I could hear that familiar sound. Gemmia was crying again. Cradling her in my arms, I scolded Damon. Through the tears he continued to inform me: "Baby no cry, Mommy. Baby no cry!" He spent an hour in the corner. Gemmia took a nice long nap and woke up without a sound. Whether it was the shock of almost choking or some mysterious healing power of the copper, I would never know, but from that day forward, Gemmia was a model child. That is, until she learned how to dress and undress herself.

Gemmia was both a picky eater and a neat freak. When she learned how to feed herself, she ate one grain of rice or one green pea at a time, and she chewed everything according to the dietary recommendation—50 times. On most days, she would just be finishing lunch when it was time to start dinner. She didn't mind sitting alone in her high chair, chewing and entertaining herself for as long as it took to complete her meal. Any meat on her plate had to be presented in neat little squares. If the edges were jagged or if the food was piled on her plate, she would not touch it. Gemmia did not eat anything with her fingers because she would not, under any circumstances, get food on her hands. And if for any reason she ever dropped food or gravy or spaghetti sauce on her clothes, she would take them off and deposit them on the floor next to her chair.

We had a lovely front yard, and often I would put Damon and Gemmia outside to play while I washed dishes or hung laundry on the clothesline. Checking on the children every ten or fifteen minutes, I frequently found Gemmia in the yard stripped down to her panties. All it took was for her to get a drop—and I do mean a drop—of popsicle juice or a smudge of dirt on her shirt or shorts. She just couldn't stand it! She would take all of her clothes off and put them in the trash can or the bushes.

Some mothers might be concerned about some of the weird behaviors Gemmia displayed. I was just glad that her legs were still straight. However, when she started eating her hair, I must admit, I got a bit worried. She had the habit of sucking two fingers, the pointer and the third finger. While engaged in deep sucking, she would grab hold of one of her braids and twist back and forth until it broke off in her hand. When it did, if I wasn't watching her closely, she would pull off one or two strands of the hair and eat it. Now, that was weird! Before I actually figured out what was happening, my baby girl had bald patches all over her head. Once I did figure it out, I didn't know what to do about it. Gemmia's godmother, my best friend at the time, Ruth Carlos, figured it out during one weekend of babysitting.

Ruth discovered that Gemmia didn't always eat the hair. Most often she rolled it into a tiny ball and massaged it with her finger-tips. Ruth called it fuzzy. Gemmia loved fuzzy! The bad news was, we never figured out why she wanted it. The good news was, we discovered a wide variety of sources for fuzzy—old blankets, sweaters, even carpet, if picked or shaved, produced lovely little balls of satisfying fuzzy stuff. I shaved every old sweater, sock, and blanket

I could find and kept those balls in a plastic baggie that I carried everywhere in my purse. When the fingers went in the mouth, a fuzzy ball came out of the bag. Like a Motrin works on a headache, Gemmia stopped pulling her hair out. Nine months later, she also stopped sucking her fingers. I kept the fuzzy just in case.

You might ask why I went to such great lengths to indulge a child in such a nasty habit as pulling out and eating her hair. My first response is that I remembered how many of my childhood needs went ignored and unmet. I was determined to give my children whatever they needed to feel welcomed, wanted, and loved. My second response: *guilt!* Having come as close as I did to aborting my child only to have her turn out to be such a joy in my life, I felt guilty each time I looked at her.

Gemmia was truly my precious jewel, despite her weird habits. She was affectionate and gentle. She was quiet and reflective. She had a memory like a steel trap, and she was potty trained in less than a month. She got along famously with her brother, and when my third child, Nisa, was born, Gemmia was her surrogate mother—holding her, feeding her, watching over her like a hawk. And Gemmia also took great care of me. She loved to rub my feet and hands and kiss my cheeks. She was the only one of my children who would crawl into my bed and cuddle with me. She learned her alphabet with little or no help from me by watching *Sesame Street*. Damon taught her how to count, which she mastered before first grade.

Gemmia never talked much. Even as a child, she was not chatty. As an adolescent, she limited her responses to three or four words. The most I heard her say to her brother or sister was "Leave me alone!" or "What are you doing?" Or the classic "Get out of here!" In fact, she was so quiet, I frequently repeated things I said to her, unsure if she'd heard me the first time. "I heard you," she would say. But it wasn't snippy or curt. It was simple, soft, and matter-of-fact: *I heard you.* It was classic *Gemmia-ese.* Her manner was always gentle, easy, and pleasant. I recognized early that there was something really special, masterful, about her.

It wasn't until much later in her life that I realized there were a lot of things I did not know about Gemmia. It wasn't that I wasn't interested. It wasn't that I was being neglectful—or was it? It was just that my own life was often so chaotic, I never thought to ask my children about their likes or dislikes, their needs or their desires. Damon and Nisa were very vocal. They had so many questions and opinions; they would not be denied my attention. Gemmia, the middle child, often seemed to get lost in the melee of my life and the needs of her siblings. She didn't present any problems, so I didn't look for any. She was also the dependable one. I could always count on her to do exactly what I asked her to do, when I asked her to do it. In that way, she was very much like my brother. Unlike me, he rarely, if ever, got disciplined for not following instructions.

When my life became unbalanced, Gemmia became the assistant mommy. She was more than willing to help with dinner or housework. She was also the one that the other children would listen to; using as few words as possible, she would reason with them and convey the importance of what she was saying. I often heard her say things like "You know what she's going to say" or "You know how she feels about that." I assumed she was referring to me. Those were the same words my brother had often used to warn me about Grandma. However, I knew when Gemmia spoke them, it was not from a place of anger or fear about what could happen if things did not line up with my expectations. She was speaking them, I thought, from a place of loving concern. Gemmia offered me the support I had never had in my life. I leaned on her the way I imagined Aunt Nancy leaned on me. *Oh my God! The pathology!* The patterns! I was just beginning to recognize them, and now they were spreading throughout my life. My children living through what I had lived through. It was totally unacceptable! And I was totally unequipped to do anything about it. Instead, I did what I had been taught to do, what I had seen done all of my life. I acted like I didn't see it, could not hear it, and did not know what was going on.

On the way to get away from where you are,
you can run so fast that you miss the blessings
along the way. By the time you realize that
you have missed them, a major portion of
your life has taken place without you.

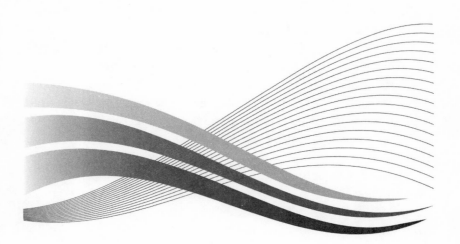

CHAPTER 6

THE DIVINE SETUP

Like so many people, I had done a great deal of living before I recognized my own healing needs. For the better part of my life, I had no clue that my beliefs about myself, men, money, and almost everything else on life's menu were playing out as the experiences I lived. It was as if I couldn't believe in or receive anything good in my life. When it did show up, I was usually the one who did or said something that was sure to make it go away. And nowhere was my inability to create and sustain solid relationships more evident than with my children. I was a great provider, and at the same time, a horrible mother.

My children were two-year stair steps. When Damon was six, Gemmia was four and Nisa was two. This chronology had its benefits. Damon could talk and explain what his sisters were doing, while the girls were close enough to share clothes. As they got older, it also meant that they could look out for each other. I ran our household like a boot camp—the higher rank was responsible for the lower rank, everyone had specific duties, and when one got in trouble, they all got in trouble. There were routines and we always followed them. We ate breakfast, lunch, and dinner at the same time every day. We shopped on Thursday, we did laundry on Saturday, and we ironed our clothes on Sunday evenings. In my mind, thanks to Grandma, it was just the way things had to be.

If we were going on a family outing or an errand, the children would get washed and dressed first. In the winter, they would sit in the living room and watch television while I got dressed. In the spring and summer, they could go outside in front of the building until I was ready. There were two rules they had to follow. The first was, do not get dirty. Dirty children did not travel with me! The second rule was, do not let me look out of the window and not see all three children together. Disobedient children did not get to go anywhere with me.

One hot Saturday, I decided the beach would be the best place for us. I made sandwiches and laid out everyone's clothes. Following the routine, the three of them got dressed and went outside. I got caught up in a telephone call and took longer than expected to get myself ready. After showering, I peeked out the window to see if they were in place. They were not. I didn't think much of it at the time; after all, they had been out there over an hour. But when I was dressed and went to the window again, none of the Vanzantlets were in sight, and I could feel the rage brewing. I loaded up the car, then issued an ear-piercing yell and waited: 30 seconds, 60 seconds, 2 minutes. No response. Now I was really pissed! Not only had they broken a rule, but it was hot and I was ready to go. I walked around the building in the blazing sun, screaming their names one at a time. After ten minutes, I snatched the bags and blankets out of the car and stormed upstairs. *We're not going anywhere! If they think I am going to spend my time and money on them having fun when they can't do what I say, they are crazy!*

Finally, I decided to go and fetch them, knowing there would be hell to pay. I walked around the block twice. No one had seen them. I walked to the park on the corner. They weren't there either. This was defiance, pure and simple, and it was going to cost them! I wiped the sweat from my face and neck, trying to figure out where they had gone. They must be in someone's house! Which of the neighbors would they go to? I was walking back toward the building, trying to compose myself enough to knock on the neighbors' doors, when I saw it: Nisa's foot, sticking out of a row of bushes in front of the building. I recognized the little white sandal with pink flowers on the front.

Those crumb snatchers have been hiding from me! How dare they! I stomped my way over to the bush ready to grab an ear, arm, foot, whatever I could get my hands on. This was no laughing matter! I was ready to do battle with these three little children, who were eight, six, and four. It would have been a slaughter, a verbal slaughter, because I never spanked them. I did far more damage with my mouth. Parting the bushes, I was prepared to let them have it when I noticed that it wasn't just Nisa. All three of them were lying on the mulch behind the bushes, asleep. Damon jumped up first, his eyes as wide as saucers. When he stood up, Gemmia's head, which had been resting on his legs, hit the ground with a thud. She popped up from the ground like a jack-in-the-box and smashed her body against the wall. Having parted that bush as if it were the Red Sea, I was not at all prepared for what was staring back at me. I saw the terror, the sheer terror in their eyes. In that moment, I realized that my children were afraid of me.

It took me less than ten seconds to realize that while waiting for me to get off the telephone, they had sat down on the cool mulch behind the bushes to get out of the sun and had fallen asleep. Damon knew he had to say something, so he did. "We're not dirty, Mommy. Nobody bothered us. Did you think something had happened to us?" His words cut through me like a hot knife through butter, because the thought had never entered my mind.

I believe there are some things about mothering that are innate. Then there are those things that you must be taught in order to know how to do them. Mothers are meant to nurture and support their children. These were things I did not know how to do. I did know that those in your care had to be fed and kept from harm. I did know that children needed to be disciplined and that they had to do what you told them. I knew that children's needs, their safety, and their well-being had to come before all of the common craziness that often occurs in the lives of adults. I had no clue that an encouraging word and a positive affirmation was required to keep a child's heart and mind open. I thought the most positive thing I could tell them was everything they were not supposed to do and everything they did wrong.

I thought I was being sensitive by *not* doing the things that had fractured my own childhood. Instead, I talked them into the ground. One false move, one mistake, one thing left undone or half done meant you would get a lecture—a 20- to 30-minute lecture about how hard my life was, and why it was absolutely necessary for you to do whatever it was I was ranting about. I did not call my children names, but I know that the tone hurt more than the words.

Perhaps they put up with me because no matter how crazy your mother may be, she is still your mother. Perhaps it was because the food was good, the beds were always clean, and above all else, they felt safe and wanted. Or perhaps my children made it through my rough years because of what Gemmia told me many years later, one day when I was beating myself up about all I had not given her.

"Yeah, you acted a little crazy, but sometimes you had to. I know you think you didn't do a good job with us, but I don't see it that way. I saw you as beautiful, proud, and strong. I saw you as trying to raise us alone, working hard to make sure we had food to eat and someplace to live. I knew that no matter what was going on, you would never let anything happen to me, and that was enough for me. What I didn't know was how much you had to learn to do as well as you did."

My first husband met Gemmia for the first time when she was just 15-months-old. It was a brief reunion. Because of his brushes with the law, rather than risk prosecution, he relocated. The next time I saw him, Gemmia was 12-years-old. By the time she was two, I was in a physically abusive relationship. I can only imagine what my children must have thought and felt when they witnessed their mommy being slapped and pushed around and hurt by the man they had been taught to call Daddy.

Gemmia was almost four years old when the beatings began. If the children were in the room, I would tell Gemmia, "Go and get the baby. Take her into your room." She would move immediately, ushering her older brother and younger sister to safety. I tried my best to keep Damon away from my husband when he was being abusive. Damon would often try to protect me. I was afraid that my husband would turn on him. Then, when the violent encounter was over, our lives would continue as if nothing had happened.

When the last violent encounter came, Gemmia was about five years old. I was frying fish for dinner when my husband came home after being gone for three or four days. As soon as I heard his key in the door, I braced myself. The children were just glad to see him. They ran to him, all six feet, two inches of him, and hugged him around the knees. He was focused on me.

"Where did you get the f——g money to buy food?"

I wanted to be amenable, but I was too pissed off.

"Don't you worry about it. It didn't come from you." As soon as the last syllable rolled off my lips, I knew it was a mistake. "Go in your room!"

Confused but obedient, the children scampered back down the hallway. This pushed me from mildly pissed off into *high pissosity.*

"You don't get to yell at my children when you haven't come home in three or four days!"

At that, he started toward me. I kept my back to him and continued tending to the fish. I knew this pattern. I knew he was trying to take the focus off of his absence.

He snatched my hair and pulled me toward him at the same time I was flipping a beautifully browned piece of whiting. He yelled that I thought he was stupid, and that *he knew* I was screwing some dude—which, of course, he'd made up. He promised to take the children and leave me with nothing.

"Nothing? You are nothing! If I was screwing somebody, you ain't home enough to know about it!" That was the best I could muster, and it was too much.

He let go of my hair and grabbed me by the neck. Instinctively, I picked up the hot frying pan and threw it back over my shoulder. Although most of the hot fish grease missed his face, a great deal of it landed on his beautiful black cashmere coat. I tried to duck past him out of the narrow kitchen, but now the floor was covered in fish grease. I was slipping and sliding, he was screaming and swearing.

"Look what you did to my coat! You tryin' to burn me! I'll burn your ass!"

As he lunged toward me, he slipped and fell backwards against the refrigerator. This gave me time to make it into the hallway. I was halfway to the bedroom when he grabbed me by the hair again. I could see the children standing in the doorway of their room when the first blow hit me in the face. I went down. The next thing I knew he was on top of me, choking me. My ears were ringing. I could see dark spots intermingled with bursts of light. *He's trying to kill me. He is going to kill me.* As these thoughts passed through my fading consciousness, a miracle occurred. He started wheezing and fell limp. My second husband suffered from chronic asthma.

Still, I couldn't move, because all 210 pounds of his body were now dead weight on top of me. Damon was at the end of the hallway, crying. Gemmia, standing next to him, looked paralyzed by terror. As soon as I could catch my breath, I whispered, "Get Daddy's medicine. Get Daddy's medicine from my room." Gemmia ran and retrieved his inhaler from the dresser. As she handed it to me, several huge tears fell across her face.

"It's okay, baby. Mommy is okay." But it wasn't okay; that look in Gemmia's eyes was not okay.

As best I could, I got the aspirator up to his mouth and pumped it. He was able to take a long, deep breath, which lightened his weight, and I wriggled out from under him, leaving him lying on the floor gasping for air. I gathered up my three children and hurried them into their bedroom, where I barricaded the door. We all piled on the bed and cried. I guess they were crying for me. I was crying for the horror my life had become.

It took me almost a year to leave that relationship, and throughout that year, I never forgot the look in Gemmia's eyes. I would never have considered myself a woman who put a man before her children, but that is exactly what I had become.

I knew this was a dangerous relationship. Although he accepted, cared for, and often provided for my children, he was jealous and violent as well as unfaithful and deceptive. I had wanted my children to have a father, some father, and he had shown up appearing willing to engage in my fantasy. *What the heck was I thinking?* I was thinking that I could give them what I never had. I was not thinking that I was showing my daughters what they should and could expect from a man. I was not thinking that I was showing my son what men could and should do. I was thinking that I was worthless and unworthy, and I should be glad that some man, even this violent man, wanted me.

‡‡‡

Gemmia was seven years old when I entered college. This opened an entirely new world to me and my children. I worked during the day while they were in school. At 6 P.M., when the after-school program ended, I would pick them up and take them to school with me. My small community college, Medgar Evers College in Brooklyn, was child-friendly. While I was in class, my children would sit on chairs in the hallway, playing or doing homework. This lasted until the middle of my sophomore year, when Damon and Gemmia insisted they were old enough to take care of themselves. They had too much homework and wanted to stay home in the evenings. Damon was 11 years old, Gemmia was 9, and Nisa was 7. With the help of a good neighbor, it seemed possible.

Thus began my experience of parenting by telephone. I would get up every morning, make breakfast, and prepare dinner in advance before I went to work and the children went to school. After school, they would ride the bus home, lock themselves in our apartment, and call me at work. When I arrived at school, I would call home and instruct Gemmia to serve up dinner. My neighbor would check on them to ensure that all homework was done and that they didn't burn the house down. I would get home at 10:00 or 10:30 to find the kitchen clean, the children in bed, and the pots empty. Rarely did they save any dinner for me.

In my junior year, I was elected President of the Student Government Association and spent more time than ever at the college. Around that same time, I also secured a position as dance instructor at my children's school. I got to spend three afternoons a week teaching my own children about the love of my life—dancing. Damon and Nisa had the rhythm and caught on easily. Gemmia, at age 11, had two left feet and a long, angular body that refused to cooperate with the beat. No matter! We made it work.

By this time, my father had left Nett and had four other children; five if you count the one his mistress brought into the relationship. He and his new family lived walking distance from the school. Many evenings after dance class, I would drop the children off at his house while I went off to my night classes. I was grateful that they got to spend time with their grandfather. All of them loved it, especially Gemmia. She was his favorite, and he was the love of her life.

The good news was that it gave my children aunts and uncles they could relate to, and none of them seemed to mind that my father doted on Gemmia. He always wanted to know what she wanted for dinner. He always made sure Gemmia did a little something extra for her homework. He taught her how to type and helped her with her math. If the weather was bad, my father would say, "Leave the kids here tonight." This gave me a much needed break from cooking. It also gave me an opportunity to really get involved in the activities of my office as President of the SGA.

I was working full time, raising three children, and doing all I could to meet the interests of the students at the college—and I was an honors student. For the first time in a long time, I felt really good about myself. I had a 4.0 GPA. I thought I was finally putting my intelligence, talents, and skills to use in a worthwhile endeavor that was sure to have far-reaching benefits for my children. I really thought that, for the first time in my life, I was clear and stable—and that I mattered. The other competing truth was that sometimes I had no idea of who I was or what I wanted. And, at an even deeper level, too often I was still unconscious of the parts of me that were doing everything to gain the attention, acceptance, and approval of my father, who still didn't notice me at all.

I didn't realize what was really going on until I graduated from college, summa cum laude, President of the Student Government, and valedictorian. My three children walked across the stage with me. They had eaten enough frankfurters, pot pies, and crock-pot concoctions over the course of three and a half years to be there. Grandma was there. My stepmother, Nett, was there. My father was not, and neither was my brother. The two primary men in my life and my heart disappointed me again.

Gemmia sensed that something was wrong. Both she and Damon kept telling me how pretty I looked. Later that night, as I lay weeping in my bed, Gemmia came and cuddled up next to me. In her typical quiet voice she said, "I sure wish Grandpa could have been there today. He would have been so proud."

I entered law school when Gemmia was 13. By then, my children were old enough to be excited about what this meant for us all. Damon's assessment was simple and to the point: "Are you really going to be a lawyer? We'll be rich!" I assured him that I first needed to finish law school, and then maybe I would get a decent-paying job. It did mean that we could move out of the projects one day.

Law school was a lot harder than college, and it would take a great deal more of my time. Gemmia told me if I taught her how to cook, she would make dinner. She had picked up a lot by watching and helping me, and although I was not ready to give her full responsibility for the family meals, it just sort of happened. On the weekends, she and I shopped and did the laundry. We discovered together that you really can get a lot of reading done in the laundromat. Things were going along pretty well until November.

Nothing good can come of a 5 A.M. telephone call. It was my stepmother. She felt deathly ill and needed me to come right away. Within 90 minutes we were in the hospital emergency room, where we would remain for another ten hours. The diagnosis was sketchy, and they wanted to keep her for more tests. Thank God for the ragged little Fiat that I had gifted to myself as a college graduation present. It only cost $800, and for the next several weeks, it got me to school, to the hospital, and back home while the doctors pondered over Nett. They had no idea what was wrong.

By the middle of December, the children were practically living with my father. All of my days I spent in law school. All of my nights were spent in the hospital. I talked to the children, especially Gemmia, three or four times a day, assuring them that their Nana was getting better. But it wasn't true.

I dropped out of law school during the Christmas break. Nett was not improving, and the doctors had no idea what was wrong with her. By January, she had had two cardiac arrests, the last one so intense that her two front teeth were broken off as they forced the respirator tube down her throat. Day after day, and through most nights, I sat watching and listening to that machine pump life into Nett's body. I kept praying that she would not die. She was my one guiding light, the only one who ever encouraged me. I couldn't bear the thought of my life without her.

Nett was still in the hospital in March when my father died. When I told Gemmia, she crumpled into a heap on the floor. Losing her grandpa meant that she had lost her first love. Damon was pounding himself in the head, insisting that it was not true. Nisa was clutching me, crying, as I tried to pry Gemmia off the floor. Trying to console my children opened the floodgates for my own tears. I cried with them and for them.

Gemmia became quite a young lady after my father's death. She was pleasant and kind to everyone. She was dependable and self-reliant. And she was the assistant mommy in our household. They listened to her when they wouldn't listen to me. I was a yeller, always in a rush, always frantic about something. Gemmia always seemed calm, stable, and in control of herself. One day, as I watched her helping Nisa with some difficult homework, I realized that not only was this child kind and patient, she was brilliant. It was then that I also realized I had missed most of her development. In fact, I had missed most of her life.

When I think back, my participation in Gemmia's life was like taking snapshots at a picnic: You get a lot of unrelated pictures that have no connection to the whole. I do remember that she loved to read. I can see her sitting somewhere in the house reading whenever I called her to do a chore or run an errand. Damon was always pulling on her or poking her to try to get her nose out of a book. Yellow was her favorite color. Blue was her next favorite. She loved chicken, but she absolutely hated peas. As an adult, she often teased me about the psychological and emotional damage I caused her by forcing her to eat so many peas.

Looking back, I can see that Gemmia loved anything and everything that I loved. I loved music. She loved music. I loved to sew, and although I never took the time to teach her, she learned on her own and would make her dolls clothes from the scraps of material I left. I loved to cook and Gemmia was my assistant. She knew how to shop for the brands I liked, the things I liked, in the places I loved to shop. I rarely had to tell her anything twice. It was as if she anticipated what I would think, say, or want, then made it her business to see that I was satisfied with the result. She not only stepped in to assist me when I was up to something good, she quickly learned how to step up when I fell down. After the few rocky months at the beginning of her life, ours seemed to be a maintenance-free relationship. With all of the other craziness in my life, that was exactly what I needed—a relationship where I could just be.

I am not sure when it began, but Gemmia was close to 14 when I noticed it—she was sleeping all of the time. She would go to school, come home, do her homework, then go straight to sleep. On the weekends, she would just sleep. At first, I thought my worst fear had come upon her—*she's pregnant!* Then, after talking to her brother and sister, I realized that this had been going on for more than a year. I had no awareness of the symptoms of depression, so that wasn't even a consideration. Instead, I threatened, bullied, and eventually forbade her to stay in the bed. Being the obedient child, she did what I asked: She stayed awake and sullen, responding to everything with the whisper of "I don't know" or "I don't care." She wasn't being defiant or rebellious. It seemed to me that she was in a place of deep despair, and I had no idea how to help her.

One day I was at the hairdresser having my hair braided when my dear friend Tulani shared with me that she wanted to teach young girls the art and science of natural hair care. Tulani thought that if girls knew how to braid, twist, and care for their natural hair, fewer of them would opt for relaxers or the hot comb. Almost as a joke, I told her that Gemmia could be her first student. She told me to send her to the shop the next day. The result? For the next two and a half years, Tulani raised Gemmia. She not only taught Gemmia how to care for hair, she taught her how to run a business. She taught her how to dress herself and create a style for herself. Tulani had an eye for what makes a woman look and feel good. I had no such skill or inclination. As a creative person, Tulani spoke a language that Gemmia understood, whereas I had no clue! We want so desperately to be where our children are, to understand what they feel, to do everything possible for them. However, we must know our limits. Often there comes a point when we simply do not have what our children need. I did not have what Gemmia needed, and it took a good, close sister-friend to step in where I could not.

Around the same time that I noticed the sleeping, I noticed the boy. He was always around, so I thought he was one of the kids from the neighborhood who had befriended my son. Then I noticed that when Damon wasn't home, this guy was still around. One day, I seized the opportunity to make a motherly inquiry.

"So, what's up with you and Pook-A-Doo?" She knew exactly who I was referring to, but she had to ask.

"Who in the world is Pook-A-Doo?"

"You know who I am talking about."

"No, I don't. You always have these weird names you call people. Why do you do that?"

"Don't change the subject. Is that your boyfriend?"

Nisa could not resist the temptation to tell on her big sister.

"You know she's talking about Jimmy, and you know he is your boyfriend."

"Shut up! He is not!"

"Yes he is! You know he is! I saw you kissing."

My mouth suddenly went dry as I realized I had not yet shared the facts of life with either of my daughters.

"Do you like him?"

"Yeah, he's all right."

"I hope he is more than all right if you are kissing him." She had to smile at that one. "Have you two done more than kiss?"

Nisa was stifling a scream of laughter.

"No!"

"Do we need to have the birds-and-bees conversation?"

"Oh, please, I have had that conversation a million times."

"With who?" I was horrified that someone had spoken to my child about something I had forgotten.

"With everybody—Grandpa, Mama Tulani, everybody. You adults are so afraid of sex, you keep talking about it like I am stupid or something."

"I am not afraid of sex. I am simply afraid of what can happen to you if you have sex. But that's not the point. The point is you have a boyfriend I didn't know about, and I want to make sure you are safe."

"I am safe and I am not having sex."

Nisa was beside herself.

Later that evening I called Tulani. She informed me that they had been seeing each other for months. According to Tulani, he seemed nice, was very polite, and he absolutely adored Gemmia. But I had to ask myself, *Why didn't she tell me?* Was I available to her? I was not. Was I accessible to her? I was not. The realization reduced me to tears. I was so wrapped up in myself and my affairs, I had neglected the needs of the people who meant the most to me in the world—my children. I didn't sleep much that night. As soon as I heard Gemmia stirring in the morning, I ran into her room and confessed my transgressions.

"Gimmi, I feel like I have failed you. I feel like I have not given you what you need. I am so, so sorry." She looked at me as if I had lost my mind. In some ways, I had.

"I mean, I am your mother. I should have known you had a boyfriend. I should have talked to you about sex. I should have let you know how important you are to me." I was rambling. Gemmia was not impressed.

"What in the world are you talking about?"

"I'm talking about you and me and my not being there for you." I was quite annoyed that she did not understand what I was trying to say to her.

"Mumzie, you are always here for me. You are going to school. You are working. You are putting food on the table and clothes on our backs. What more do you expect from yourself?"

Wait a minute! Was my daughter lecturing me? Yes! And it was exactly what I needed to hear. Then why was I so pissed off?

"You don't have to tell me what I'm doing! We are talking about what you are doing without me!"

"No, we are talking about your guilt." Gemmia didn't talk much, but when she did, it was a mouthful.

"Guilt! What guilt? I'm not guilty about anything I've done."

"I did not say you are guilty. I said you are feeling guilty. You are feeling guilty that you are not here for us because you don't understand that we understand what you are doing and why. We really do, and we are so proud of you."

Now we were both crying. I didn't ask her why she was crying, but I was crying because I felt guilty! I felt guilty for underestimating my children. I felt guilty for underestimating myself and what I had taught them. I felt guilty because, although I was busting my butt, I was not honoring myself. Now here I was being called out by my child. It was all too much at 6:20 in the morning.

"Ma, I would never disappoint you by doing something like getting pregnant. I am not you. You did that, which means I don't have to do it. Okay?"

The only thing I could muster up was "Okay. Thank you."

‡‡‡

On a balmy September Sunday, I left New York and my children behind to move to Philadelphia to practice law. Of course, I left Gemmia in charge. She was 16. Damon was staying permanently in New York; he had completed high school and was living with his father, who had shown up after 18 years of silence to take him in. Nisa had just begun high school and was adjusting fairly well. I had to go to Philly not only to start work but to find a place for us to live. Four months later, Gemmia and Nisa joined me in a quiet residential neighborhood in West Philadelphia. I enrolled them both in West Philadelphia High School, and we began a new life.

Guilty though I may have felt, as emotionally absent as I told myself I was, I always did something special for my children's special days. When Gemmia's high school prom came around, I was more excited about it than she seemed to be. And I was proud. In the fall, we would be sending her off to college. She had won a full four-year scholarship to Morgan State University.

I made her dress: white satin, strapless, with a pearl and brocade bodice. I did her hair in an upsweep 'do and put white flowers along the side. I wanted her to carry the purse I carried when I got married the second time. She said it was too big. I spent my last $15 and bought her a white satin clutch. She refused to allow me on the second floor of our home while she was getting dressed. She said I was annoying. I believed her, and instead, I sat poised in front of the sewing machine in case I needed to do any last minute adjustments.

Jimmy arrived on time with a beautiful orchid corsage. We waited together until Gemmia descended the stairs—and I wept! That quiet little girl with two big left feet had been transformed into a beautiful young woman. She had beautiful legs. She had beautiful boobs. Her skin was beautiful. Her hair was gorgeous. Before I could really get my cry on, Gemmia ordered me to stop crying and get the camera, which I did obediently. She was standing before me, a vision of loveliness. Once again, I felt that I hardly knew her at all.

When you feel unprotected, unsupported and unprepared to take care of yourself, your insides will feel as if you have been through a train wreck. The best way to describe the experience is that you are having a head-on bloody collision between your wannabe *and your* can never be.

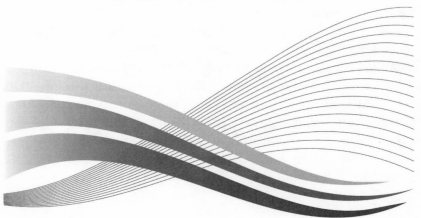

CHAPTER 7

AIN'T NOBODY'S PRISONER!

When I left New York and moved to Philadelphia, I thought I was leaving the bad times and bad people behind. I wasn't aware that I was carrying more baggage than the 12-foot moving truck could possibly hold.

I actually thought that a new job, in a new profession, in a new city would evoke in me feelings of accomplishment. From the poorhouse to the courthouse was a major accomplishment. Instead of celebrating that, I focused on the fact that my daughters and I were sleeping on mattresses on the floor. I beat myself up for leaving behind the broken-down furniture, because I thought my new salary in the public defender's office would be enough for us to buy new things. Now I realized that my salary was barely enough for us to eat and keep the lights on. Instead of feeling good about living in a real house, in a neighborhood that had no unsavory persons hanging out on the corners, I obsessed over the fact that I had no family or friends to celebrate my accomplishments. Instead of studying for the bar, I beat myself down because of what I thought was missing in my life. My inner saboteur was in a death match with my past. This fracture was so deep in my soul that no amount of good fortune or Godly grace seemed capable of dethroning the lies I was capable of telling myself about myself. At times, I seemed hell-bent on being the nothing Grandma told me I would be, even though there was amazing and tangible evidence to the contrary.

There are times when we can become so involved with our physical lives that we forget we have a spiritual life. Let me own that by saying I was so overwhelmed by the events of being human that I forgot to give care to the needs of my spirit. Though I wasn't much of a churchgoer any more, I knew how to pray and did so frequently, but I usually prayed begging prayers. I would beg to a God outside of myself to fix what I thought was wrong with me and my life.

Several years earlier, I had been initiated as a Yoruba priestess. I was a minister in the ancient tradition of my matriarchal lineage. I was a cultural custodian of an ancient civilization, possessing knowledge that allowed me to use my spiritual heritage as a resource, rather than just a reference. I wish I could tell you I stepped into this role with great pride and as a matter of choice. I cannot. Although I knew about my culture and the spiritual tradition of my ancestors, I fell into the priesthood chasing after a man—a man who had left me. I thought I loved him too. When he decided to leave me and our five-year union, a friend suggested that I see a spiritualist and get a reading to help me through the grief.

Grief will make you do some very different things. The spiritualist told me that I had lost him and all of my luck because I was not following my calling. My calling was to be a priestess and to guide other people on their spiritual journey. *Yea! Right!* With eerie detail she told me things about my life that I had never spoken aloud to anyone. She also told me about the misery I could expect if I did not get on the right track. Then she told me what I wanted to hear. She told me that the only way I would ever be with the man of my dreams was to surrender my life and become a priestess. One year and six months later, I was initiated. The man never came back but—it is clear that his departure got me to where I was intended to be—in service to God.

As a result of my initiation, I knew intimately the power and necessity of ritual and ceremony. Ritual was something that my African soul cried out for and flourished in, when I participated. I knew the power of pouring libations to my ancestors and welcoming their essence into my consciousness. I knew the need to call upon the names of powerful women from within and without my family lineage. Once I called upon them, I knew how to sit and listen for the wisdom of their lives to flood my mind.

Ceremony was something that both my African and Native American essence was intimate with and grew from, when I took the time to be present. There was a time in my life when I would light a candle for my deceased parents every Wednesday. I would sit and listen for what I had come to know as their voices whispering in my heart. I could hear my daddy reminding me, "Sit down, shut up, and listen." Many times, I would see a pretty brown lady in my mind, beckoning me to come near. It wasn't until my aunt showed me a picture that I realized the image was Sahara, my birth mother. There was a time when I would light incense and candles in my office or whatever room I was working in at the time. I would call upon the angels of God and the spirits of my ancestors to guide my every word and action. I was intimately familiar with the effectiveness of disciplines that inspired me to listen, pray, and approach my life in a humble and spiritually grounded way.

Then I moved a man into my house and gave his shoes the space that once housed my altar. In order to accommodate him, I lost track of the things that kept me sane and grounded and safe. I lost my commitment to the principles and practices that made my spirit whole, and it was then that I became confused and consumed by the events of my life.

Somewhere between my first breakup with Eden, which sent me running to the church, and my entering the field of law, I had fallen into the belief that spiritual work was unnecessary and, quite frankly, not fruitful. All my praying had not brought *him* back into my life. All the candles and incense had not made me any richer or smarter. At the time, I did not understand that challenges and difficulties are opportunities to deepen your faith. I thought I had been faithful doing part-time worship and expecting full-time rewards. I had no clue that when God gives you something to do, you cannot do just the parts you like, the easy parts. God had given me gifts and talents that I was wasting chasing a forbidden fruit. God had kept me alive and sane in the midst of unspeakable abuse and neglect. God had something huge in store for me, and I needed to allow him to prepare me. Yet, too often in the swirl of a downward spiral, I would misinterpret my life and decide it was just a series of mishaps and devastating events that would never change. Trying to change what I did not believe could or would change rendered me exhausted. Rather than turning to my spiritual practices for discipline and strength, I turned to and learned to rely on what I could do by sheer brute human means and methods. That was actually wrong move but, I didn't know it then. I hadn't yet heard the saying *God can only do for you what God can do through you.*

As far as I was concerned, breaking up with Eden meant that I was leaving the dysfunctional, unfulfilling relationships with men behind me in my hometown of Brooklyn. No more married, separated men! No more men who wanted to mess around with my head, fool around with my heart, or sleep around with other women. I wanted someone who was willing and ready to be with me just for the pure joy of it. I had learned quite a few things about men and about myself in those relationships. They weren't spiritual things. They were just things that I thought I needed to know. I was determined to move beyond the pain of loving into the joys of being loved.

After my move, I got back into my spiritual discipline. I started writing in my journal again. I started each day with prayer. I even began sharing what I knew about the Yoruba tradition with my first set of godchildren, people who looked to me for spiritual guidance, support, and training. I had long been a student of the Bible; now I was studying the Word again and, without much difficulty, making a profound connection between what I was reading there and what I was practicing as a Yoruba. I recognized and understood that the Bible, with its many twists and turns, shalts and shalt nots, was actually the ancient foretelling of my life, of everyone's life. Sure, it had been distilled and watered down and many parts had been changed or omitted for various reasons. However, I recognized that the ancient stories and parables that my ancestors used to prepare young men and women for the trials of life were hidden in its sacred lines. I loved the warnings and the lessons and the promises as they were revealed in the Bible, because it was all that I had left of those ancient stories.

Somehow, those practices and beliefs were coming alive within me. I could see, feel, and understand the oneness of all things spiritual—not religious—but spiritual. The lines that separated African from Christian, ancient from New Age, and right from wrong had become blurred for me. I saw and felt Spirit. I sought and honored truth. I made a connection between the old-world ways and my new-world needs. In the midst of it all, my spiritual eyes were opened and my spiritual identity was renewed.

✛✛✛

I really thought I would love practicing law. However, before you pass the bar, you don't get to practice law. You get to fill out paperwork—lots and lots of paperwork. Because I had not taken or passed the Pennsylvania bar exam, I couldn't actually represent anyone in court, though I could appear at bail hearings. Mostly, what I could do was interview clients in the office and fill out their paperwork. I also interviewed clients at the courthouse and filled out their paperwork. I went to the jail, the stinky, hot jail to meet with clients and fill out their paperwork. Then I went back to the office and distributed the paperwork to the people who had passed the bar exam. The senior lawyers loved my paperwork. In fact, one of them assumed I was already practicing because of the details and nuances in my paperwork. When I told him I had not yet passed the bar, he said, "Damn! I thought you had it going on, but you're just a highly paid law student." Then he burst out laughing. I had to really work with myself not to eat his face off.

Every now and again, the paperwork would turn out to hold a real story. Those were the people I really wanted to help. Those were the people I thought I would be helping after I passed the bar exam.

One woman, Patricia, had gotten into an altercation with another tenant in her apartment building. There was a knife involved. The other tenant got stabbed, and Patricia was arrested. When I first saw her paperwork, I assumed she would get bail, go to court, and get probation and I would never see her again. Case closed. I had put my paperwork in order and was standing at the vending machine when a short woman tapped me on the back.

"Are you the public defender?"

Oh Lord! Another story?

"Yes, ma'am, I am."

"Are you going to handle the case for Patricia Muller?"

There was something about this woman that I liked. While she was very soft-spoken, I could feel an energy coming from her that I recognized but couldn't quite explain—yet.

"That is my pastor's daughter, and I am here on her behalf."

That's it! This was an old church mother. One of those powerful women who sit around and pray all day. I knew that energy because I had felt it so many times as a child when I went to church with Grandma. These women felt welcoming. They rocked. They hummed. They moaned. And they could pray the paint off the walls.

"Is she going to have to go to jail?"

"No, ma'am. Not if you pay the bail."

She explained that the pastor and his wife were on the way up from South Carolina, and it was going to take them at least eight hours to get here. When would she need to have the money?

"They will probably call her before the commissioner within the next hour. If you can't pay the bail then, you will need to pay it later and then go to the detention center to pick her up."

"The Lord knows the way."

"I am sure he does."

The next group of defendants came up within the hour. Ms. Muller was not among them. When I looked over my shoulder to give the church mother a reassuring nod, her eyes were closed and she was rocking from side to side. By the time the third group came up without Ms. Muller, I was laughing to myself. *This woman's prayers are affecting the entire legal system.* I called the defender's office and told them I would take the next shift. Although it meant I would be on my feet for 16 hours, I almost felt obligated to see this case through to the end.

As soon as I sat down next to the church mother, her eyes flew open. Before I could get my mouth open, she asked me if I would go and let Patricia know that Mother Carol was here and her parents were on the way. I explained that I was not allowed to speak to the prisoners before they came into the court room.

"Prisoner? Patricia ain't nobody's prisoner!"

"I mean the defendants. I am not allowed to speak to them while they are in police custody."

"You are the lawyer, right?"

"Yes, ma'am. I mean, I'm not actually a lawyer because I haven't passed the bar exam, but I can stand before a commissioner."

"You're going to pass the exam, but today I need you to go and tell Patricia that I am here."

It was worth a try. I knew the officers on duty, and they teased me about being a New Yorker. I had never made such a request, so maybe—just maybe—they would be nice to me.

I went down into the basement where the defendants were held in lockup. I walked the long and narrow hallway that never seemed to end. When I stepped up to the window of the cage, I noticed that Patricia was alone. I knew from the paperwork that there were at least 212 defendants in the cage, but Patricia had a cage all to herself. She was sitting on the floor, in the corner. She had been in lockup for 11 hours. I tapped on the window and gave her Mother Carol's message. She began to weep.

"Why are you crying? Your parents are on the way, and Mother Carol has this entire building on lockdown."

"I am so scared."

"Scared of what?"

"I didn't do what he said. I didn't stab him."

"So what are you afraid of? You know what to do."

"I don't know what to do!"

"You mean to tell me that you are a pastor's daughter and you don't know what to do? Girl, you better get to praying."

She looked at me as if I had lost my mind. I started her off:

"The Lord is my shepherd."

She continued, "I shall not want."

We prayed Psalms 23 and 91 together, aloud. Then we just prayed. The only thing that stopped us was the officer letting me know that court was about to begin. As I left, prisoners in the other cages were screaming through the windows.

"Pray for me too! Miss. Miss. Please pray for me too!"

Two hours later, the pastor and the first lady arrived. Ten minutes later, Patricia Muller entered the courtroom. When the commissioner attempted to set her bail at $5,000, I reminded him of how long the prisoner had been held—14 hours by this time, 2 hours longer than the maximum. I glanced into the gallery. Pastor Muller, the first lady, and Mother Carol were all standing, all rocking from side to side. The commissioner released Patricia Muller on her own recognizance. When she came upstairs an hour later, the pastor thanked me and invited me to church. I went.

Over the next few weeks, I realized I was in the right place, at the right time, doing the wrong thing.

All of a sudden, after many months of agony and much prayer, I knew in my soul that I was not meant to be a lawyer. I knew that my destiny was not aligned with man's system of law. It was my destiny to find and teach the process of being in alignment with God's law. After 21 days of fasting and purification, I left the defender's office without a goal or a vision. I knew I had made the right choice.

‡‡‡

He was absolutely delicious to look at, and he saw me first. I was walking through the halls of Temple University, trying to find the Religion Department. I was going to pursue a doctoral degree. Apparently, I had passed his classroom several times on my many trips around the corridor, and when class was over, he decided I needed help.

"Are you lost?"

"I sure am. I'm looking for Dr. Stewart's office and I'm late for my appointment."

"Well, I guess so. You're on the wrong floor. Come with me."

He looked good. He smelled good. He was willing to help me find my way. This was turning into a very good day.

"I am Fahim Majid. And you are?"

I am. He said, I am. That is a powerful way to introduce yourself, but he must be Muslim. That could mean that he had four wives and nine children.

"I am Iyanla Vanzant." We had arrived at our destination.

"Hey, Doc, I brought a very beautiful lady to see you."

I introduced myself, and my escort excused himself.

After my meeting, I headed toward the elevator. To my pleasant surprise, Mr. Smell So Good You Want To Bite Him showed up while I was waiting.

"Are you following me?"

"I sure am."

As we walked to my car, he told me all about the Ph.D. program. He too was a religion major, one class away from his dissertation. He had served as the imam in a Connecticut community for many years before he simply burned out. He had left his mosque and his wife and had spent the past two and a half years trying to find his next steps. I left him with my telephone number and I had his.

For the next three months, we talked every day, several times a day. Once I started the program, we saw each other every day. He was everything I imagined a good man could and should be. He opened the car door and every other door. He listened when I talked and answered everything I asked him. Even better, he was completely accepting of my views on things religious and things spiritual. We didn't always agree, but he gave me the space to share and practice what I believed.

By the time we were heading toward the ninth month of dating, things were starting to get serious. We both tried to deny it. He broke first.

"I think I have fallen in love with you, and that is not what I want."

"Really. What do you want?" I wasn't ready to declare anything.

"I'm not really sure."

"Have you prayed about it?"

We were both students of religion. Prayer was our first line of support and defense.

"I did more than that. I talked to my imam about it."

"What did he say?"

"He told me to keep praying until I received an answer."

"Okay, so what is the problem?"

"No problem. I just wanted you to know what I was thinking."

"Well, thank you. I appreciate it."

This man was too good to be true.

Over the next few weeks, any time we were together, we had the same conversation. He would list all of his reasons for not wanting to go to the next step. I would listen and reassure him that I had no expectations. Then one day we ended up in his apartment and I spent the night. The next morning, he went for a jog and left me in the apartment alone, with a mind full of questions. Did I snoop? Well, of course I did. Did I find anything? Absolutely! I found panties in the dresser drawer. I found notes and lists in a handwriting that was not his. It was the Tampax under the bathroom sink that sealed the deal for me.

By the time he returned I was good and heartbroken. He kept asking me what was wrong, and I kept denying there was anything at all. He dropped me off at home, kissed me goodbye, and headed to New Jersey to see his children. I spent the weekend trying to figure out why this was happening and what I needed to do next. I thought to myself, *Look, he has not made a commitment to you and you have not made one to him. What is the big deal?* The big deal was that I was standing at the threshold of a recurring and calamitous pattern in my life—meet a man; sleep with a man; fall in love with a man; get dissed by the man. I knew that I did not want to participate in yet another man-sharing opportunity.

I prayed about it and received the guidance I needed—*Stop looking for love outside of yourself.* I didn't like that guidance, so I went back to being human. I intended to produce myself on his doorstep bright and early Monday morning and tell him what I had found. I sat in my car in the parking lot for at least 15 minutes, waiting for my legs to stop shaking. It was just long enough. As I put my hand on the door handle, I looked up and saw Mr. Wonderful coming out of his building with a woman. They kissed. He got in his car. She got in another car. They both drove away, leaving me in the parking lot with my mouth hanging open.

By the time I got home, he had already been there and left a note. I must have sat with one hand on the telephone for hours waiting for him to call. He did.

"You're not coming to school today?"

"No. I had a few other things to do."

"Okay. You want me to stop by later?"

"No. I will probably be out."

"Okay. Are you okay?"

"Yes. I'm fine. I'll talk to you later."

Damn it! I'd punked out.

But by that evening, I was over it. Although I still didn't quite buy into my spiritual guidance, I couldn't believe that he was my attempt to find love. My relationship pattern was playing out, and I was no longer angry. I was no longer hurt. I was complete with him and with the pattern.

There is something about knowing the truth that makes you responsible for determining what you do next. What I knew was that I was no longer willing to participate in my own heartache and disappointment. I was no longer willing to pine away over a man who had a different agenda than mine. I was choosing to say no to something that I knew would eventually blow up in my face.

Finally, thank you Lord! I had drawn my line in the sand, and I was not willing to back up and draw another. Lesson learned. Pattern disrupted. Amen and Ase!

Those whom the devil would tempt,
He tells not a lie, but
a lesser truth.

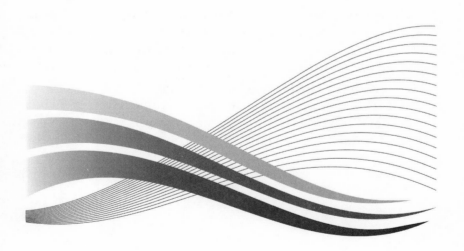

CHAPTER 8

THE PERSONAL LIE

When I first moved to Maryland, it was more than a new beginning. It was a divine opportunity for me to catch up with myself and begin to practice some of the things I had learned and begun teaching in the world. My first book had been published and was selling with great success. *Essence* had published my story, and I was recognized as an energetic and popular speaker. My Philadelphia family was close enough that I could still feel and receive their support.

Then there was home. My son was in prison. My youngest daughter was pregnant for the second time, and I was raising her son. Gemmia was expecting her first child with Jimmy, and although she refused to marry him, theirs seems like a solid relationship.

I was moving forward but struggling within myself. I felt guilty about my son being in jail. I felt ashamed about Nisa having two children with no husband or formal education. At the core of my being, there was this gnawing belief that I did not deserve good things and that the not-so-good things were going to swallow me up.

When Simon and Schuster published my second book, *Acts of Faith: Daily Meditations for People of Color,* my life took off at warp speed. On my first book tour, I traveled to 16 cities, stayed in first-class hotels, and spoke to audiences who seemed to admire me.

I was in Charlotte, North Carolina, when Gemmia called me at 10 P.M. to tell me she was in labor. I could not get a flight out until 7 A.M. the next morning. I got to the hospital 15 minutes after my granddaughter, Niamoja, was born. When I looked into her eyes, waves of Mommy guilt and failure flooded my body. This had been one of the most important days of Gemmia's life and I had missed it—by 15 minutes. Jimmy hadn't been there either. He had left Gemmia to take a friend to rent a car. By the time he got back to the hospital, the baby had been born. *Who the hell goes to rent a car while his child is being born?* Men who are emotionally unavailable that's who! I glimpsed the family pattern. I saw it. I felt it. I denied it.

Shortly after my granddaughter was born, I was named Best New Non-Fiction Writer by the American Booksellers Association. They flew me to Chicago, put me up in a four-star hotel, and gave me my award in front of more than 1,000 people. Just before I stood up to receive the award, I put my finger on the problem: I was numb. I didn't feel proud or excited or happy. Something had taken over my mind and my body, leaving only a void.

I offered some words of gratitude to the people who had helped to make this possible, and I took my seat. I was truly grateful, I think. Yet I was unable to accept my own worthiness. For a very brief moment I toyed with the idea of investigating what was going inside of me. Then I thought better of it.

My next book, *The Spirit of a Man: A Vision of Transformation for Black Men and the Women Who Love Them,* was a download, an inspiration from something or someone on high, in response to the guilt and shame I was feeling about my son's incarceration. I had tried so hard and wanted so badly for him to be different from my brother and my father. I wanted him to be living proof that I had not failed as a mother, even though I had had him when I was 16 years old. Every collect call from the Virginia prison destroyed that dream a little more. In the world of dashed dreams, my youngest daughter, Nisa, had given birth to her own son at age 16, and my oldest daughter, Gemmia, was basically raising her daughter alone.

All of these disappointments and failures clouded over my growing success. Learning about Damon's experiences behind prison walls, glancing over at my daughters who were struggling but making it, ripped open something inside of me. *I had to know why this was happening to me; to them; to us.* I had to unearth the damaged puzzle pieces, the life-threatening patterns I had passed to them.

The book began with a very simple prayer that I now recognize as a cry for help.

"Lord, what is going on? Why is this happening to me and my children?"

I sat on the edge of my bed, repeating this one phrase over and over in my mind. When I heard the first words of what I now know was God's response to my plea, I wasn't sure what to do. As the thoughts and feelings continued to spill forth, I got a pencil and started to write them down. Within a few hours, I had written pages of information, some of which I understood, much of which I did not.

I remember Gemmia and the baby coming into my room. I tried rather incoherently to explain what was going on. Gemmia knew that I had a gift that I did not yet fully embrace. In the calm and loving way that only she had, she said, "It would probably be good for everyone, including you, if you would put that in the computer instead of on that hotel message pad."

I followed her advice. I sat at the computer typing whatever I heard without worrying whether or not it made sense. Gemmia made sure that I had plenty of water, fruit, and something to eat. I stayed in my room for three weeks. In the end, I had a manuscript and a completely new way to tap into the Divine Spirit of God.

My agent loved the manuscript and believed that my current publisher was not offering a competitive advance. She initiated a book auction, and Harper San Francisco bought *The Spirit of a Man* for $150,000. I now had lucrative contracts with two different publishers. Simon & Schuster recognized that my next book could be huge and pushed me to deliver it quickly in an attempt to beat Harper San Francisco to the marketplace. *The Value in the Valley: A Black Woman's Guide Through Life's Dilemmas* was born to great reviews and successful sales.

The Spirit of a Man was a great book that confirmed that most men do not read self-help. Its failure left me doubting whether I had a communication line to God at all. It didn't matter. I had to keep moving. Within a year of publishing *The Value in the Valley,* I wrote *Faith in the Valley,* a book of potent inspirational messages for women designed to get them to the other side of life's difficulties. The publishing world, like most entertainment businesses, loves to duplicate success. *Faith* sold decently, but it was not the mega-hit that Simon and Schuster had anticipated. Back to the drawing board for them. Deeper into numbness for me.

When I tell you I was moving *fast,* I put the emphasis on fast. I was writing and flying all over the country speaking. I had begun to teach classes and conduct workshops in Maryland and Washington, D.C. Gemmia was my second in command. She managed my business and encouraged me to charge for my classes and workshops. She orchestrated my first makeover by changing my usual traditional African-inspired garb for more contemporary attire accented by African-inspired jewelry. She braided my hair, and when that became too much to manage, she encouraged me to cut my hair off.

It was Gemmia who encouraged me to create a prayer team to staff every class and every workshop. If I was going to call my work spiritual work, it had to be deeply rooted in the basic spiritual practices that had saved my life, such as prayer and meditation. I asked around, and this family member asked that friend; that friend brought this friend, and before we knew it, there were 14 of us working as the team we called Inner Visions.

Twenty-five years ago, when the spiritual movement was a virtual embryo, there was no money in it. Or perhaps I should say that if you were a person of color, there was very little money in it, unless you were a preacher. I make that distinction because my career emerged around the same time Marianne Williamson and Deepak Chopra both began to appear in large venues across the country before sold-out crowds. Although I had published and sold more books than either of them, I had yet to be invited to be a guest on the *Today Show* or *Good Morning America,* and *Oprah* was simply out of the question. I contented myself with doing things on a much smaller scale. I told myself that because I was doing good work, it didn't matter. Somewhere inside, however, there was a cesspool that kept pumping *not good enough* into my brain.

When you do not believe that who you are and what you do is good enough, that message will contaminate everything you do. People coast to coast would tell me how this book or that class had changed their lives. I heard the words, but I could not receive what they were saying. Deep down, I thought they were either mistaken or out-and-out lying.

Comparisons are a form of violence. When you believe you are not good enough, you will compare yourself to others. I constantly compared myself to other spiritual or self-help gurus. I compared my income and their public acclaim to my lack of the same. I became more and more numb to the good things that were happening in my life. I beat up on myself for not doing the right things, in the right way, to make the money I needed to live a comfortable life. My classes were filled. The workshops were in demand. I was busy, busy, busy. And I was broke, broke, broke.

I kept wondering when my time of prosperity would come. I had no idea that I was sitting right in it. I couldn't see it, because my thoughts and beliefs about myself had not changed. Somewhere in my mind, part of me still felt like an impostor, the ugly, worthless teenage mother on welfare, pretending she had it all together. Deep down inside she was *shit,* she came from *shit,* and the *shit* she was doing would never make anything any different. Of course, I didn't share this with anyone. I just went about my business. In the bliss-filled moments when I was serving those who came to receive the gifts that I'd been given, I was a genuinely wonderful vessel, but offstage I was more and more numb.

In the publishing world, I had become a cash cow. I discovered how lucrative my work had become when my first publisher reissued my first book, *Tapping the Power Within,* with a cover so closely resembling the best-selling *Acts of Faith,* that you might mistake one book for the other. Not long afterwards, the same publisher decided to publish *Interiors,* a manuscript written years earlier for the women in my life-skills program. After I began the editing process, I realized that writing that book was for my healing alone. It was not for the world. But the publisher ignored my request to table the manuscript. The book was released anyway, with my face plastered on the cover to seduce my one-million plus readers. I'm not sure what the readers did. I sued that very small, independent, black-owned publishing company for breach of contract and copyright infringement. It was a terrible ordeal. It was a betrayal of the highest order. I refused to acknowledge the book, autograph it, or allow a copy of it to enter my home.

I got new representation and my new attorney retooled all of my contracts with Simon and Schuster, who reissued *Acts of Faith* in hardcover and paid me a sizeable advance. My agent, attorney, and publisher then began to reshape my publishing career. Everyone seemed to feel that my message was universal and I was limiting myself by staying "black." They said my message had worldwide appeal. It was decided that I should "cross over" to the larger self-help market that was booming at the time.

I wasn't sure what to think or how to feel. Here I was suing an independent black publisher, and now they wanted me to drop "black" from my titles. It was frightening. Finally, though, Gemmia and I decided to roll with it. We determined there was nothing wrong with me expanding my work to the broader market. There was no danger of me being confused with anyone else. I was Iyanla, pure and simple. The question was, *Who the heck was Iyanla?* Or better yet, *Who had she become?*

‡‡‡

When doubt is present in your consciousness it indicates a much more profound problem. The real problem is the *personal lie.* Everyone has one: It is a story that we tell ourselves about who we are and what we do and do not deserve in life. *Your personal lie is a function of all of the broken pieces of your puzzle—all of the elements of your history, all of your experiences, all that you have been taught about yourself merging with all that you have made up about yourself.* Your personal lie circulates throughout your entire being and determines how you move, or if you can move at all. It is a function of what is stored on your internal landscape, your perceptions and misconceptions about life and how you fit into the scheme of things.

In the modern world, the personal lie is also known as your core belief. The way the personal lie operates in your consciousness is that it becomes the lie about yourself that gets projected onto other people and into the environment. When the lie is projected, we see in others exactly what we resist, avoid, or deny about ourselves. If your lie is that you are bad, you will see others as bad, and at the same time, you will be unable to acknowledge that there is or could be anything bad within you. If your personal lie is that you are stupid, you will see others that way and imagine that you are better than or smarter than those "stupid" people around you.

As we project the lie outward, we experience a great deal of internal conflict. Unfortunately, most of us are not aware of the lie. We have no clue that we are being driven by an unconscious thought working against our best interests and greatest efforts.

My personal lie, my foundational belief, was that I was *not good enough.* As a result, nothing I did was ever good enough. This made sense to me. It was what I had learned throughout my childhood. As an adult, I felt a lingering dissatisfaction with everything I did. I always felt that I had to do more, give more, and be more because nothing was ever good enough.

From welfare to law school wasn't good enough. From self-publishing and selling books out of the trunk of my car to six-figure advances and being one of the most sought-after speakers in the country still wasn't good enough. The only thing that gave me some modicum of peace was when someone who had read a book or heard a tape told me her story and thanked me for helping her. In my work, I was deeply Spirit-connected and able to share from the deepest place of my being. When I heard how people had learned from me, and how I had helped change their lives, I could breathe a sigh of relief, believing that maybe I was finally becoming good enough to matter. But the feeling was always short-lived.

It has been almost four years since I had heard from Eden. By the time he reached out to me, he was living in Atlanta. He needed some information, and I kept the conversation short. I had finally started breathing again. I was no longer a frightened little girl in a woman's body. I was all grown up, living in another state, writing books, and speaking all over the country. *Iyanla had arrived!* At least that was what I told myself.

When Eden called me again, the conversation was lighter and longer. This time he wanted me to speak at an event he was hosting. It meant there was a possibility that I might see him face to face. This time I wasn't afraid. I had an inner clarity that I had worked my little buns off to achieve. I had prayed and healed, grown and changed. I liked myself a lot more now. I loved what I had become and what I had made of my life. I knew that somewhere in my being, I was still in love with the man I fell in love with when I was a young girl. But I went to Atlanta anyway.

I still liked the way he looked and the way he smelled, and I still refused to think about it. When I got back home and he started calling once a week, then every other day, then every day, it felt really good; but I refused to think about it. I refused to think about him being engaged to someone else and breaking it off just as we began to talk again.

There was just too much at stake. My life. My work. My sanity. My heart. I was no longer desperate to love or be loved. I no longer needed to prove anything to myself or anyone else. The one thing I really had to get a handle on was the way I could feel my eyes light up when he walked into the room. Now that was a problem.

Six months into the calling back and forth, I found myself in Atlanta, in his bed. This time we talked about it. This time we made a plan. This time we both agreed that we were meant to be together. On his next trip to the Washington area, he took me to dinner at a small Mexican restaurant. When the waiter brought the food, he also brought a small black box. I didn't see it at first. When I did, I held my breath. Just like the first kiss, he was *asking* me. I said yes over chicken quesadillas.

‡‡‡

Our marriage began with an elaborate spiritual ceremony in Nigeria. Because I had been initiated as a priest in the Yoruba tradition, it was required that he also be initiated so that we would be "equally yoked." We spent seven days going through a series of rites and rituals designed to clear our past transgressions and open the way to a harmonious new beginning. He slept on a cot on one side of a bare brick room, and I slept on a similar cot on the other side.

Early each morning, the women from the village would take me to do my ceremonies. When I returned, we would spend the rest of the day talking about the past and preparing for the future. On the third day, while I was gone, the men came to take him to do his ceremonies. As the women ushered me back to the room, I saw a parade of men walking across the second-floor balcony of the compound. There was my godfather with several other village men surrounding someone who looked vaguely familiar. He waved. I waved back and asked one of the women, "Who is that?"

She laughed a hearty Nigerian laugh and said, "Who is that? That, my sistah, is your husband!"

I looked again. The men had shaved off his beard. I had never seen him without a beard. He was wrapped in a white sheet from the waist down, with a white towel draped over his head. All of a sudden, my heart began to pound so loudly that I could hear it in my ears. I had an overwhelming urge to cry. It was as if my heart was breaking, but I did not understand why. At the same time, there was a voice screaming inside my head:

I can't marry that man! I don't know who he is!

It was such a startling response that I froze in the middle of the courtyard. One of the women was nudging me along. I swallowed the tears that were starting, turned away from the stranger on the

PEACE FROM BROKEN PIECES

balcony, and let the women escort me back to our room. I sat on the edge of the bed as they danced around me in celebration.

"Your husband is being prepared for you. Your husband is being prepared for your life. Dance, my sistah! Dance!"

I tried to stand, but the shock of what I had heard left my head spinning. Perhaps it was the ceremony the women had just performed on my head. When the women left the room, I wept. When I saw him again, it was two o'clock the next morning. His ceremonies were complete. He, like me, was now a Yoruba priest. The voice in my head was gone, and I tried to convince myself that all would be well. I was going to have a beautiful wedding as I once again married a man I did not know.

I told myself that the man I was marrying—who had cheated on me during our first relationship and left me once for another woman, and who had come back to me at a time when he was down on his luck—was the brass ring, the prize that would prove to me and everyone else that I was worthy of my father's love. The truth is, everything about him reminded me of my father. I had a tremendous amount of unfinished business with my unavailable daddy. The men that I married were the souls who volunteered to spend time in my life so that I could work through that learning agreement.

I was beginning to claim success in my life, but emotionally, there was a piece of me that still felt like a failure. To the naked eye, I looked amazing. I was earning more money than I ever thought possible. I was traveling the world and doing things that I never imagined I could. My children were grown and making it on their own, with the broken pieces of myself that I had given to them. I loved God but I didn't really know God, not then, not yet. I was transforming from who I had been into who I was becoming, but I still wasn't quite sure of who I was.

Finally, I had a home and a husband. I thought that would make me feel whole and complete and make everything all right. I was wrong.

✝✝✝

Love does not die easily.
It is a living thing. It thrives in the
face of all of life's hazards, save one—neglect.

My brand-new husband was critical of me, my life, and how I did almost everything. I am sure that was not his intention. In fact, he probably thought he was being helpful and supportive. However, when you grow up the way I grew up where *everything* you did and said was wrong, you can hear disapproval where none is meant or offered. That was not my case. My husband had a way of saying things in his soft, gentle tone that left me feeling criticized and wrong. Things like, "Why do you always . . ." Or, "Why don't you stop . . ." Or when I was really upset or concerned about something and would turn to him for support, a curt "Oh, please!" Or "Why do you always have to make such a big deal out of everything?" These remarks would leave me doubting myself and feeling crushed.

But it was what he didn't say that shook me to my core. It was the way he looked at me without opening his mouth that let me know that what I was thinking, feeling, or doing was unacceptable. It was the way he would answer my question with a question that flung me face first into the vicious cycle of self-criticism.

There was this certain way that he fell into silence that alerted me that he had some information, some opinion, that I wanted. "What's wrong?" was usually how I would start the conversation.

"What makes you think something's wrong?"

This was not an answer.

Just the way I used to gauge whether it was safe to ask Grandma for something I wanted, now, in response to his response, I had to make a choice. Either I would share my observations about his behavior, which he would dismiss, or I would lie and say, "Just checking." I usually went with the first option. Whenever I questioned him about the emotional distance I felt or his unwillingness to share what was on his mind, it would lead to an argument. We had those snipping, biting little arguments where each of us would try to get in the last word on the way to being right. We became very good at it. So good, in fact, that by the end, all we could remember was how bad it had been.

I now understand that we simply didn't see things the same way. He saw life as a series of fun-filled adventures that you moved through one by one, making no plans or provisions for the future. I saw life as a battlefield on which you had better be prepared to meet the most deadly of forces moment by moment in order to stay alive. He saw home and family as a safe haven with a revolving door, where people could come and go to share in all that you had. I saw home as a temporary refuge at best, where the people inside could be as dangerous as the people outside. A place where you had to make yourself as comfortable as possible in the moment, because you never knew when your refuge would be disrupted or destroyed. For him, home had been a safe but lonely place. For me, home had been a dangerous and unhappy place.

He saw *our* home as *my* home because he had not contributed financially to secure it. Despite the fact that he had his own office, a 52-inch television where he could watch all of his favorite sports events, and a wife who loved to cook for him, he said he felt out of place in our home. When he moved from Atlanta, a huge project he was working on had just gone bad and he was deeply in debt. I saw our home as the fruits of my hard work, something that I deserved, that I wanted to build and share with him. I wanted us to be comfortable. I wanted us to be happy, *damn it!*

He saw money as a necessary evil that you used when you had it; when you had none, you borrowed from other people. I saw money as my ticket out of misery, a way for me to fill all of the holes in my soul; it was something you had to plan to have, work hard to get, and intend to hold on to. He saw me as a workaholic, a dramatic and controlling woman with little time for what really should matter: spending time with him. He saw me as wanting him to work for me rather than with me, and that, he said, disrespected and dishonored him. I saw myself as a successful entrepreneur working diligently to build something I had never experienced: personal and financial freedom. I saw him as my partner, someone who had benefited from—and therefore needed to support—my intentions and my vision.

In the beginning of the second time around, he lived in Atlanta, in his element as a community organizer. He brought the right people together to make things happen. In Maryland, I too was in my element. I was teaching classes, conducting workshops, traveling for speaking engagements, and writing books. We talked about everything on the telephone. We shared our thoughts, hopes, and dreams. What we did not do was plan our life together. We knew we were coming together, we knew we would be together, but we never discussed a shared vision. He told me what he wanted, and I told him what I was already doing. Rather than building a life together, we brought our two lives into one place and tried to make them fit.

He brought his belongings to my home. I did my best to make room for him, but some of his things just didn't fit—they didn't fit in the space and they didn't fit the decor. There were things he had that were important to him that looked like junk to me. There were things he wanted to put into places where I simply did not want them. It felt like he was seizing territory, and as an independent woman, I could not, would not, submit to being taken over. What I didn't see was how his belongings left in those boxes made him feel unwelcome, like a boarder rather than a partner.

He brought his many years of organizing expertise into an established business. He brought his ideas into a system that was already in motion and moving rather successfully. He brought his masculine energy into an organization that was predominantly female. His vision was to create for men what I had built for women: a process and a safe place for personal and spiritual empowerment. The challenge was that I had done the work—the arduous internal and external work to master my craft and build my brand. He was just beginning. He had not done the work. He had, for the most part, watched it be done around him.

Did I have some personal issues that I needed to work through? Absolutely! Yes, I spent a lot of time on the telephone and on airplanes and in hotels, but I was manifesting my vision and building an institution that would serve the world long after I had left it. My work had grown into an opportunity for me, for us, to create a life we enjoyed and a future for our children and grandchildren. We just saw it differently. We responded to it differently. And we argued about it very differently.

His way of arguing was to shut down and shut me out. I now know it was the very same emotional abandonment I had experienced with my father and, quite frankly, with my brother. My husband's approach was to grow deadly quiet. If the silence went on too long, he would ask if he could share his thoughts and feelings with me. By then, I was so hurt, so afraid, and so furious, I would say, "Of course," knowing that I was just waiting for the right moment to verbally attack him. And boy, could I attack. Venomous assault was a skill I mastered in childhood.

Often, in the midst of a silent standoff, I would busy myself with work and shopping. I would buy things that I didn't need or want just to have something to do rather than go home. When we did speak, he would tease me about being a "workaholic" and a "shopaholic." He would criticize me for having too much of everything or for trying to do too much. I suspect he had no idea that I overshopped and overspent because I was afraid that I would not have what I needed when I needed it. I guess it would have been too much to ask him to consider that I kept my cupboards overrun with food because of the fear of being hungry. A childhood of deprivation and denial will do that to you—cause you to expect lack where none exists. My husband had no idea of the conflict and chaos my success stirred up in my mind.

✤✤✤

My husband and I had puzzle pieces that fit together, but painfully; patterns and pathologies that seemed to get tangled up in each other. We had a knack for bruising each other in our most vulnerable places. His parents were divorced. Mine were never married. After the divorce, his mother became a working mother and he became a latchkey kid, alone and lonely at home. I grew up in homes where someone was usually at home and usually wanted me to do something for them. We both grew up believing we should not, could not, ask for what we wanted, and that it was essential for us to make do with whatever we had.

He had the experience of women being soft, gentle, and demure. I had the experience of women being hard, tough, or beat up. He had come to believe that women were meant to support and satisfy the needs of men. I had come to believe that women should *expect* men to leave, and that when they were around, it was your *duty* to do whatever was required to keep them happy. This was one place where we kind of saw things the same. But there was one problem—*it was an affront to my spirit!* I hated feeling like it was my responsibility to carry a man and do all of the work, all of the time. Unfortunately, I was so deep in denial that I didn't know how much I hated it.

When we were married, I was renting a house on the way to purchasing one. My second book, *Acts of Faith,* was selling very well, and I was squirreling away the money I needed for a down payment, although I had spent a big chunk of it on the wedding. I needed another six to nine months to amass what I thought we would need. Since he wasn't working full-time yet, I took it upon myself to find ways to get and save the money. We didn't talk about it. I guess we both assumed I would do it. In fact, I had talked to the landlord about buying the house we were living in at the time. He was willing and accepted a $1,000 deposit to seal the deal. The agreement was that I would pay an additional $200 per month toward the down payment. In a year, I would have 10 percent of the asking price. We shook hands on it.

Then one day, out of nowhere, the owner's wife showed up on my doorstep to inform me that I had 30 days to get out of her house. There was an ugly back story about her philandering husband, but the bottom line was that my lease was up, she knew nothing about the lease-purchase agreement, and she wanted me out—period. We had been married for about two months when we faced the possibility of being houseless. My writing career was just taking off. I had several lucrative speaking engagements scheduled. My classes and workshops were filled to capacity, and I was about to be out on the street. It just didn't make sense to me. In his gentle way, my husband would simply say:

"Something will turn up, don't worry."

Don't worry! Doesn't he know that this opens all of my childhood wounds about being moved from place to place, not belonging anywhere, being put out? Don't worry? He is out of his mind. Of course, I didn't say this to him. I acted like I thought he could make it better. Yet someplace inside of me, I knew nothing could be further from the truth.

The first thing I felt was shame. *Here I am! Miss Iyanla! Inspiring the masses, and I won't have a place to live.* Then, fear. *People are going to know! People are going to find out that I got put out of my house, and they will talk bad about me.* Next, a major mental meltdown about the thousands of dollars I had just spent on a wedding. Then I thought about the children. Gemmia and her daughter were living with me. My son had just been released from prison and was living in my basement. Nisa was still living in Philadelphia, but what if she needed to come home? My children had to have a place to live. Even if my own life was falling apart, I had to take care of my family.

So I got busy. I signed myself up to work anywhere they would have me. I scheduled three more classes at my center. I had 30 days to find a place. We looked at houses and apartments to rent. We were willing to settle for anything we could find. The challenge was the number of people in the family. There were six of us and only two had verifiable income. In addition, my credit score at the time was just below acceptable. In fact, it was actually unacceptable to every apartment complex where we applied. With five days left, I was hardly sleeping or eating. My husband seemed totally unaffected. He ate. He slept. When we talked about it, he always had the same deep insight:

"Something will turn up, don't worry."

When there were three days left, we decided to put the furniture in storage and move into a hotel. By then I was scared to death. We had referred a great deal of business to a local hotel where out-of-towners would stay when they came to take a class with me. We asked them for a weekly rate, and they were more than happy to support us. Then I had a brilliant idea. Rather than put the furniture in storage, why didn't we store it in the back room of our office building? That's right, I was renting an office building. Two stories. 7,500 square feet with three empty rooms we had not renovated yet. Everyone, including my husband, agreed this would be best. After all, it was only temporary. Surely we would find something in the next week or so.

My husband rented a truck. I mean, I gave him the money to rent a truck. On a bright and sunny Saturday morning, we loaded all of my household belongings and transferred them to the first floor of my office building. Between moving the furniture on and off the truck, I cried. When everyone was sitting around eating pizza on a break, I was in the bathroom puking my guts up. Of course, I didn't say a word to anyone. But every once in a while Gemmia would cuddle up to me and say, "It's all right. Remember what you taught me. You can do anything for a little while. This is just for a little while."

Really good friends always know what you are feeling. And in that moment I thought she was right. I was wrong.

We lived in the hotel for two weeks to the tune of $1,100 per week. Searching for a house or an apartment to rent had become a full-time job. My husband and I made a wish list of what we really wanted. He closed his eyes and told me what his ideal home looked like. I wrote down everything he said. Then he did the same for me. Each day, as we thought of things, we would add them to the list. It was a beautiful experience and one of the few times we really worked together to create something for our shared life. But we also realized that spending $1,100 a week was pushing the dream further and further away. I was still the only one working full-time, and sharing a hotel room with a six-year-old was wrecking havoc on our sex life. We were about to embark on our third week in the hotel when I had another brilliant idea; at least it seemed brilliant at the time. Since our furniture was in the office building, why didn't we live there also? We could pull out everything we needed at night and put it away before the staff arrived in the morning.

My son had found an apartment three blocks away from the office so we could go there to shower. Brilliant! Everyone thought it was a brilliant, although uncomfortable, way to save money and expedite finding a real home. We left the hotel that day.

The first night of living in my office, my husband made us a lovely pallet on the floor of my office using all of the sheets and blankets he could find. Gemmia did the same in her office. We put the children in the conference room with the television so they could entertain themselves. Gemmia put sheets across the conference table and made a fort. She played with the children until they fell asleep, and we both retreated to our offices to lie on the floor with the men we loved. I would have been fine had my husband not acted like he wanted to make love. The moment he started to make sexual gestures toward me, I think I lost my mind. No, it wasn't then. It was later, after I submitted to him and he fell off to sleep.

At that moment, I didn't recognize the pattern, and I couldn't believe what was happening. When you are in the midst of the healing, you can't recognize the pattern because if you did, you would stop yourself.

I lay on that pallet on the floor of my office reviewing my life. I had survived unimaginable horrors in my childhood to emerge a reasonably sane individual. I had worked my way off welfare, through college and law school, to practice law, leave law, and emerge an up-and-coming motivational specialist. I had raised my children for the most part alone, and they were all what I would consider good people. I thought about the people I had helped as a lawyer, a writer, and a regular person. I thought about the cities I had traveled to, the thousands who had heard me speak. Now here I was, lying on a pallet in the floor of my office next to the man I had loved and wanted all of my life. He was perfectly content, sexually satisfied, and sound asleep. I, on the other hand, was realizing that somewhere along the way I had lost myself.

Something happens in a woman's heart and mind when she realizes that she cannot lean on the man she loves. Three months into my marriage I found that I was losing respect for my husband and it was not okay. Nor was it okay that he was okay with us sleeping on the floor of the office I had worked so hard to create. It was not okay that he would get up each morning, fold up the sheets, stash them away as if they did not exist, and walk down the hall to his office. It was not okay that he was on my company's payroll and seemed totally uninterested in finding any other work, knowing as he did that we needed money to buy a house. It was not okay that I had married a man who could not and did not seem to want to take care of me or our family. Of course, I said nothing while my heart began to harden against him. And, of course, he said nothing when I snapped at him or ignored him throughout the day.

It took almost three weeks of sleeping on the floor and showering in my son's basement apartment before I had another flash of brilliance. I walked into Gemmia's office, where she was busy working as usual. She thought I wanted to talk about my schedule. Instead, I told Gemmia that perhaps it was time for her to leave home. I reminded her that she was 25 years old with a perfect credit score, and that there was no reason to allow the mess of my life to fracture hers. I let her know that I had no problem with her and her family moving out of the office and into their own place. We would still see each other every day because we worked together. When she started to object—she didn't want to abandon me—I apologized for holding her captive to my craziness. It was not, I told her, her responsibility to take care of me.

This was one of the heart-to-heart, woman-to-woman, friend-to-friend talks that made my relationship with Gemmia so rich. I could talk to her in a way I wanted to talk to my husband, but couldn't; and she could talk to me the same way. This was my turn. Both of us had tears in our eyes, but we didn't do the touchy-feely stuff. Instead, we sat, two strong women trying not to cry in each other's presence, until Gemmia broke the silence:

"You, Iyanla Vanzant, are a remarkable woman, and he does not deserve you."

Four days later, Gemmia had a beautiful apartment and a moving truck, and I had a place to live. Her apartment had a loft. My husband and I not only helped her move, we moved in with her. As frightened as I was by the feelings about him that were brewing in the pit of my stomach, having him there made what we were going through seem doable. I wish I had understood that his silence was not indifference. He was just happy to be with me, no matter where we were. He felt that the love between us was all that we needed to make it through to the next step. But I felt alone, on my own, and abandoned. With a different kind of father, perhaps I would not have entertained so many fearful thoughts about my husband not doing right by me, would not have wondered when he was going to leave me. Not if, but when. I wish the women in my life had taught me about sharing, cooperation, and the strong one carrying the weaker one until they regained their strength. I wish I had known what to say and how to say it to him so that he would understand I was afraid and ashamed. In fact, I had one such friend—but to her I said nothing. How could I? It might mean that I had married the wrong man, and that was not a mistake I was willing to acknowledge. Denial takes on many forms. Silence is one of many.

We lived with Gemmia for three months, while I worked to amass money and we hunted for a house. We refined our wish list almost daily and used it as the measuring rod for every property we visited. We were about to make an offer on a house that was *almost* perfect when I had yet another flicker of brilliance. I needed to pray.

I was a meditative woman. I was a praying woman. There were only a few things, a very few things in my life that I would do without first engaging in deep, contemplative prayer or knowing that I had received divine guidance. That is what made me who I had become! That is how I had healed so many of the deep wounds in my soul. But in the period of upheaval, I lost sight of who I was.

Since the wedding, since welcoming a husband into my life, I had done very little praying and even less meditating. Sometimes it is like that—we fall in love and forget what sustained us prior to the fall. My husband and I often prayed together, but it did not feed my soul the way deep, contemplative prayer did. For that kind of prayer, I had to be alone. I had to get still. I had to surrender my thoughts, my feelings, and my will. I told myself that I couldn't or shouldn't pray that way with my husband around. Don't ask me why. I made it up. By the time we moved into Gemmia's loft, I had broken the discipline of my daily practice. But now, facing this monumental decision that would affect the rest of my life, I knew I had to pray. My husband respected my space by leaving the room or sitting quietly beside me.

God doesn't do anything halfway. When you lay your heartfelt desires before God, he will bring them to fruition in their fullness. When you trust God with your dreams, they will materialize *better* than you expect. Within a few days, I had the answer I needed: This was not a house we should settle for. When I shared this with my husband, he agreed and we kept looking. That was one thing I did love about him. He honored who I was when I was on my game.

It didn't take long after I prayed about it. The very next weekend, a friend gave me the number of a private Realtor. We told him what we were looking for, and he drove us out to an area in Maryland that we had never seen. We walked into the perfect house. The Realtor brokered a private sale between us and the owner. I had to come up with a bigger down payment, but our credit was not an issue. In fact, the deal was so private, the closing took place in my office conference room. All of the parties involved met there, in the same room where my grandchildren had slept on the floor in a fort made from sheets three months earlier. When you are in alignment with the desires of your heart, things have a way of working out.

The hard part is keeping track of what you learn along the way. I learned that I really can do *anything* for a little while. I learned that even though I thought I had been a bad mother, my children really did love and respect me. I learned that I still had many unhealed wounds from my relationship with my father and the women who raised me. I learned that I had married a man who had a very different view of life than I did. More important, I learned that I was afraid—afraid that I had made a mistake. *I had married the wrong man for the wrong reasons.* Or, the *right man* for the *wrong reasons.* Or, the *wrong man* for the *right reasons.* It really didn't matter which it was. All that mattered was that I had done it and that I would be judged for it.

When God looks in my direction,
change is on the way.
He proves my strength behind the scenes
before putting me on display.

— Iyanla Vanzant Journal
February 1994

CHAPTER 9

PUSHED TO THE BREAKING POINT

There was a period of about three years in which I simply was not fully present to what was going on within me or around me. The re-release of *Acts of Faith,* coupled with the simultaneous release of two new books, *In the Meantime* and *One Day My Soul Just Opened Up,* took my work to the *New York Times* bestseller list and put me in such demand that I was traveling four or more days a week, every week, month after month for more than two years.

And it was during this time that Spirit and I became all but strangers. On most days, I lost track of my spiritual practices and my faith. I prayed and I meditated, but I was no longer sure what I believed or how I felt about what I believed. The thing that saved me and kept my faith alive was when I sat to write, stood before an audience to speak, or coached another person, I could feel the living presence of Spirit in my being. These were the times when the failure of my marriage and my feelings of unworthiness didn't matter. When I was on purpose, doing my work, I knew without a shadow of doubt that God had my back. Yet, for some reason, I slipped out of the Presence when it came to handling my personal life. Then, in the midst of my human madness of living out my personal lie, I got the telephone call that would change my life forever. I was invited to be a guest on *The Oprah Winfrey Show.*

✜✜✜

Long before the young Eminem penned the lyrics, some part of me knew *"You only get one shot, do not miss your chance to blow!"* I got my hair and nails done, put on my best suit, and flew to Chicago to seize the opportunity of a lifetime. I was going to be on the show to talk about love and relationships. Lesson number one: Never talk about stuff publicly that will be broadcast around the world unless you are really clear that *you mean what you say.* My relationship with God was hit and miss at best. My marriage was on the verge of being a mess. My relationship with myself was a complete disaster, and I was slated to appear on *Oprah* to talk about things that I was still trying to master.

I was totally numb until I walked through the door of the studio. In that moment, a fleeting thought caught my attention:

She is going to do your show.

What show? I don't have a show.

Then the security officer beckoned me forward and the moment passed.

Everything went beautifully on the set. I connected with Oprah, and I felt that she connected with me. I sat across from her, sharing what I knew to be true about love and relationships, even though I had not mastered it in my own life. Then I left the studio the same way I had entered it: numb.

Back home, Gemmia was beside herself with joy. She knew, in a way that I did not, that something magnificent had been set into motion from that one appearance. She was always right. Within a few months Oprah premiered what she called Change Your Life Television, with a faculty of experts that included Dr. Phil, Suze Orman, and John Gray. I was invited to be a part of that faculty. It meant that I would appear on the show once a month. My area of expertise would be love and relationships. Oh joy! Oh rapture!

Working with a few of the show's different producers, I appeared in several segments that were widely popular. One, which told the story of my life, was particularly meaningful to many viewers. Many of them knew my name, but few knew my story. With my entire family in the audience, I shared things about myself that had been healed but not exposed to public light.

Oprah, an excellent interviewer, asked me a number of probing questions. The one that really caught my attention was "How do you know when you have healed an issue?"

From a deep place within my gut I responded, "When you can tell the story and it doesn't bring up any pain, you know it is healed."

In that moment, on that stage, I was being as authentic as I knew how to be. I would not discover until much later that my personal lie was running my life and using my mouth.

One of the best shows during my time with Oprah was the men's show. On one side, the producers gathered a group of men of all ages, my husband among them, to talk about their challenges with women. On the other side was a group of women who were ready and willing to talk about their disappointments with men. My job was to help both sides get on the same side of the table. It was meant to be insightful, inspiring, and instructional, and it seemed pretty innocent—until one of the men made a comment about women only wanting men for their money and what they could provide. I offered several counterarguments, but he and a few of the others were intent on arguing me down. So, to make the point, I put another nail in the coffin of my marriage. With all of the sincerity I could muster, I stood there on national television and said:

"That may be true for some, but it is not true for all. I love my husband and he doesn't have any money. What he has is a huge heart and a lot of love for me. That is what really matters."

As I spoke, I pointed at my husband. The camera zoomed in on him. He looked fine to me, or perhaps I needed to believe that my announcement about him would not have any effect on his masculine ego. Meanwhile, the man I was talking to told me that I was special and that most women were not like me. Oprah saved me by bringing in another point of view. It was innocent. It was a disaster. We never talked about it, but I learned from friends that my husband was devastated. What I had said was true, but he was still devastated. Although I apologized several times, he never really recovered from my unintended humiliation.

It really is true that being on *Oprah* can make or break you. While in one sense that appearance was the straw that broke the back of my marriage, it also injected a hot shot of adrenalin into my career. Everywhere I went, I became "the lady on *Oprah*." People were mobbing me for photographs and autographs in the airport and Target! My books were flying off of the shelves. The publisher was printing more to keep up with the demand.

Every organization that had anything to do with love, relationships, saving the environment, or anything else wanted me to speak. My travel schedule tripled. My office telephones were ringing off the hook. My husband and I were barely speaking, and I was, for the first time in my life, beginning to believe in myself. At last, I was loved and I mattered. I had something to say and people were listening. I could pay my bills on time and I had something left over. I could buy things without looking at the price tag. People knew my name when I walked into a restaurant or store. And yet I was always preoccupied with the next thing.

‡‡‡

The first book royalty check I received after a season of appearing on *Oprah* was so large, I was afraid to touch it. I made a copy of it. I wept over it. I deposited it in the bank and could hardly sleep, thinking that the money would not be there in the morning. It was.

Gemmia told me that I needed to buy myself something special to commemorate the achievement. I thought about it for more than a week. I decided that I would buy two peach colored armchairs. I wanted to be able to sit in and on that money! I had them custom made and I still have them today.

The chairs were just the beginning. When my husband and I bought our home, I was determined to make it everything I ever wanted and more. I had started with the kitchen, which had to be torn down and rebuilt. Next, I wanted a sauna room with a hot tub. I decided to wait, and instead I built a sun room onto the side of the house. My husband was all for it until the work began. Then he got quiet. I asked him what was wrong. I asked three or four times before I got an honest response.

He said, "This is your house, not our house." He felt bad that I was paying for everything and he could not contribute. I reminded him that we were partners and that I didn't consider the house or the money mine. It was ours. I felt that my job as a wife was to make our home as comfortable and beautiful as possible. I wanted him to participate, and it did not matter to me who paid. The truth is that he had to participate because I was never home.

Since he was unhappy anyway, I decided to proceed with the construction of my sauna room. He bought into the idea and even suggested that we build a stairway from our bedroom down to the sauna room so that we wouldn't have to walk through the house if we wanted to use it late at night. While construction was going on, I kept traveling and working.

During the summer hiatus after my first season on *Oprah,* I recorded my first spoken word album. It was a collaboration between the recording company and my publisher to put the message of the book *In The Meantime* to music. The producers understood my vision and pulled together a team of artists who could deliver the sound that supported the essence of the book. Working on that project gave me something that I had not felt for a long time—*joy!* I flew all over the country and met musicians who were my all-time favorites. The maestro himself, Mr. George Duke, crafted the title track, which was sung by Howard Hewett. Donnie McClurkin came into the studio to record, then flew to London to record a track with the London Tabernacle Choir. Maxi Priest sang the opening track, which was a remix of a Bob Marley song. Yolanda Adams gave us permission to use one of my favorite songs, "Just A Prayer Away." Donald Lawrence served as the music director and produced a song with Kelly Price and Tulani Kinard. It was all so magical. It was divine.

At the same time, I had begun negotiations to make my role on Oprah's show more regular. Of the Change Your Life faculty, Dr. Phil and I were the only two invited back for the next season. I remember the day my attorney and I went to the office for a meeting with Oprah and her attorney. This time, rather than just going to the studio, I got to go upstairs to the office. It was magnificent, dogs and all. The conference room was warm and comfortable. Oprah was gracious and very down to earth. We talked about my plans and my vision for the future. Oprah asked me if I wanted to do my own show or if I wanted to wait. In the back of my mind, I heard the message that I had gotten on the first day I walked into the studio: *She is going to do your show.* Now it made sense.

I also heard: *Just who the hell do you think you are to be sitting here?* I tried to ignore that voice.

"I will wait," I answered. "I want to be ready." So we agreed that I would be a recurring guest every other Tuesday with Dr. Phil.

When something unbelievably phenomenal is happening in your life and you don't believe you are good enough to have it, you will consciously or unconsciously find a way to sabotage your dreams come true. My sabotage was totally unconscious. My life had changed so much, I hardly recognized it or myself any more. I was going through the motions with no real emotional connection to any of it. My saving grace was Gemmia and my incredible staff. I had attracted a group of women, sister-friends who absolutely loved and supported me. They, along with Gemmia and my grandchildren, kept me sane. They ate chicken wings and drank Pepsi with me. They encouraged me when fear and doubt crept in. They answered the telephones and the mail. They supported the hundreds of people who flocked to my workshops and classes. They kept reminding me of the importance of the vision I had to build an international spiritual institution. They became the family I always wanted and thought that I never could have. They became the soft place I could fall as I realized that my marriage was falling apart.

Between recording sessions and speaking engagements, I would fly home. I remember the time I landed in my home-sanctuary just before the sauna room was complete. It was so beautiful! The walls were all glass, and from the hot tub I would have the perfect view of the three and a half wooded acres that surrounded the house. The one solid wall was built of blue marble that matched the tiles on the floor. The inside of the tub, also blue, was lit with rotating lights. The sauna was made of cedar, which gave the room an earthy smell. There was a spiral staircase up to the new redwood deck outside the master bedroom and a French door that led into the living room. It was just about done. By the next time I came home, my husband and I could float in the tub together and perhaps find our way back to each other.

I left for a three-day trip to finish up the album. When I called home the next evening, I got no answer. Several calls, still no answer. I didn't worry; I knew my grandson was with my husband, so there was little chance for hanky-panky on his part. He called me back after midnight. They had been to dinner, he and my grandson and his best friend. Then, because the hot tub was finished, they had all gotten in. I suddenly felt as if someone was trying to pull my eyeballs through my ears.

"Who was in the hot tub?"

"Me, Oluwa, and Jerry. It is really nice. I know you'll love it."

"Are you telling me that you let Jerry into the hot tub with my grandson?"

"Yes, I did."

"Are you crazy?"

"What do you mean?"

Jerry has AIDS. Jerry has full-blown AIDS! He has no business in a hot tub, and he has no business in that hot tub with my grandson or my husband."

"Well, he is my best friend and I don't have an issue with it."

"Well, you should!"

"You can't catch AIDS like that."

"Did he sweat?"

"I guess so."

"Well, my love, sweat is a bodily fluid and that is how AIDS is transferred. You must be crazy."

"No, I'm not, but you are!"

I am not sure who hung up first. I just know we both did.

Now I knew that my husband either had left or was about to leave our marriage. The man with whom I thought I would spend the rest of my life was communicating to me in a passive-aggressive display the depth and breadth of his rage. I had no clue how to address it. So we did not address it. When I arrived home the next day, I called the contractor and had him come and drain the hot tub. By the time my husband returned, there was fresh hot water bubbling in the tub waiting for us to immerse ourselves. He went to bed. I sat in the tub alone and wept.

Once the album was complete, I embarked on a 16-city tour to promote it. The plan was to debut the album on my first fall appearance on *Oprah* and begin the tour the next day. In each city, I would be joined by one of the artists who appeared on the album. I would perform the spoken word, they would perform the music. The producers at Harpo, Oprah's production company, wanted the exclusive right to promote the album and announce the tour. I was fine with that until I learned that it meant they did not want me to make my annual appearance on BET with my friend Tavis Smiley.

Tavis and I share the same birthday. Each year, I would appear on his show on our birthday, and we would discuss our plans for the coming year. The producers wanted me to forego it that year so that my first appearance for the season would be on Oprah's show. Tavis and I discussed it, and we agreed not to talk about the album. I told the producers, but either they were being overly cautious or they didn't believe me. They insisted that I not do the show. Numb as I was, though, I was not quite ready to have people tell me what I could and could not do.

Oprah sent me a message that it was my birthday and I could do whatever I wanted to do. Though I was delighted to have her support, I also sensed that something had subtly shifted. The producers seemed a little less cordial and a little less amenable to my suggestions for the show. I decided to pray about it and hoped that everything would turn out for the best. Little did I know that I was revving up to sabotage everything I had dreamed of and worked for. Lesson number two: You do not get full-time blessings for part-time devotion.

The album debuted on *Oprah* as planned. Shortly thereafter, I got a hand-written note from a vice president at Buena Vista Television. I read the note in total amazement. The VP praised my work and wished me good luck. She gave me a telephone number and invited me to lunch at any time. So I picked up the telephone and called the number. Perhaps I thought I would leave a message letting her know that I had received her note. Perhaps I thought that it was good business to have the private telephone number of a television executive. Perhaps I just didn't think. My personal lie of not being good enough simply could not pass up such a self-destructive bonanza.

I was completely unprepared when she answered the telephone on the second ring. When I introduced myself, she squealed and thanked me for calling. She said she'd been trying to contact me for some time but had been told that I had a six-figure deal with Harpo. You would think that, knowing I did have a deal on the table at Harpo, I would just keep my mouth shut. You would be wrong. Instead, I helpfully explained that while I had a wonderful working relationship with Harpo, I did not have a six-figure deal.

A few days later, she called me. Her boss had an idea for a television show on relationships that she thought I could help her develop. She assured me that all they wanted to do was pick my brain. When she told me her boss's name, my mouth dropped open. Why in the world would *Barbara Walters* need my advice? Apparently they were getting nowhere with the show, and Ms. Walters felt that I could help them find a new approach.

This is me, I thought, a poor, ugly, unworthy girl from Brooklyn, talking to an executive of a major television network who, on behalf of Barbara Walters, is asking me what to do. This could not be happening to me! But it was. I was amazed. I was scared to death. I was primed for self-sabotage.

I had become so busy, so self-directed, I had lost touch with my inner voice and my sense of self. My marriage, my most intimate relationship, was failing. What better way to boost my sagging ego than to have the two most powerful women in the television world talking to *me,* courting *me,* wanting to make a deal with *me?* That was not my first thought, but I must admit, it was a thought. Beneath it all, I now realize that I was still trying to heal the poor, dysfunctional, ugly, bad girl who needed to prove to herself and everyone else that she really was good enough. Someone once said that those who are buried alive do not die. They smolder. They steep. They emit a lingering stench that invades the most secret parts of your life. They stimulate the pathology and ignite the patterns. The only reason I could even consider living beyond what I was feeling was because I remembered to pray—*Oh God! Please help me! Please! Tell me what to do!*

The network flew me to New York and put me up at the Plaza. Over a lovely meal of food that I could not spell and did not recognize, Barbara Walters and three other network executives plucked my brain and stroked my ego. Back at home, I got the first in a series of telephone calls from the network asking that I consider an offer to host a new show. My response was, "No, thank you. I am happy where I am." The executive said she understood. She just wanted to ask in case I had changed my mind. There were changes going on at the network, she said, and they needed to make some decisions very soon. If I changed my mind within the next week or so, I could call her. She gave me her home telephone number. That bothered me, but it was also intriguing. *Why are these people so hot on my tail? What do they want from me? What do I have that they want?*

Until and unless you know that you are enough just the way you are, you will always be driven to look for more. Knowing that you are enough is a function of consciousness. Your enough-ness develops in direct proportion to the relationship you have with your true identity. Until you wholeheartedly believe in your own worth, in spite your of accomplishments and possessions, there will be a void in your Spirit. I had more than a void. I had a gaping hole that no amount of achievement, money, or acknowledgment could fill. *I'm not good enough, and I will never be good enough to deserve this kind of attention.* It was the personal lie, the core belief running my show, encouraging me to blow up my life just to prove once and for all that I wasn't good enough to have or keep what was coming my way. There was a part of me that knew that I was on purpose, the same purpose the spiritualist had made me aware of so many years before—ushering other people on their spiritual journey. I wanted to do just that, be of service and support to others. There was, however, a part of me that refused to believe I could be that valuable.

After the fourth or fifth telephone call from the executive, I concluded that the offer warranted my attention. I knew there was a lesson I needed to learn, but I had no clue what it was. I decided to reengage my spiritual practice of prayer and fasting. I committed to pray and fast for seven days or until I got the direction I needed. The issue at hand was whether to stay at Harpo or leave and start my own show. My preference was to stay put, but I had that black hole in my Spirit to be filled.

On the sixth morning, I awakened with the thought, *The time is now.* I shot straight up in my bed and spoke aloud, "I am not leaving Harpo." As if someone were whispering in my ear, I heard it again, *The time is now!* Time for what? I concluded that the message meant that it was time for me to stand on my own. Then I came face to face with the belief that I was not good enough to stand on my own. That meant I was avoiding the offer because fear was driving my choice. But I *really* didn't want to leave Harpo; it was the opportunity of a lifetime. Why would I walk away from a blessing as huge as the one on my plate? Then I had one little egotized *show me that I am good enough!* thought. The thought was: *Tell Oprah what is going on and ask her if she would be willing to back my show.* Seemed like a good idea at the time.

I followed the thought into action, with a few minor and perfectly devastating adjustments: I did not reveal to Oprah who had made the offer. I just said it was someone very big in the television world. I shared with her—honestly, I thought—why I should move forward with my own show now, even though I had said just the opposite in our meeting. I asked for what I thought would be an appropriate next step—to create a pilot project for a show I would host. Oprah seemed to receive my request with gracious consideration. The executive producer asked me who had made the offer. I told her that it was not important. What was important for me, I said, was to listen to the guidance I had received after praying and fasting. Instead of pressing me, she simply said that I would hear from Harpo soon. Oprah remained silent.

A week later, I heard that I should accept "the offer," because it was evident that I was not moving in the same direction as Harpo. My attorney received a similar curt call. He too was shocked and confused, since I did not actually have a firm offer from the Walters camp. Yes, there had been inquiries, but we had dismissed them, saying that I was happy with Harpo. Not one to give up on a dream that easily, I pursued the executive producer for a better explanation of why they had decided to drop me. When I finally got her on the telephone, she let it rip!

"We were offering you the chance of a lifetime. We were offering you something that not many have been offered, and you have the nerve to tell me that someone 'big' made you an offer. Someone big! Who is bigger than we are? Because you prayed and meditated, you think that someone big can do more for you than we can? I'm not sure what you want, but we must not have it."

For the next two weeks I could barely eat or sleep. I waited and I prayed, but there was no more information forthcoming. Not a word, a note, a card from Harpo, and only self-condemnation from my own mind. How could you be so stupid! *Now look what you've done! You have totally and royally f——d up!* Each thought made me more nauseous than the one before it. While I had often been numb to the excitement of appearing on Oprah's show, I was intensely aware of the pain I felt at being put off it. Pain was something I had learned to anticipate and expect. Joy was a completely unfamiliar emotion in my life.

When your life starts to fall apart, it doesn't always happen all at once. One fell swoop of the universe's backhand across your face might be more merciful. I had no idea that this was just the beginning of a collapse that would span seven years. It was October 1999 when the *Oprah* pebble landed, sending an unmistakable ripple through the river of my life. It was December 25, 2003, when the proverbial brick hit me in the head. And it didn't stop there.

When you don't know who you are,
Chances are you don't know what you want.
When you don't know what you want,
There is no chance for you to get it.

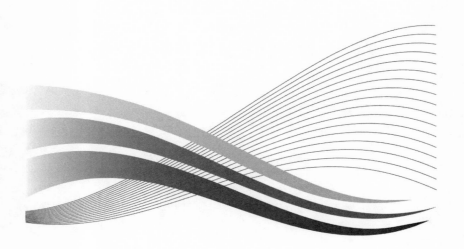

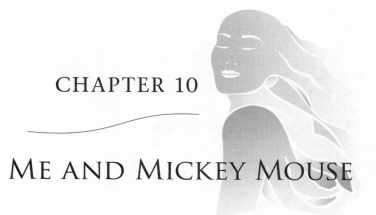

CHAPTER 10

ME AND MICKEY MOUSE

Almost a year had passed since I had last heard from Harpo. Other than a few close friends and Gemmia, no one knew the pain I carried in my heart and soul about what happened. Greater than the pain, however, was the shame. How do you explain to people that Oprah Winfrey kicked you to the curb? I had a bizarre kind of loyalty to her. I wouldn't talk about what had happened, because I didn't want anyone to think ill of her and I was ashamed to admit my role in it. Instead, I convinced myself and everyone else that I had left of my own accord to do more writing and, perhaps, my own show.

Then I received a call from Buena Vista saying that since I was no longer on *Oprah*, they really would be interested in talking to me about launching my show. It put a smidgen of truth in my fabrication. It gave me something to focus my energy on. It forced me out of the house, away from my depression and sadness.

The contract negotiations went quickly. I was about to make more money than I had ever imagined. With the deal inked and ready to go, Gemmia and I started planning for the future. I still had most of the huge check I had received from my *Oprah* appearances. I did something that Gemmia and I had been planning for years. I bought a building. Finally, I was going to have a spiritual center, a place where the work could continue long after I had ceased to be. We decided to pay for the building outright and borrow the money to do the renovations. We created a business plan, established a board of directors and went to the bank. With the promise of future income in my contract, the bank gave me a loan for the amount I had paid for the building, $1.3 million. They put the money in escrow and struck a deal whereby I would pay only the interest for five years. They would roll the cost of the building into the overall loan for $3.5 million.

The sight of that many zeros on one line, attached to my name, made my head spin. But Gemmia was totally comfortable; she had a business acumen that I had never developed. I was afraid to have money and afraid that if I had it, it would go away. She believed that money was just a means to an end, and our end, as we had envisioned it, was a good one. Her calm gave me the tummy comfort I needed to move forward. She and my business manager handled all of the details. I just showed up and signed wherever they pointed.

I was so proud of myself. In fact, when I sat and thought about it, I could feel a bit of joy brewing inside of me. Everyone at Inner Visions was totally elated. One of my board members had a canvas sign made with my picture on it. It read, "The future home of Inner Visions Worldwide." He had it hung on the side of the building. I was smiling in that picture, and for the first time in a long time, I was smiling on the inside. Many nights on the way home, I would drive past the building and stare at the picture of me smiling at me. I would allow myself to think about how far I had come. I had a very lucrative contract from a major television network. I was about to start a new project for my publisher. I owned a building that was about to become my dream come true. I had money in the bank. All systems were go in every area of my life, *except at home*. There, we were coasting cautiously. I didn't say much to my husband about the building except to talk about a space for his men's program. The bigger my life became, the more I could intuit his fear and resentment. True to my pattern, I mastered the art of growing very small in his presence.

‡‡‡

Nineteen-ninety-nine was a huge income year for me. That meant that 2000 would be a huge tax year. I had no idea how huge until I sat down with my longtime accountant. It was just a few weeks after we had purchased the building, so the joy was still brewing when he informed me that I owed the federal government $1.3 million. That was the exact amount I had paid for the building, the same as the amount I had put in escrow in order to get the loan to renovate. It was also the exact amount of money I no longer had in the bank.

I was still functioning with a paycheck mentality: Someone else took the money out of your check and sent it to the government on your behalf. What I learned that year was that as an independent contractor, I needed to pay quarterly estimated taxes. My accountant and business manager, with Gemmia's input, worked out a payment plan with the IRS. What none of us had anticipated was the amount of income one guest expert appearance on *Oprah* would yield. I had landed in an entirely new tax bracket. I was still thinking like a pauper and driving a Honda when in fact, I had become a millionaire. *Who knew?*

✣✣✣

Buena Vista spared no expense in getting the *Iyanla* show off the ground. The production office was in the high-rent district of Upper Manhattan, with the studio directly across the street. I had an assistant, a hairdresser, a make-up artist, an apartment, and a chauffeur-driven car on call. I worked with executive producer Bill Geddie and my supervising producer, Mindy Moore, for weeks before I arrived in New York. We discussed the theme of the show, the look and feel of the show, and most important, a vision for the show. I was just beginning to get excited. In no time at all, I would be living out a dream I had held on to for many years.

I was assured that Mindy and Bill as well as Barbara Walters and the executives in Los Angeles understood my vision and were committed to making the show a success. I was their latest and greatest find. The day I arrived in New York, I realized that things were not as they seemed.

The first clue was that I did not have a space of my own in the production offices. Mindy had a huge office overlooking the West Side Highway. They reminded me that most of my time would be spent in the studio, where I did have an office and a dressing room. In the interim, there was a small alcove outside of Mindy's office, and I could set up there.

The second clue was that all of the producers had already been hired without the consultation I had requested and expected based on our many conversations. The problem was that several of the producers could not pronounce my name and only one of the six had ever read one of my books. *Somebody shut the front door!* This show was supposed to be based on my books! How was that going to happen if the producers had no idea what was in those books? No problem! I called Gemmia and instructed her to ship me six sets of all of my books and a variety of my audio tapes. I went office to office and presented each producer with a set of my work, encouraging them to become familiar with my language and style. They seemed grateful.

Another challenge was that of the six producers, only one was an African American. Of the remaining five, only one was older than me. I wasn't sure if they knew anything at all about life as I saw it and had lived it. I knew that Bill Geddie, a 40- or 50-something white male, had no clue about my reality, and Mindy had spent most of her career in the newsroom. Something was incongruent with the original discussions that we had, but I didn't know how to address it. So I didn't.

My office and dressing room quickly became my sanctuary. There, with Jeff my assistant, Channel my hairdresser, and Lydia, a dear friend I hired to be my audience eyes and ears, I would retreat each day to discuss, eat, and pray. All the important work took place in the production offices—the "big house" as we called it—where the production meetings were held in Mindy's office or in the conference room. It didn't take me long to figure out that prior to most meetings, Bill and Mindy had already met. Their job at the meetings was to get me to agree to their decisions. Sure, they asked for my opinion, and of course they solicited input from the producers, but in the end, Bill's best idea always won. My job was to read the teleprompter to deliver the message. It was nothing like I'd imagined.

I was constantly reminded that daytime television was geared for housewives in Middle America, rather than the urban viewers and readers who had heretofore been my primary audience.

The women who watched daytime television wanted to see makeovers, learn about parenting issues, and have their secret questions about relationships answered. They wanted to escape. They did not want to watch me solve problems specific to the African American community. This was my opportunity to cross over to a much larger and more lucrative audience. There were those words again, *cross over.* I thought I had already done that. I was confused.

Bill and Mindy assured me that if I gave the show one season according to their formula, by Season Two, I could start introducing the subjects I had written about. My show needed experts so that I didn't come across as a know-it-all. We couldn't do an entire show on one topic, they said. Too difficult to hold the audience's attention. We needed a magazine—two big topics and two small topics—to keep people tuned in. "Appointment viewers." That's what we wanted, and we had one season to get them hooked. We would not be showing my books on television. People might think I was being too black. We didn't want that at all.

I was groomed for daytime television by the industry's best speech coach. After years of speaking publicly to thousands of people at a time, on the first day of my show, I froze. I talked too loud. I laughed too much. I was uncomfortable in my clothes, and I kept forgetting to look in the teleprompter. *It was a mess! I was a mess!* After the show, Barbara Walters gave me a good talking-to. She was sweet about it, but she gave me some very clear instructions about what I was never to do again. She advised me on how to keep myself calm and focused, and what to say even if I forgot to look in the teleprompter. I took everything she said to heart and put it into practice the very next day.

Unfortunately, according to the coach, I was still way off the mark—still too loud and unsure. He advised me to say things a certain way. He gave me tips on how to stand and which way to look. He said it was all about the camera and making myself believable. It took about three sessions before I realized that *it was about changing who I was into who they wanted me to be.* By then, I was convinced that I didn't know anything and that I was destined to fail. Gemmia was with me in New York that first week, and she could sense my fear. She kept saying, "Just be you and do you. If they don't like it, you can come home to your life."

Her words made sense, but she had no idea how much they disturbed me. I couldn't tell her that I no longer had a clear concept of who I was. I couldn't tell her that I felt like I was drowning in a glassful of water. I didn't dare speak that to anyone. There was too much riding on this venture. Too many people had put their hopes and dreams on my success. I was willing to do whatever it took to make the show a success, even if that meant following Bill and Mindy's exact orders. It wasn't just difficult. It was, painful. But it was, I thought, absolutely necessary. Going home every weekend was just another reminder of how lost I actually felt.

Looking back, there were some bright spots on the *Iyanla* show. My proudest moments were the shows I did with Deepak Chopra, Dr. Wayne Dyer, Marianne Williamson, and Dr. Michael Eric Dyson. These shows by far overshadowed the many makeovers and cooking shows I had to do. But I still shudder to think that I agreed to seat Dr. Dyer in the audience rather than on the stage. They told me it was to make him seem more approachable. Later, I discovered that one of the network executives didn't like him. The bright spots were often dimmed like that by the nastiness going on behind the scenes.

Although it has been almost a decade since *Iyanla* ended, I still remember the day Bill Geddie spit on me. He didn't actually spit saliva, but he might as well have. I had done a show about mothers losing control of their children. I had a real in-your-face, Iyanla-style talk with one mother. Although she got the point and seemed to respond, Bill decided that I had attacked her. I assured him that I had not. "Please trust my instincts," I said.

Standing over me, cigar in hand, he whispered in the hissing way he had: "That's just it. I don't trust your instincts. They seem sort of off to me."

It was like spit in my face, and it was all I could do to hold myself together. The part of me that responded was not the fighting girl from Brooklyn who didn't take mess from any body; apparently, she had left the building. The figure who emerged was the broken teenager who desperately wanted to prove that she was good enough to be on television, that she was worthy of all she had accomplished. The Brooklyn fighter would have had a few choice words for Mr. Geddie. The broken teenager barely made it to the bathroom before she wept her heart out.

Why couldn't I stand up for myself? Why couldn't I stand for what I knew to be true about me and within me? Why? Because I had never been taught how to do it— that's why. Because I had never, not once in my life, been told that I had a right to stand in my power, to affirm my knowing and, to be proud of the gift God had given me. The gift of seeing and hearing beyond the physical world that was the undergirding of all of my work.

Every ugly thing that had ever been said to me, every vicious thing that had ever been done to me, every hurt I had ever experienced rose to the surface, and I cried every tear I had ever swallowed in my entire life. It was a purging to prepare me for who I was becoming. Unfortunately, in that moment I didn't know that, so I still felt like a wounded victim. Lydia, who had never seen me cry, went into an angry panic. Channel cried with me. Jeff, who really would have liked to punch Bill out, sat down and prayed instead. When I was able to pull myself together, I knew that something had to change. I couldn't tell Gemmia, because she would lose it and possibly make a scene. My husband was not in the habit of defending me. I couldn't walk out of the show for fear of being sued. Looming over my head was a million-dollar debt to the IRS that I was paying at the rate of $30,000 per month. Let me be perfectly clear: I needed my job. Yet I understood that if I didn't get some help and support really soon, I would never make it through the season.

The day after the Bill Geddie meltdown, I hired Steve to coach me—Steve Hardison, a brilliant man who is extraordinarily sensitive and downright psychic, although he would never represent himself as such. We had met during our master's program in spiritual studies at the University of Santa Monica. Steve could see directly into my heart. I flew him to New York to get the lay of the land.

Bill was extremely suspicious of the tall, good-looking white guy who wanted to follow me around for two days. I explained that Steve was my coach and that he was there to help me adjust to the world of television. Within the firm boundaries Bill set, Steve talked to everyone he could and got familiar with the day-to-day operation of the show. Before he returned to his home in Mesa, he gave me his impressions and outlined our work together. This is what he said:

"Iyanla, these people do not know who you are. They do not know, because you have not told them. Most of them respect you and they respect work you did on *Oprah*, but they do not know your vision. If this show is going to work, you have to let them know who you are, get them enrolled in your vision, and make this process life-giving for you, or you might as well walk away. If this process does not give you life, it will steal your life, and nothing is worth that."

Over the course of three months, Steve coached me on how to stand up for myself within myself, and how to take a powerful stand on my vision for the *Iyanla* show. It was one of the most powerful experiences of my life. It is the reason the *Iyanla* show did not live beyond Season One.

During the third week of filming, the 9/11 tragedy destroyed the World Trade Center. We didn't tape for three days. I had some ideas about what we could do to support people through the tragedy, but neither Bill Geddie nor the network executives thought much of my ideas. Only after I spoke to Ms. Walters—which I did only when something was really important—was it agreed that I could go into the street and talk to people. It was a week after the bombing had occurred, and the state of the city made it difficult to get a studio audience. People were afraid to come into New York, and those who did come weren't there to attend a TV taping. It was then that the decision was made to hire actors to fill the audience. No one told me about the decision. I found out purely by accident when a producer let it slip that the crazy guy in the front row should not be hired back. I didn't get suspicious until a month had passed and I kept seeing the same people in the audience. When I asked about why it was still going on, I was told it was necessary to diversify the audience, because my core audience was black. Not only were they black, but they had a tendency to come dressed in African clothes, with the large head wraps. We needed to be careful not to give the impression that the *Iyanla* show was a "black" show. I was floored.

I had been working with Steve about a month when I had my second deadly encounter with Bill Geddie. After some persuasive insistence on my part and a little support from Mindy, it had been agreed that we would do a series of shows based on the principles in my book *In the Meantime*. These once-a-week shows would focus on relationship issues, and I would bring in an expert on the topic so it didn't appear that I was trying to do and know everything. I was so excited about finally using my own work on the show, I missed the point that I myself was an expert on the principles of healthy relationships—I didn't always live it but I knew all about it and that is what mattered for television. It was all the other the stuff they had me doing that was beyond my expertise. In any event, I flew in an African American husband-and-wife team from Michigan whom I had worked with before. The show went well, but like everything else, since there was no clear vision, it needed to be tweaked. That was the mandate of the production meeting where whole the team would be present, the meeting where Bill Geddie reigned supreme.

The meeting got off to a good start. The producer was enthusiastic as we discussed how to make the *Meantime* show more exciting. The ideas were flowing, and we were just about ready to settle on a plan when Bill dropped a bombshell. He was the only one in the room who was not seated. Instead, he walked around the table, offering his point of view here and there. He was walking up behind me, just about to pass me, when he turned and said:

"We're going to change the experts."

"Why?" I asked. "That's not what we had discussed previously."

"Well, I think we need a little more variety."

"Okay, but you said I could choose the experts since I would be working with them."

"Yeah, but those experts didn't really work."

Now I was getting a little pissed. I knew this couple and their work. In addition, they brought some diversity to the stage.

"Why didn't they work?" I turned to the producer. "Did you think they worked?" Unfortunately, that producer, like all of the producers, she remained mute. I did not.

"Bill, you seem to forget that I am the one who has to work with these people, and I still haven't heard why you think they didn't work." I had him backed into a corner and he had to tell the truth.

"I don't like them. They are boring, and they sound like you with all of their psychobabble. We need to get somebody else, that's it."

The comment moved through the room like a giant vacuum cleaner, sucking all of the air out of the producers. Thanks to Steve's coaching, the wounded teenager in my consciousness didn't even react. Instead, the fighting Brooklyn girl was alive and kicking. I had a vision for the In the *Meantime* shows. There was a part of me that was ready and willing to stand up for that vision.

"Bill, this really isn't about what you want, it's about what works for the show. I think this team of experts works, and I want to move forward with them."

He had made it all the way around the table again and was almost behind me as I spoke. Instead of walking on, he leaned over me, all six feet, four inches of him. He leaned over me and hissed:

"Let me tell you how this works. I am the executive producer. I am the one who gets to say who and what goes on this show, and I am saying that I don't want them back."

Looking up into the face of the large white male leaning over me as he sputtered his command, I wasn't sure what was happening, but I can now identify it as *a Middle Passage experience.* It was a fight for survival. This was another man using his size and position to bully me into doing what he wanted me to do. There was a part of me that wanted to scream and claw his eyes out. Another part of me knew that my *life* as the host of a nationally syndicated talk show was in danger. Was I going to sacrifice myself to please him? Or was I going to take a stand?

It was then that I realized something deep inside of me had shifted and been healed.

Very often we claim to know something. We get an idea about what to do or not do, yet, for some reason our behavior doesn't change. At times, we just can't seem to do what we know. This is known as mental healing. Something has shifted in your thinking, but it has not reach the other levels of your being—the heart and the spirit. Mental healing occurs quite often, and it is not a complete healing. It is not enough to shift or change the long-standing influence of an inherited pathology or way of being. In order to change your response to a pathological form of behavior, healing must take place on three levels of being—intellectual, emotional, and spiritual. Not until this level of healing has occurred will your behavior change. I had been healed!

In the back of my mind, I could hear Steve's voice: *If this does not give you life, it will steal your life.* My voice in the production of the show was the only way my vision could or would have life. The vision was the most important thing in that moment. The air was thick with silence. I knew I needed to back down, but I also knew I needed to stand up for myself. Scanning the room, I saw ten deer in headlights. Mindy, next to me, was fidgeting with paper. I was on my own. This was my flight to freedom!

In that moment, another part of me came to life. A real live wise woman, a warrior woman, sprang to life within me. She wasn't a soldier or street fighter engaging in a battle just to stay alive. Oh no! She was a well-trained and majestic warrior ready to do battle to advance my total well-being. I could feel her energy, power, and confidence move up my spine. Her presence slowed my heartbeat to a normal pace and calmed the shaking in my body. When she spoke, it was a shock to me and everyone else in the room.

"I'll tell you what, Bill. If you want another team of experts, you work with them, because I won't."

"Oh, so now you want to sabotage the show?"

"No. I don't want to sabotage the show. I want to honor my word to the experts I have chosen, and I want to hold you to your word, because you said I could choose them."

"Well, I'll tell you what; we just won't do the shows any more. We will drop the *In the Meantime* shows."

Oh, no! You can't do that! I'm sorry! Please don't do that! I recognized that internal voice as the not-good-enough part of me. The part of me that was ever ready to give up and give in. The part of me that was not willing to stand up for what mattered to me. The part of me that had done the wrong thing again, and now some man was angry with me. The part of me that was about to die a natural death.

The wise woman spoke again. "That's fine with me, because at the end of the day, it is my name on the wall. This is the *Iyanla* show, and there must be some part of Iyanla in the show."

How does a room full of women recover from the attack of a powerful man? Let me tell you, it ain't easy! Mindy finally broke the silence by introducing another topic. Bill, who was now beet-red, left the room. It was done, but it wasn't over.

I went across the street to my sanctuary. This time it was not the weeping little girl who shared her experience with Jeff and Lydia. The wise warrior woman explained what had occurred and what she planned to do about it. She asked Jeff to pray with her. While he was praying, the wise woman called the executive in charge of the show at the Buena Vista offices.

"I will not work with Bill Geddie. He needs to be removed from this production. Working with him would be like smiling in the face of the man who raped me as a child, and I refuse to do it."

The executive was silent for a long moment. When she did speak, she told me she would look into it and get back to me.

I asked her when. She promised to call back later in the day. I thanked her and hung up. Jeff was still praying.

Within a few moments Ms. Walters called. She had already heard the news and wanted to apologize. She did her best to convince me that Bill's bark was worse than his bite and that I did not need to feel threatened. To me, she was speaking for all the women in my life who had shown me that it was okay for the men in my life to abuse, deny, dismiss, and demean me. She was Aunt Nancy. She was Nett. She was the frightened little girl in me who was afraid of doing the wrong thing. I listened to her but I could not hear her. I was polite as I told her "I will not work with him." Iyanla was back! She had been resurrected from wherever she had been buried. In fact, this was an Iyanla even I did not know. She was clear. She was courageous. She knew that no matter what happened or how it happened, she would survive.

Thanks to Gemmia and my incredible staff, Inner Visions remained up and running while I was in New York doing the *Iyanla* show. I went home every weekend to see my husband and my grandchildren and, usually, to teach classes. Before I could go home or teach, however, I would go into my office at Inner Visions and weep. Except for that early meltdown, I didn't dare cry in New York. Crying there meant that Jeff would want to beat someone up and Lydia might curse someone out. Nor did I cry at home. My husband told me I needed to be grateful. He told me I was being too dramatic and should try to get along for the good of the show. He was clueless!

Half-truths and contradictions create an atmosphere of doubt, suspicion, fear, insecurity, and instability and all of it was totally familiar to me. At that moment, I didn't recognize the pattern and I couldn't believe it was happening.

Sometimes when you're healing your patterns and pathologies, the people watching you mistakenly come to the conclusion that there is something terribly wrong with you. There is something wrong; it's just not what they think it is. Few of us understand how hurtful it is to be judged and criticized when you are on a learning curve or in the midst of a healing crisis.

You would think that those closest to you would want to be helpful, supportive, nurturing and encouraging. Instead, because they don't know what they are looking at, they make snide comments, offhand jokes, they talk about you in front of your face and behind your back and because you are healing you can't just shake it off. Very often the very thing they judge you for is the very thing you're healing and their insensitivity only makes it worse.

When you are alone and scared in the midst of people who are trying to make you into what they want you to be, it is pretty hard to be grateful to them. My husband just didn't—or wouldn't—understand. So, rather than have yet another argument about the flaws of my personality, I cried in my office, surrounded by the women I knew loved and respected me. Then I could go home and act like everything was just fine. It was self-destructive. It was exhausting. It wasn't going to last much longer.

I didn't see Bill for quite a while after our confrontation. Mindy communicated with him by telephone. She and I began to form a tighter alliance, but I suspected that Bill was still pulling the strings. Meanwhile, I began to seek out people who could give me insight into the television-production maze and how to make the show viable. One unexpected blessing was the note I got from a producer at the Discovery Channel. He said that if there was anything he could do to help me, I should give him a call. I did, and he became my secret angel. I told him that I was scared and exhausted. I remember saying to him that I was doomed to fail because I didn't know how to do television. His response was the bucket of cold water in my face that I needed.

"You don't need to know how to do television. That's why you have producers. You just need to know how to do Iyanla."

Those were just the words that I needed to hear. I had turned my television show into a replica of my family environment where I thought it was my duty to do what they wanted me to do; to please them, to avoid confrontation, and to keep everyone happy. This is a challenge we all face in life; to become aware of when we are engaging the pattern of our pathology rather than addressing the people and issues at hand. Somehow, when I wasn't paying attention, Bill Geddie had become my father and all the men in my life, and the staff had become all the women. I was trying to be a television host and had forgotten to be myself: a powerful, insightful, compassionate spiritually grounded coach, well versed in spiritual principles and the laws of the universe. And because I wasn't paying attention, I was enslaved to the pattern rather than being empowered by the purpose. My purpose was to usher others on their spiritual path. It was not my purpose to do makeovers and soak almonds on national television!

Steve and I had been working diligently to clarify my vision for the show so that I could share it with the powers in charge. Without their buy-in, I would be forced to walk away. During the holiday hiatus, I began to put my vision for the show on paper. The plan was to give a copy to all of the executives at the season's end and let them know that unless we could agree on a clear direction for the show, I would not continue. In the meantime, Mindy was my only ally. We grew closer and closer to solidifying a direction.

My first breakthrough with Mindy came when she tried to convince me to do a show that included a segment on how to remove egg from a linoleum floor. I refused. She told me that her reputation was on the line because she had used her contacts to get this particular expert on the show. I reminded her that it was my name on the wall and my reputation was on the line as well. The second breakthrough occurred when a producer booked two guests who had written a book of their own based on *In the Meantime*. They were both 23. On the teleprompter, there was a question I was to ask them about why women stay in bad relationships. As I was reading the question, I had an epiphany, right there in front of the guests and the audience.

Why is Iyanla Vanzant asking these two people about something she has been writing about for 15 years? Why am I asking these people these questions that I already know the answer to? I wrote the answers to these questions!

The words flew out of my mouth before I knew what had happened. The guests were shocked. I was horrified, not because I had said it but because I realized, in that very moment how I had diminished my sense of self. I realized, in that very moment, that I had trained these people to play to my weakness, my not-good-enough weakness, rather than to honor my strengths, my intuitive spiritual strengths. I cleaned it up and kept the show moving. Later that day, I told Mindy that I would not entertain any more experts unless they had published at least half as many books as I had or were talking about a subject on which I had written nothing. She was very resistant to the idea.

That evening Mindy and I had a long and very tearful dialogue. It was an eye-opening conversation. It revealed the backroom deals that I knew nothing about. Mindy said she didn't know why she felt so bad. I told her it was because we both knew the writing was on the wall. She really believed in the show and wanted it to work. I assured her that if it was in the divine scheme of things for the *Iyanla* show to survive, it would. I told her that this entire mess was my responsibility. I had for too long given away my power and my voice. I had aligned myself with a process that did not honor me. I had trained people to believe that I would go along with anything just to be on television. I asked her to forgive me and told her that if the show had to end, I would be okay and so would she. Two days later, I was given the opportunity to stand in those words.

The first season of *Iyanla* was about to end when I gave my written vision to the executives. I asked for a meeting to discuss what I had submitted. I never got a response. Instead, we got a slew of e-mails from viewers complaining that the show was no longer airing in Los Angeles. No one in the office, including Mindy, knew anything about it. When I called the Los Angeles office, the executive claimed that she was trying to find out what was going on. L.A. was one of our biggest markets, and without it there was no way the show could survive.

The next day I got the call. I learned there was to be a conference call with all of the executives, including Ms. Walters, the following afternoon. The wise woman warrior was calm. That part of me knew that my life and my sense of value and worth was more important than a television show. The little girl in me was hysterical. That part of me felt that people were mad at her and she was going to get in trouble. She was particularly upset because, once again, she had failed to get her daddy's approval. Iyanla, the woman, mother, and wife went back to the apartment and started packing. That part of me was trying to make sense of what had happened, why it had happened, and what I was going to do about it. That part of me was finally strong enough to look at all of the pieces of the puzzle, knowing there was a way they all could and would fit together.

The call was brief. The network was dropping the show. They were sorry but the ratings just didn't justify continuing . . . they had fought for the show but . . . blah, blah, and blah.

I expressed my gratitude for the opportunity. Then I excused myself so that I could go talk to the staff. The new television season had already been set. That meant that everyone on my crew, the technicians, and the producers could be unemployed for an entire season. I ran across the street to the production office to talk to Mindy. I arrived to find her and Bill Geddie in the conference room talking to all of the producers and production staff. While I had been tied up on the call just finding out what was happening, they had broken the news to the staff. I took one look in the room, turned around and went back across the street to inform the technical crew. Those who were still there already knew.

When I called Steve, he wasn't surprised.

"We always knew that it was a possibility that they would not buy into the vision. You cannot be concerned about their response to your request. Now, you can create this in a way that gives you life, rather than takes life from you. Can you be okay with that?"

I wasn't sure if or how I was going to ever be okay again, but of course I said yes. First *Oprah*, now this. I wondered if I was the only person who had ever been kicked off of two television shows in two years. I didn't know what to feel, and now it seemed as if the wise woman warrior had left the building too. In her absence, I consciously willed myself to be numb. Before I could figure out the puzzle, the pathology kicked in.

We finished out the week of taping. After the cameras shut down and I left the studio for the last time, I never saw or heard from Mindy or Bill. Ms. Walters called me at home that evening. What she shared was very revealing.

She said that she was sorry things had turned out the way they did. She had inferred that because I was doing so well with Oprah she felt badly that now everything was falling apart for me.

"Well, it was my choice to be involved, and I am grateful that I had this opportunity. I really am."

Ms. Walters praised my talent and gifts but acknowledged that she had never really wanted to do *Iyanla*. She wanted to focus on *The View* and her specials, but Bill wanted to do this show with Mindy after she had done so much work to get *The View* up and running. He seemed so committed to doing *Iyanla*, that as his partner, Ms. Walters felt she had to back him.

She went on to affirm that I really should have my own TV show. But she believed that I needed to be in a place where I could do *pure Iyanla*. Like a television evangelist without the religious part.

"Well, I am sure if that is what I need, that is what I will get one day."

I stared into space vacantly. Suddenly the missing pieces of the puzzle fell into place. It was my family pathology all over again. *Iyanla* was never about me or my vision.

Then, I remember hearing Ms. Walters's final words.

"If I can ever help you, Iyanla, please promise me that you will call. Do you promise?"

"I promise, but do you promise that you will answer the telephone?"

"I will always answer if you call. That is a promise."

With that, I ended my relationship with Buena Vista, Disney Television, and Barwall Productions. I realized that the *Iyanla* show had never been meant to last. It had been a learning experience. I had just received a $10 million education in the art of television hypocrisy and the power of the pathology of my family of origin.

I had to laugh to myself. Mickey Mouse had paid $10 million to teach me a powerful lesson. Something good had to come out of this. It just had to. The key was that I would need to pay closer attention to who I was and want I was creating in and for my life.

I pray that from his glorious, unlimited resources
He will empower you with inner strength
through his Spirit.

— Ephesians 3:16 (NLT)

CHAPTER 11

BE STILL AND KNOW

Gemmia and several of the Inner Visions staff drove up to New York to help me pack up my office and my apartment. On one hand, I was grateful to be leaving what often felt like a hellhole; on the other hand, I felt like a total failure. On one hand, I was glad to be going back home to Maryland, where I was loved and respected for being just who I was. On the other hand, I was going home to a failing marriage and a $30,000 IRS payment due the first of every month. And I was now unemployed. My lifestyle was about to undergo a radical change, and I didn't have the first clue about what it would look like or how it would feel. I could only pray that when it unfolded, I would be ready and able to handle the changes.

It was time to think about how I was going to jumpstart my career and put my life back on track. The problem was, I was physically, emotionally, and mentally drained. Between leaving *Oprah*, going on the CD tour, and starting and leaving the *Iyanla* show, I had had three, maybe four good nights of sleep. I was running on adrenaline and fear. I was eating once every two or three days and gaining five or six pounds a month. I felt fat and ugly and alone. Gemmia knew it. She became my soft place to fall, my voice of reason, and my lifeline. No wonder my husband was jealous of her. We did everything together. And, she knew more about my business than I did.

Steve and Ken Kizer, my breath coach, were both trying to help me work through the maze of emotions I was stuffing down, denying, and trying to avoid. So much had happened so quickly, I couldn't give voice to what I was feeling. When Gemmia and I talked about it, I got upset, and then she got upset, so I would hold back just to keep us both sane. Her first thought was *f—— them.* We would re-create the show and do it somewhere else. I said I wasn't sure I was cut out for television. We agreed that it was time to get back to the business of building Inner Visions.

Unfortunately, business was very bad. Requests for speaking engagements were becoming fewer and fewer. In addition, since I was no longer on television, I could no longer command such a big fee. Several months after the show ended, I had to cut the staff. Several workers refused to leave; they said they would take half of their salary or even work for nothing. When I cut ten, I only lost three. When I cut the next seven, I only lost two. Those who could stay did stay. Those who could not became our wonderful volunteers.

Gemmia had a brilliant insight one day. She reminded me of how much money I had made for other people. Whether publishers or television networks, anyone I worked with or for had made money because of me. She wanted me to think about how I could turn my energy into making money for myself. She wanted me to understand my own value and worth. Why, she asked me, did I think I needed someone else to endorse me, promote me, and pay me? If I was truly self-employed, then I needed to make my name and my knowledge work for me. Gemmia said that I needed to apply for a job with God, Inc., and let that be the focus of my labor.

She was absolutely right. I was still operating with the mentality of a welfare mother who believed that someone else had to issue me a check. But I had learned that businesspeople do not spend money unless they know they are going to make money. If the publisher and the television network were willing to pay me a million dollars, it had to mean that they stood to make two or three million. I wasn't sure how they would make it, but I knew they weren't paying me because they liked me. They were making an investment in a valuable commodity—*me!* Why had that been so difficult for me to accept?

I took the question to both Ken and Steve. They both had different words that explained the same thing—somewhere along the journey of my life, I had given my inner value away in order to be accepted. Ken said I was so beat up about being who I was, I decided to be "less than" in order to keep myself safe. I felt guilty about being powerful, intelligent, and clear because it made the *big people* in my life so crazy. I had to play the role of being helpless, confused, and dependent because I had learned that if I wasn't, I could get hurt.

Steve put it another way. He offered that I'd been taught not to like myself, because the people around me didn't, for whatever reason, like me. I accepted the things I was told about myself and the things I made up about myself in response to what I had been told. Nothing that I'd been told had ever affirmed my power. If you add the issue of racism, the extent of the abuse I had endured, and the number of separations and losses I had experienced, it was a wonder that I could tie my shoes and spell my name. According to Steve, I was a bona-fide miracle, and God had created me for a very special mission. All I needed to do was learn to love myself, make self-honoring choices, and accept my true identity. Boy, did that sound good! It felt good too! And the wise woman within me reminded me that if I weren't already taking small steps in that direction, I would still be doing Mickey Mouse TV.

"Where are you to start, Iyanla?" Steve asked.

"Well, of course, I must begin within! But—I have done that. I have explored the depths of my mind, heart, and soul, and this is where it has gotten me."

"There is always more to do, Iyanla. There is always more to do."

I had done a great deal of inner work and studied almost everything the master teachers had to offer—and yet *I had come to the end of everything I knew.* I thought I knew a lot, and on some level, I did.

But I had to remind myself that when you cannot embody what you know, maybe you don't really know it. There was one thing I had come to realize. All the time that I was engaged in my childhood battle of seeking out my father's acceptance and approval from my husbands, I had missed the "Father's" true presence in my life. Ken, Steve, my producer friend, and several other men had come into my life to provide for me the support, guidance, and protection that I longed for and craved. Yet, because I was so busy looking for it in one place, I had missed the fact that it had always been there. I have had some great male friends in my life who have loved me unconditionally, and I didn't have to sleep with them to get their support or approval. The Bible says that God always has a ram in the bush. I was so busy trying to chop down a huge tree that I had totally ignored the powerful presence of the male bushes all around me.

With that realization came the truth that I had fallen off of my spiritual center. I had surrendered too much of myself to *doing things* and not enough to *being* myself. On the emotional level, I had fallen into a pattern of terrorizing and brutalizing myself with my own thoughts. Before anyone else could, I would make myself wrong; before anyone else could, I would begin to doubt myself. It was the pathology of my early life that had been so engrained into the fibers of my being that I no longer recognized my habitual thoughts and behaviors. I knew better or at least, I thought I should know better.

None of this stopped me from doing great work in the world. I knew the spiritual principles; I knew the spiritual laws that made life work. Even when I did not practice them consistently, teaching them and sharing them with other people reinforced their extraordinary value. The question was: What kept me from practicing them in my own life, every day? The truth? *I had become spiritually lazy.* Because I knew the principles on an intellectual level, I pretended that I could backslide and fall down on my own daily spiritual practice. What I was able to admit to myself was that when you are entrusted to usher others you have to stay clear and clean. This means that God will shine light on your internal landscape to show you what has been hidden from your view. It's not meant to be a punishment. It is all about fine-tuning your self-awareness. Nothing happens outside of you that isn't going on inside of you. That is how the law of Cause and Effect operates.

Gemmia felt the same way. For days, she and I discussed the ways we had slipped out of our practice. We vowed to get on track. For her, that meant better time management. For me, it meant cleaning up, or perhaps cleaning out, my house.

Every 24 hours, the mind and the body need to eat, work, rest, and play. But in our fast-paced lives, we are living on borrowed time. We borrow hours from one day and put them into another. Some days, we work long hours and don't get enough rest. On other days, we eat more and do not play enough. On most days, we work and eat and forego rest and play. After decades of doing that, the mind and the body become confused and no longer function at maximum capacity. These imbalances result in dis-ease: mental, emotional, and physical breakdown. I think the same is true in the heart.

What people commonly call stress, I believe is the rebellion of the heart. The heart can only take so much pain, disappointment, or upset. The heart is communicating to the mind, Hey! *You better chill or else.* My heart had been screaming to my mind for years, and for some reason my mind just would not listen. I had trained myself to push up the mountain rather than take the lift. Things only counted if I suffered. For far too long I had been willing to be beaten up and beaten down and pop back up smiling. If the mind and the heart are the foundation on which we create experiences in our lives, my foundation was crumbling and I needed to do something about it.

The wise woman was back. She reminded me of all the things I did know and encouraged me to put them to use. At the same time, I recognized someone else standing up within me. It was the warrior. She was not trying to fight; soldiers fight. Warriors had another level of honor to uphold. The warrior was ready to do battle within and without to save the kingdom. The kingdom was my mind and my heart. The warrior's ultimate work was to protect my soul.

Driving home on the day I first experienced the warrior woman within me, I called my husband.

"Hello."

"Do you still love me?"

"Wow! What brought that on?"

"Do you still love me?"

"Yes, I do."

"Do you want to save our marriage?"

"Yes, I do, but I just don't know how."

"Do you need to know how? Or are you willing to do whatever it takes?"

"I want to save our marriage, and I am willing to do whatever it takes. Do you still love me?"

"Absolutely. You are the first man I have ever loved, and I want to save our marriage."

With that, we both burst into tears. I was crying so hard I had to pull over to the side of the road. He was weeping from a place that I had never heard before. For the first time in a long time, I had an intimate moment with my husband. It was both powerful and frightening.

"When are you coming home?"

"I am on my way right now."

"I'll be here."

Knowing as I did that I had come to the end of everything that I knew, I understood that I couldn't go any further on my own. The wise woman spoke: *Iyanla, your best intuition got you here.* I waited. I prayed. What I needed to do was whispered into my heart.

Sitting on the side of the road, wiping my nose with the hem of my skirt, I called a sister-friend of mine. She and her husband pastored a church in Washington, D.C. I told her that I was in trouble; that my marriage was in trouble. I asked her if she and her husband would be willing to counsel me and my husband, to teach us how to be together. She said she would talk to him and get back to me. I asked her to pray with me and she did.

The next call I made was to Ken in Richmond. I asked him if he would be willing to work with my husband and me together so that we could clear whatever was going on between us. In typical Ken style he responded:

"Hot damn! Let's kick some psychic butt! Come on down, honey!"

For the next 15 minutes I sat in total stillness. I was startled back to reality by the telephone ringing. It was the pastor's wife. "We're in. We can do Wednesdays. What time will work for you?"

I was crying again. I put the car in drive and headed home. I so wanted to call Gemmia, but I knew I couldn't. I couldn't be sure she would agree with what I was about to do, because she was having issues of her own with Jimmy.

Gemmia had one boyfriend her entire life. She met him when she was 15 and dumped him when she was 30. She was in the middle of that separation when I was leaving the *Iyanla* show. As with almost everything, Gemmia kept her challenges to herself. She did tell me that she had had enough of him and his lies. What lies? She wouldn't say. I could sense her sadness, but she, like me, knew how to hide her emotions. She, like me, refused to let anything take her down. She kept many things to herself. What she did do was write in her journal. Whether it was a good thing or a bad thing, Gemmia wrote what she really felt in the safety of her private pages.

Most people thought that Gemmia was quiet and shy. Shy she was not. Quiet, I'm not sure. My experience was that she chose her words very carefully. She was observant and wise beyond her years. Her wisdom had certainly saved me many more times than I care to remember. Gemmia was grounded and centered in a way that I often longed to be. She had always said that when she grew up, she wanted to be like *me,* clear and spiritually on purpose. Yet, in her presence, I felt that she was the master and I was the student.

What Gemmia had that I did not was an absolute shut-off valve. When she was done, she was done. The day that I stood up to Bill Geddie at Buena Vista was the day she knew she had to make a decision. If I could take a stand like that for myself and risk everything I had ever worked for, she said, surely she could tell a mere man that she no longer chose to endure his bad behavior.

I had no idea that my adult child was inspired by me. I knew she deeply loved and profoundly respected me, and yet to think that my behavior encouraged, instructed, or supported her was something I hadn't considered. In fact, we often joked that she was the real mother and I was her child. Gemmia taught me so much about myself, life, and how to be my most conscious self.

Gemmia was an avid fashionista and once told me that I looked like I was stuck in a 1960s time warp. Shortly thereafter, we took a field trip to Bloomingdale's, where she taught me how to dress. I had to admit, the outfits Gemmia chose made me look ten years younger.

I taught her how to cook. She raised the basics I had taught her to new heights. I taught her how to fry chicken. She taught me how to oven-fry it. I taught her how to bake a cake. She produced a different flavor cake, in a different shaped pan for Niamoja every holiday. While I stuck to the basics and mastered them, Gemmia ventured out, experimented with different spices and herbs, and gave her meals more depth and dimension. It was the honey glaze on the turkey and the apples in the cornbread stuffing that let me know she was ready to take over Thanksgiving dinner. When Gemmia turned 29, we shifted Thanksgiving Dinner to her house, but I retained the privilege of doing Christmas, which was her favorite holiday. There was just something about putting up the tree on Christmas Eve, wrapping presents until the wee hours of the morning, and watching her mother cook that made Christmas a joy for her. I shared that joy with her as my children became adults and their children slept over on Christmas Eve.

There were so many things Gemmia knew that I did not. I often watched her deal with angry and upset people with a smile on her face. She was an expert at handling people. She rarely responded to their upset with anything other than a smile. Someone once said to me that anytime they spoke to her, it sounded as if her words were smiling.

Gemmia was also an excellent mom—way better than I had ever hoped to be. She was patient and gentle with Niamoja, her one and only princess. She made a point of having specific days when she and Niamoja did special things. Tuesday was baking day. I always got the benefit of their Tuesday-time on Wednesday.

Most Fridays, when Gemmia wasn't working or traveling with me, were movie nights. They popped corn and slept on the living-room floor in front of the big-screen television. They also went to the theater and museums together. Sometimes they would invite me. Most times not.

One day I asked Gemmia where she had learned to be such a good mom. Without batting an eye she said, "I only had one mother. Where do you think I learned? You always focus on what you did wrong, but I am alive because of what you did right." I left the room and wept.

If you asked me, I would have said that I taught my daughters absolutely nothing good about relationships. Gemmia would beg to differ. Every now and again she would remind me of something I had said about men or done in my relationships with them that had taught her a powerful lesson. I expected to be perfect. Gemmia accepted that I was human. According to her, she had learned a great deal from my humanness.

Gemmia told me she knew that standing up to Bill Geddie was a stand for my independence, not from men or from domination, but from fear. Fear that I would lose something; fear that he would hurt me; fear that I could not make it without him. She said that those were her fears also. Those were the fears that she had been dealing with in her relationship with the only man she had ever been intimate with. She loved him, and she knew that his behavior kept her in bondage. When I pressed for details, she gave me her Gemmia look and changed the subject.

Gemmia, my daughter, mother, teacher, and best friend, opened my eyes, heart, and mind in a way that few people ever have. It was very strange to know that my daughter and I had come to the very same place in our relationships with men, and that I didn't know how to guide her or myself to the next step.

✞✞✞

I arrived home to find my husband sitting in one of the two rocking chairs in our bedroom, in front of the fireplace. As I entered the room, I realized that we had rarely sat there together. He must have had a different realization. For the first time in a very long time, my husband grabbed me and held me. It wasn't an *I want sex* holding, and it wasn't a *let me get this over with* holding. It was a deep, sincere *we are in this together* embrace that nearly made my knees buckle. The way he held, rubbed, and rocked me made me feel hopeful and a bit excited. When we finally separated, he told me he had been thinking about us all day.

I told him about my side-of-the-road breakdown and how I had been guided by the Holy Spirit about what we needed to do. But before I could tell him the plan, he said that the Holy Spirit had spoken to him also. Quickly, I had to decide if I would speak or if I would let him take the lead. Remembering how he had just embraced me, I yielded.

"I have to leave, Iyanla. I have to go and find my vision, get my life on track, come back and court you, and start this marriage all over."

What the hell are you talking about? I thought it, but I did not say it.

"I've been resentful because I'm not contributing to our marriage. I'm not standing on my own. If we are going to make it, I have to be able to stand on my own."

This does not sound good! Another thought I did not speak aloud.

"I really feel that Spirit is telling me to take the time to order my own life so that we can have a life together."

I couldn't hold the silence any longer.

"What spiritual authority are you relying on for your guidance?"

"What do you mean?"

"I mean, when you get guidance from the Holy Spirit, you have to test the Spirit by the Spirit. You have to make sure that what you are hearing is coming from the Holy Spirit and not just any spirit passing by on the way to McDonald's."

"I'm not following you."

"I mean, is there a scripture, is there a section of *A Course in Miracles,* is there anything that you can turn to that ensures that what you are hearing is divine guidance?"

He was on the defensive now. "You are not the only one that Spirit speaks to, you know!"

"I am not doubting you, but I know that when the Holy Spirit is working, everything that is given to everyone involved lines up, and what you are saying to me does not line up with what I have been given. That makes me suspicious."

"Well, what were you told?" It was going to be a competition.

"I'm not denying that is what you heard, it just doesn't line up with what I got and what has been confirmed for me."

"So tell me what you heard. I'm open."

I shared the plan for counseling with the pastor and his wife and breath work with Ken.

"I'm not feeling that," he said, "and I really need your support. This isn't just about you. This is about what I need to do for myself, so that I will be able to do better for us. You always talk about finding a vision. Well, I don't have one and haven't had one for a long time. I need to be able to look at you and know that I am an equal partner in this relationship. Right now I'm not."

He said some more words that I couldn't or didn't hear. I was too busy listening to my heart echoing in my ears. This was it! The end had finally come. He asked me a question that I did not hear, so I did not answer.

"See how you dismiss me and my feelings!"

"Forgive me. I was trying to listen."

"So what are you hearing?" He knew that there was a zone I could enter to get information when I needed it.

"What I am hearing is if you leave this house, you're never coming back."

"I don't believe that! I believe this is what I must do to save this marriage. I must find my vision. I must court you. I will be back."

He really believed what he was saying. There was nothing I could do that would change his mind. But I decided to make one last-ditch effort.

"You are talking about separating. That is not from God. God is about unity. God is about holding on and breaking through. We don't need help to love each other. We need help in learning how to be together. That is what the pastor and his wife can teach us. That is what God wants us to learn."

"I don't believe that. I am asking you to trust me."

Just then, one more piece of guidance was whispered to me.

Let him take the lead. It was as if a dear friend were whispering in my ear. *Let him take the lead.*

Then the telephone rang. It was the pastor's wife. My heart sank as I explained that my husband was not open to the counseling. She said she would pray for us.

We spent the rest of the day talking and packing. He didn't know where he was going. We talked about our mistakes and our misgivings. Sometimes we stopped to dry our tears. Him first. Then me. He shed tears because he was afraid he was making a mistake. I shed tears because I knew he was. But I had to encourage him. I did so by promising I would wait for him, no matter how long it took. He wanted a year—a year to find his vision and come back to me.

I asked him to forgive me for anything I had done to undermine his confidence. I acknowledged my coldness and my meanness. I tried to explain my fears, the ones that had multiplied after we'd slept on the floor of my office together. He started to remind me of all of the uncaring things he thought I had done and said; then he caught himself and stopped.

It wasn't until he started putting his clothes in the car that it really hit me. Thirty-seven years of my life, of loving this one man, were about to come to an end. Oddly, while I was falling apart, he seemed energized. He looked taller and seemed clearer.

‡‡‡

The first four months after we separated, we spent more time together than we had living under the same roof. Things felt lighter between us; the pressure had been released. We were no longer forcing ourselves to stay together. Instead, we were choosing to *be* together. We spoke several times a day. We went out to dinner. We spent many intimate nights together. When I needed him to stay with my grandson, he would. And when he was around, he continued with his household chores: the trash down the hill, raking and blowing the leaves, and helping me with the groceries. We went from being husband and wife to being boyfriend and girlfriend.

Only my closest friends knew about our trial separation. Most of them stayed mum on the topic. Most did not include Gemmia. When I told her, she simply said, "It's about time." She apologized, but she didn't really mean it. She told me not to worry about how or when or whether he would come back. What I needed to worry about was that I didn't have a prenuptial agreement.

"He doesn't want anything from me. He would never accept anything from me."

"Of course not," she said, "he already took everything he could get."

"What do you mean? He hasn't taken anything from me."

"Well, I guess if your dignity and self-respect don't matter to you, then he didn't take anything."

After Gemmia's observation, there were more nights than I care to remember when I would sit on the edge of my bed and wait to see the headlights of his car coming up the driveway. It took me about nine months to get used to the fact that he was not coming home.

‡‡‡

I have heard many times that a breakdown is an opportunity for a breakthrough. The breakdown of my marriage led to a breakthrough in my spiritual life. I had to pray to stay focused. I had to meditate to stop my mind from plotting murder. I had to read the masters, searching the ancient texts, to find some understanding of what I was experiencing. My Spirit was growing strong. Good thing! Because I was in a royal battle with my flesh. I could not accept that the marriage that I had put so much into was over. I found the last, definitive sign in the last place I expected.

Was it really a marriage? Well, maybe not. And at the same time, it was as good as—if not better than—any marriage I had ever seen. He didn't beat me. For the most part, I always knew where he was, and when we were together and not fighting, he was always a gentleman. I could always depend on my husband to do what he said he would do; unfortunately, that wasn't too much. But then again, that is what I had learned to expect from most, if not all of the men in my life. I did, however, feel certain that he provided a good example for my grandson. I was mistaken.

When my husband and I got married, Gemmia offered to take my grandson Oluwa and raise him. When I told him about Gemmia's offer, he said, "Absolutely not!" Oluwa would stay with us. He wanted the opportunity to do for him what he had not done for his own sons. Raising him, like our marriage, was a blessing, an opportunity from God for a second chance. There is no doubt in my mind that my husband loved Oluwa. Unfortunately, he was so old-fashioned in many ways that his love was a more Spartan than generous love.

He would take Oluwa with him to meetings and gatherings where there were no other children and expect him to sit quietly. Oluwa just wasn't that kind of child. My husband was extremely impatient with modern children. In his exasperation, he would box Oluwa's ears or knuckle him on the head. Oluwa hated it! I was caught in the middle. I wanted Oluwa to be raised with a male influence, so I rarely interfered.

When we were alone, I'd suggest a kinder way to discipline him. I thought we were co-parenting. I thought we should talk about things and come to an agreement. He charged that I dropped Oluwa off on him because I didn't want to deal with him. Oluwa didn't see it that way and neither did I.

One day Oluwa and I were in the mall when he announced:

"Yeye, I am going to find you a husband."

"Really!" I said with some interest. "Why would you do that when I already have a husband?"

"Baba doesn't act like he wants to be your husband. He treats you mean, and I don't like that. He treats me mean too."

"Really? I thought you loved being with him. Why do you think he treats you mean?"

He went into a long explanation about the ear-boxing and the head-knuckling, the long meetings and the boring things Baba did.

"But he always came to your games when you played ball."

"Yeah, and then he stopped coming and never even said he was sorry."

"Well, Baba loves you, Oluwa. Maybe you should tell him how you feel."

"No. I'll just find you another husband, one who treats you and me better than he does."

My heart sank, but that was before he dropped the bombshell.

"You need a husband who treats you like he treats Ms. Brenda."

"Who is Ms. Brenda?"

"She's Baba's friend. She always comes by the office to help him. He talks real nice to her, and he is always smiling at her. I think he likes her and that's why you need a new husband."

I couldn't believe that he would take my grandson around another woman. I didn't want to hear any more, but Oluwa had more to say.

"And you know what else?"

"No, Oluwa, what else?"

"He always buys her lunch. He never buys you anything. Do you know that Baba has never bought you or me anything at all?"

"That's not true, Oluwa, he has bought you things, and he always takes you to breakfast."

"No, he doesn't take me to breakfast. He goes to breakfast because you are not home to cook. If you were home, he wouldn't take me anywhere."

"Why do you say that? I think he would take you places even if I was home."

With that, he stopped dead in his tracks. He turned his innocent little ten-year-old face to me and said with a maturity far beyond his years:

"Yeye, I thought you were a smart lady. You help people everywhere all of the time. People you don't even know, like you. I'm telling you that Baba doesn't like you, and you need a new husband."

As we walked on through the mall, I explained that he should talk to Baba about his feelings. He said it wouldn't matter, because Baba never listened.

"Yeye, I belong to you not him. He puts up with me but he doesn't want me. You do everything for me and Baba. If I had to wait for him to do anything for me, I would die. Trust me. I would be dead."

I imagined the headline: "Best-Selling Author Has Nervous Breakdown in Suburban Mall." In order to save myself, I suggested to Oluwa that we go have pizza. The truth? I needed to sit down.

Was it a marriage? As hard as it was to admit, it was not. It was a co-dependent entanglement. Maybe it was an addiction. Addiction means that you knowingly engage in behaviors that are destructive or harmful. In many instances, it is described as an obsession or compulsion. *I was obsessed with making the marriage work.* I did many compulsive and impulsive things to try to make it work, including ignoring all of the signs that it was not working. But was I going to spend the rest of my life trying to prove that I was worthy of this man's love?

I could do for my grandson what I could not do for myself: I could break the pattern of exposing children to dysfunctional relationships. The next time I saw my husband, I told him about my conversation with Oluwa. He thought it was funny. He asked me why I was listening to Oluwa. I said that his behavior was not only inappropriate, it was without integrity. He said that I was not one who should speak about integrity. I recognized the bait. He was trying to drag me into the valley of what was wrong with Iyanla, and I refused to take the trip.

Instead, I asked him for a divorce.

He asked me if that was what I wanted. I told him no, but I didn't see how anything was going to change. He let me know that I was what needed to change. We had a very brief, very nasty exchange before he got up to leave. My normal addictive behavior would have been to call him and apologize. Not that day! On that day, I decided to go cold turkey. I refused to allow myself to want somebody who obviously did not want me.

✝✝✝

The television had become my new lover. After doing my prayers and bedtime intentions, television was the way I subdued my mind, the way I kept it from conjuring up distorted images of what he was or was not doing in his apartment or elsewhere. Most nights, I would take a long hot bath, lotion my body down with some lovely scent, put on my grandma nightgown, crawl into bed, and let my lover cover me with colors, sounds, and pictures. I would watch things that I had seen 20 or 30 times as if it were a first-time experience. *The Color Purple* was one of my favorite foreplay exploits. *The Fugitive* was another. Unfortunately, the climax did not leave me exhausted or wanting more. When it was over, it was simply over. No kissing. No hugging. No giggling under the covers. Instead, I would roll over and grab the remote. I was usually asleep by the third act, waking up just in time to see the credits roll.

This particular Sunday night was no different. None of my favorites were playing, so I watched something that was sure to take me down quickly. I was awakened by what felt like an incredible weight being dropped on my chest. My eyes flew open. Then I realized I couldn't move. Flat on my back, I was pinned to the bed by something or someone that I could feel but could not see. *Oh Lord! Someone is robbing my house! They must have given me some type of drug!* I tried to listen for movement in the house, but the only thing I could hear was my heart pounding. I tried to move my legs. My arms were at my sides. I imagined that they had been strapped down, but there was no belt, no rope, nothing I could feel. *Maybe I'm having a stroke or a heart attack!* I must get to the telephone. That thought led me to the discovery that I could move my head. Craning my neck as far as it would go, I looked toward the nightstand where the telephone was resting, but I still couldn't move my arms. What I could do was see the clock. It was 12:41 A.M. My mind was racing. My heart was still pounding. I tried to take a deep breath to calm myself down. As soon as I did, I felt the overpowering weight again; this time it was pressing deeper into my chest, my stomach; now it was all over my legs. I needed to get my hands moving to that telephone!

Suddenly, my nostrils were filled with the smell of sandalwood. It was the scent my husband wore every day. Oddly enough, the fragrance was comforting. Whatever was going on had something to do with him.

Then it began. I could feel the warmth of his breath on my neck. It felt as if his hands or someone's hands were stroking and caressing my body. The pressure would increase and then decrease. Then I heard a woman's voice. She was moaning. Now he was moaning. *What is going on? Am I having a wet dream?* I turned my head again. It was 12:58. The stroking and the moaning were beginning to intensify, and I could swear the bed was moving up and down in a very intimate way. I closed my eyes, determined not to die and not to succumb to the panic I felt in my body.

It felt as if I were floating, maybe time traveling. Then the pictures began to flood my mind. I could see him and her, caressing, kissing, making love. My heart stopped pounding and sank into my stomach, setting off an intense wave of nausea. Whether my eyes were opened or closed, the images did not disappear. It all began to make sense. He was somewhere, making love to another woman, and I had inexplicably tapped into or fallen into their energy. As disgusting and unsettling as the thought was, the realization brought me to a state of calm. It was bizarre, but at least I wasn't dying.

I laid there for what seemed like forever, checking the clock every other minute. 1:07, 1:14, 1:36. The images were floating in my mind and in front of me as if they were on television. Finally, the pressure was released first. My hands flew up to my eyes on their own. My body was my own again. I screamed and rolled onto my side in a fetal position. The images stopped as quickly as they had begun. The nausea subsided. I could still detect the lingering scent of sandalwood. I looked at the clock. It was 1:57.

Shaking and shaken, I reached for the telephone. My hands were trembling, but not so bad that I couldn't dial. I called his cell phone. No answer. Before the message played out, I hung up and called back again. Still no answer. Tears were falling violently from my eyes. Between screaming and wailing, I kept dialing the number. By the tenth or eleventh call I decided to leave a message.

"I don't know where you are, but I know what you are doing. I felt it. I saw it. I could smell you and her all over me. You need to call me."

I waited several minutes, somehow believing that he would get the message and hoping that he would believe what I had said. Hell, I didn't believe what I had said. A wave of sandalwood blew past my nostrils and made my stomach turn over. I ran into the bathroom. Should I go to the toilet to vomit or to the shower to wash this mess off of me? I voted for the shower and jumped in still clad in my granny nightgown. Grabbing soap, shampoo, and whatever else I could get my hands on, I scrubbed my body and the nightgown feverishly. It was only when the scent on me had changed from sandalwood to lavender and then to lemongrass that I dared to rip the nightgown off, allowing it to fall in pieces into the tub. The sound of the shower did not muffle my screams well enough. I heard Oluwa crying out to me.

"Yeye, Yeye, what's the matter?"

The sound of his voice brought me back to reality.

"I'm okay, sweetie. You go back to bed. I am sorry I woke you up. I'm so sorry." I didn't know what I was actually sorry about—what had just happened, or making so much noise that I woke a sleeping ten-year-old.

I checked on him when I got out of the shower, smelling as if I had taken a nose dive into a perfume vat. He had gone back to sleep. I went back to the telephone. This time, I called my Yoruba godfather, Bale, in Panama. He too was having a sleepless night and answered the telephone on the third ring. As calmly as I could, between weeping and screaming, I recounted my experience. When I got it all out, he told me to make myself some tea and call him back. Chamomile. I settled for three bags of chamomile tea without any sweetener. I sat at the kitchen table and called my godfather again.

He began with an apology. He was sorry it had happened to me. Bale was also my husband's godfather and spiritual mentor. He had taken us to Africa to be married. When you are spiritually joined to another person by ceremony and ritual, he told me, you cannot conduct yourself in any manner you choose. You must respect what you have been given. He reminded me that my husband and I had not just gone to the justice of the peace. We had gone into an ancient village and been united in a very sacred way, by people who carried thousands of years of tradition in their DNA. He asked me if I knew where my husband was. Of course I did not. He told me to call him and leave a message that he was to call his godfather as soon as possible. As soon as I hung up, I did. Three days later, when I hadn't heard from him, I called him again.

I could hear the hesitation in his voice. He asked about Oluwa. I asked him if he was crazy! Had he gotten my messages? He remained silent. I asked him what was going on. He said he didn't know what I wanted him to say. I went into a rant about the sacredness of how we had been joined. I reminded him, as our godfather had reminded me, that we were not just married. I was a priestess and he was a priest. If he wanted to end our marriage or invite someone else into it, he needed to do it the right way. He needed to call his godfather, our godfather, and get some clear instructions. He said he would and then fell silent. I slammed the telephone back into the cradle.

The nighttime incidents continued, sometimes more intense than others. I was afraid to go to bed, and the lack of sleep showed on my face and in my body. Two weeks passed and he had not made the call to Panama. I was reluctant to share my experience with anyone because it was so bizarre. How do you tell someone that you can feel your husband making love to another woman? How do you explain that you can not only feel it, but you can hear it, see it, and smell it? You don't. You keep it to yourself, wondering if you have been possessed by something evil.

I prayed for relief and release but there was none to be had. Sometimes three or four nights in a row, I was made to be an interloper in the sex life of my husband and some other woman. Most nights I put the Bible in the bed with me. It didn't help.

One night, in desperation, I remembered the ways of the old-time church. I stripped myself naked, and lying face down and prostrate on the floor, I begged God, the angels, the ancestors, all of the prophets and guardians to deliver me from whatever this was that had taken over my body and my bedroom. In the old church, it is called "pleading the blood of Jesus." I did it. I pleaded and confessed and repented. I said all of the things I had ever been taught or told about the sovereign mercy of God. I laid on that floor, praying, crying, pleading with a mouthful of carpet fuzz until I could feel the release in every fiber of my being. In that moment, I didn't care to be a Yoruba priestess, a Christian, or anything else. I simply needed a Higher Power, something greater than me to lift me up and out of the experience. And it did. Something shifted. I got up, put on my pajamas, and got in the bed. For the first time in weeks, I slept like a baby.

It was several days later before I could feel the energy again. As soon as it started, I began to pray. I began to call out for divine intervention. As soon as I did, it stopped. The energy lifted. As horrible as the experience had been to endure, it took me to a deeper realization and experience of the presence of God. It deepened my faith. It opened my heart and mind. It sent me on a deeper exploration into the mysteries of relationships and sex. It helped me to understand the interconnectedness of all things and people. It also sent me to divorce court.

I filed for divorce on the grounds of irreconcilable differences and adultery. I felt almost indifferent as I handed the papers to the clerk. She stamped my form and sent me on my way. It wasn't until I was back in my car, about to turn the key in the ignition, that I broke down. I felt absolutely defeated and depleted. It felt so unfair. But then again, everything happens exactly as it needs to happen in order for us to grow. *Damn it!*

I knew he would get the papers in the next two or three days, and I wondered what he would do or think or say. But I didn't hear from him for a week, and when I did, he didn't mention anything. Then I remembered. I was supposed to send him a certified copy of the paperwork and take the delivery notification back to the court. Great! It was all on me again.

However, the morning I woke up planning to do just that, I got a clear message. *Be still. Let him take the lead.* You have got to be kidding me! *Let him take the lead?* He was leading me into his sexual exploits! Where was he going to lead us to?

Then, as if a movie screen dropped in front of me, I could see the words of Proverbs 3:5: "Trust in the Lord with all of your heart and lean not on your own understanding. Be still and know." *Oh My God!* I thought the guidance was to let Eden take the lead. Now I realized it was all about God. I was being guided to allow God to take the lead in my marriage and my life. *But, he was talking about leaving! Is that what God wanted?* I didn't understand, but I decided to trust. I didn't file the papers. Perhaps it was for him to do. Perhaps there was something bigger that I could see or know. Whatever was happening, as long as I did not have to be accosted in my bed, I would trust and keep moving forward.

I remembered that I had a powerful tool I could use to support and heal myself—the Emotional Freedom Technique or EFT.

I don't remember when or how I learned about EFT but I do remember how it helped to keep me calm in some very difficult times. Like so many things I had studied, things that would actually help me, I had used it for a while and then cast it aside convinced that I could not be helped by something so simple.

The easiest way to describe EFT is that it is a form of needleless acupuncture. Using your fingertips you tap on specific parts of your body while saying certain affirmations in order to move and remove the energy of mental and emotional trauma. Goodness knows I had experienced enough of that in my life. At this point, I was beyond being stressed out. I was becoming numb again; it was the only way I knew to protect myself. Yet, in order to move forward, I needed a clear head and an open heart. My daily Tapping regime became my ticket to a place I did not know I was headed.

Dear God:
Please untie the nots.
All of the can nots, should nots,
may nots and have nots.
Please erase from my mind the thoughts
that I am not good enough.

— Everyday I Pray

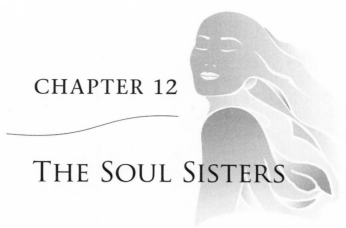

CHAPTER 12

THE SOUL SISTERS

I began to focus all of my attention on Inner Visions and the coaching institute we had begun. I needed and wanted to write a book. I needed to because my contract called for it. My last book, *Everyday I Pray,* had hit the stands two weeks after 9/11 and the sales were dismal. Two years later, I needed to get back into the publishing world. My publisher agreed, but argued that my two-year absence, combined with poor sales and the fact that I was no longer on television, meant that I no longer had the same value in the marketplace.

What I heard was that I was no longer worth the money. No, they assured me. It wasn't about my worth, it was about the audience. I would need to rebuild my audience to generate the sales I once had. I was insulted. They were firm.

We negotiated a decent three-book deal, which meant they still had faith in me. The truth is, I was ready to write and I needed the money. I also knew that I had a few things to clean up if I was going to move forward unencumbered by past mistakes.

The first thing I had to clean up was my exit from Harpo. I had learned a lot since then, a lot about myself and the world of television. Since leaving Oprah's show, I had heard stories that had shocked, horrified, and humbled me. My intention was to clear the decks between Ms. O and myself.

I wrote Ms. O a letter. I started by apologizing. I apologized for not honoring my word, the word I had given to Gayle when she told me not to let other networks trick me into leaving Harpo. I had said, "I am not going anywhere." I did not honor my word.

I apologized for being naive and not revealing who had made me the offer. Had I simply told the truth, perhaps she could have advised me differently. I told her what Ms. Walters had said to me the day the show ended. I apologized for being used as a pawn. I admitted how disrespectful it had been for me to leave her show and end up, as I did, looking like a total fake on television. I asked for her forgiveness and explained that I was in the process of forgiving myself. I assured her that I did not want anything from her. I considered her a sister whom I had wronged, and I only hoped that she would be willing to accept my apology. It didn't matter to me if she responded. I knew that I had to take ownership of my behavior if I was ever to be free of the guilt and shame I felt.

Two weeks after I sent the letter, I got a message asking me to call Ms. Winfrey. She thanked me for the letter. We talked about the *Iyanla* show and how it had been produced. I told her I was glad it had not happened on her watch. She said that it would have never happened on her watch. Before we hung up, she thanked me again. She said that I was not the first one who had been lured away, but that I was the first one who had ever apologized. She told me that it took a big woman to do what I had done. She promised that when she came into the area, we would get together for crab cakes.

When I hung up the telephone, it felt as if a hundred-pound weight had been lifted from my shoulders. I sat very still for a long time. Then I had a thought. If Oprah Winfrey thought I was a big woman, I had better start acting like one.

‡‡‡

Even in your most difficult times, God will always find a way to send you a blessing. My blessings were 14 beautiful and powerful women. They came from all walks of life, they were all different ages, and they all had two things in common: They loved me and they supported my vision. Together, we made up the Inner Visions faculty and workshop team. Together, we touched the lives of men and women all over the world, from the United States to the United Kingdom, throughout the Caribbean and all the way to South Africa. Bad, in the good sense, does not describe who we are together. In the Michael Jackson sense of the word, we were *baaaaaaad!*

We supported and encouraged each other. We worked and played together. The most important thing we did was make an all-out commitment to serve God and God's people by using our talents, gifts, and abilities, as well as anything or anyone else we could put our hands on. We were always threatening to write a book about our exploits. Perhaps we will—who knows? Without each of my sisters, I would never have made it through some of the darkest and most difficult days of my life.

I met Ebun "Laughing Crow" Adelona when I was a young Yoruba priestess living in New York. She was interested in the culture, and was raising her daughter in a quiet Harlem neighborhood. When we met, she was studying with a Native American teacher, and at the same time, seeking a deeper connection to her African roots. Together we explored both cultures, in fact, all spiritual cultures. It was Ebun who introduced me to the concept of healthy eating and the benefits of good nutrition. I attended my first meditation class with her. It was Ebun who took me to my first Inipi, or Sweat Lodge Ceremony. I supported her on her first vision quest. Ebun, a registered nurse, was deeply committed to the total healing of the mind, body, and Spirit. She was also a master at integrating scientific and spiritual knowledge. She was the elder in the group, and she was a stickler for protocol—spiritual, cultural, and energetic. If we were going to do it, it had to be done right.

When I moved to Maryland, I met Muhsinah—Mama Muhsinah, as we all called her. She was the earth mother among us, large in stature, with an ever-smiling face. Muhsinah was unflappable, always pleasant, and usually had something good to say about the worst scoundrel. She also looked after the children. Any child in the room was likely to end up on her lap or sleeping against her breasts. I was both late and lost on my way to a speaking engagement when she spotted me. She introduced herself and took me to where a roomful of people were awaiting my arrival. After that, Muhsinah would call and volunteer her time whenever

I was doing a workshop or a class in DC. The three of us became a team. Actually, there were four of us: Gemmia, Muhsinah, myself, and Niamoja. Three women and a baby. We went everywhere and did almost everything together, believing as we did that we had known each other from another life.

For many years, I had the honor of being a speaker and workshop facilitator at The African American Women on Tour Conference. I was first recommended to speak at the event by Susan L. Taylor, the former editor in chief of *Essence* magazine. After my first keynote address at the conference, I was invited back annually to conduct a workshop. Women came from all around the world to attend the conference, and many of them ended up in my workshop. The energy was high. At times, it felt almost too high to really support the women in having a meaningful experience.

I asked Muhsinah if she knew any prayer warriors, people who could hold the High Watch and pray for the participants during the workshop. I had learned about the High Watch when I was a child, going to church with Grandma. Whenever there was something big going on in the church, or if one of the members was sick or in some sort of trouble, the church mothers held a High Watch. That meant that they sat around a table or in the living room at someone's home and prayed. As a child, it was one of the most gut-wrenching experiences I had to endure. As a child, I would sit for hour after hour while grandma and the other "saints" prayed. Because I didn't understand anything about prayer and no one bothered to explain, it was like watching paint dry. Now, as an experienced workshop facilitator, I understood the absolute need for constant prayer as people engaged in spiritual healing work.

Muhsinah contacted Helen. She was a teacher and a good old-fashioned Baptist. Helen admitted that she didn't understand what she was being asked to do, but she knew how to pray. I discovered Judith on my way to the workshop room. She was a huge fan of my work and asked if I needed any help. She reminded me of my make-believe sister Bunny. As she ran alongside me, almost flippantly I asked, "Do you know how to pray?"

"I guess so."

I told her the number of my workshop room and asked her to meet me there.

Judith showed up with her friend Almasi. She was about the same height, same size, with the most beautiful complexion I had ever seen. The six of us stood in the middle of the room as the participants lined up outside. I assigned each of the women a chair in one of the corners of the room. I told them to stay in their seats and pray. They were to pray any prayer they knew over and over. They were praying for peace in the room and healing for every woman in the room. Then we all prayed together before they took their places. Helen the Baptist in one corner. Almasi the Akan in another. Judith, like me a Yoruba, and Muhsinah, a recovering Catholic who was simply delighted to be doing spiritual work of this nature. Gemmia was at the table working the music, because music is a huge element of my work. Niamoja, who did her first workshop when she was six weeks old, was asleep in her stroller. When the women began to enter the room, it felt good. We felt ready. The Inner Visions workshop team was formed.

I had met AdaRa the first day I moved to Maryland. She stood about five foot six inches, and she could not have weighed 100 pounds soaking wet. But baby, let me tell you, that woman could move. Together, she and her sweetie helped Gemmia and me unload an 18-foot truck in under two hours, and she did most of the lifting. AdaRa was an energy master. Although she worked for the federal government, she studied the way-left spiritual arts of Reiki, Bio-Energy Kinesiology, and some other things I couldn't even pronounce. She worked with light and color energy. To look at her you would never know it, but she was a true facilitator of healing and the healing arts. I asked her to join the team. She said she would be honored.

AdaRa introduced me to Janet, a registered nurse like Ebun and one of AdaRa's students. Janet was quiet; very quiet. She rarely said a word unless you asked her to pray. Janet was skilled at being still and quieting the mind. She brought another level of energy to the team.

Viviana was a massage and colon therapist, and was married to a colon therapist. They had a small office in Silver Spring, Maryland, not far from the Inner Visions home office. She also lived in the same housing development with Gemmia. Viviana hosted a monthly full-moon meditation that was open to the public. Like Janet, she was a meditation master. She had also mastered the art of playing crystal bowls as a meditation tool and enhancement. Muhsinah suggested that we invite her to hold her meditations at the Inner Visions office. The team was growing and so was the Inner Visions brand.

Lydia joined the team when I began hosting monthly lectures in New York at Aaron Davis Hall on the campus of City College. Lydia was our Puerto Rican sister. On the day of our first lecture, she was sitting outside waiting to buy her ticket. When we arrived—the three women and the baby—she asked if she could help us unload. She fell in love with Niamoja, who seemed totally uninterested in Lydia's displays of affection, until she produced her package of Tic Tacs. Asking Gemmia's permission, Lydia began to feed Niamoja one Tic Tac at a time. That was the beginning of their love affair, and ours.

Lydia had been successful in her recovery for ten years, and she was on a serious spiritual mission. We were simply the vehicle to carry her through the journey. Every month for almost four years, Lydia would show up at Aaron Davis Hall to help us unload the van, and every month she had a package of Tic Tacs for Niamoja. When we started selling books at the event, Lydia would man the table. When an attendee had a problem with a ticket or a seat, Lydia was the trouble shooter. She also became my eyes and ears, running between the front of the theater and backstage to let me know what was going on.

It took about a year of these monthly appearances before we hit a milestone. Lydia and Gemmia came into the dressing room where Tulani and I were changing to go on stage. Tulani opened every lecture with a series of songs that eventually became our trademark. The two of them rarely came into the dressing room together, so I assumed something awful had happened.

"We have a problem."

"Oh Lord! What's wrong?" We had invested so much time, energy and money in the lectures and they were just beginning to catch on.

Gemmia said: "I'm not sure what to do so I thought I should speak with you."

I was really getting nervous. I knew we had insurance, but I was beginning to think that someone had been hurt. Suddenly her face broke into a smile:

"We have a full house! We are sold out and there is a line of people outside waiting to get in."

"What?"

Lydia answered this time:

"We are sold out, Mama. There is not a seat left in the place."

This is what we had prayed for. This meant the event would now pay for itself. We were in the black! It was a miracle! No. It was an answer to a prayer. We all realized it at the same time and started to jump up and down like lunatics screaming, "We're sold out! Thank you God!"

Of course, it would be Gemmia who came to her senses first. She had left Muhsinah upstairs with the irate people who had failed to buy their tickets in advance. The management of the theater said we could probably get 50 more people in if they were willing to stand. They were. That left us with another 25 standing outside. We offered them discounted admission for the next month, but people hate to miss something when it is going on. We offered them free food and an autographed book. That calmed most of them down. It was an incredible evening, an incredible lecture, and an incredible accomplishment for three women and a baby.

Over the years, the team grew to include two massage therapists: Danni, from Detroit, and Yawfah, from Atlanta. Terri from New York and Lydia became students in the inaugural class of the Inner Visions Institute while they were working on the workshop team. Our team became so much more than a group of women doing workshops. We became a family.

We spent so much time together that we had no choice but to include all of our families in the process. The husbands, Almasi's, Viviana's, and mine, became community husbands, without the sex, of course. All of the men did school runs or bought ice cream for everyone. The children became community children: Judith had six; Almasi had five; Helen, Muhsinah, and I had three; Yawfah and Viviana had two; Danni, Ebun, Terri, and Lydia each had one. AdaRa and Janet were the childless big sisters to them all.

Parents inherited us all, and siblings became part of the crew, giving us a built-in volunteer core. For me, the team became my safety net. They took care of me, and I honored them in the same way. When Almasi's daughter had her first baby, we were all on the telephone. When Helen's son went into the service, we prayed to keep him out of the war. When one of the children or husbands was having an issue, they would get calls from several of us. When someone needed something, the need was met.

Finally, I had a family I could trust and depend on. Everyone was invested in the vision and everyone brought something valuable to the table. We built a community of like-minded people. We built a family of unconditional love.

Without the love and support of the community team, Inner Visions would not exist. It simply wouldn't. It wasn't just that they did the work; they supported me in ways most people have never experienced and cannot imagine. It was through the love and support of these women that I learned to love and honor myself.

I watched them. I talked to them. They talked to me. They watched me. When something needed to be done, they got it done. When something needed to be worked out, they worked it out. In the process, they loved me, honored me, and held me in a position of great esteem. They didn't worship me; in fact, they helped me keep my life and everything about it real. Because of them, I was able to leave my home and my business in order to travel the world. With them, I was blessed to do some miraculous work in the world. With them, I walked through some of the darkest hours of my life. And, because of them, I survived.

‡✛‡

The first class of students had entered the Inner Visions Institute, and they were an eager and lively group. Working the kinks out of the curriculum kept me and the rest of the staff pretty busy throughout the week and on most weekends. There was no way my husband could sleep in my house again, which raised a serious childcare issue for me with Oluwa. Gemmia got the support of Jimmy. Although they had separated, he continued to work for me, and their relationship remained amicable. He kept Niamoja on the weekends, and she asked if Oluwa could join them. He may have wanted to say no, but he knew he could not.

With the children cared for, Gemmia and I threw ourselves into the work of building a teaching institution. As faculty members, we each had students we were responsible for. We marked their papers and coached them through their learning process. Gemmia was an excellent instructor and a wonderful life coach. Her students were among the best in the group, and their progress was excellent.

Before we gathered for a scheduled class weekend, she shared with me that one of her students was interested in Jimmy, and she wasn't sure how to handle it. The student had asked Gemmia if she would be okay with her seeing Jimmy, who also happened to be the student's landlord. Inner Visions staff and students all knew that Gemmia and Jimmy were Niamoja's parents, and that they had been involved in a long-term relationship. Very few knew that their intimate relationship had ended. Gemmia, with her classic diplomacy, reminded the student that she had not come to Inner Visions to find a personal relationship. She had come to heal her life and learn how to be a life coach. She suggested that the relationship might need to wait until she had completed her studies.

Inner Visions was a teaching, healing environment, and there was a relationship based on trust between our faculty and students. People came to us trusting that we would support them in moving beyond the mental and emotional blockages that had stalled them in their lives. While many other psycho-spiritual programs like Inner Visions had strict rules about personal involvement between staff and students, we had not considered the need for a specific policy, because most of our staff and students were female. Jimmy was one of two male staff members. As my administrative assistant, he had access to the intimate personal history of our predominantly female student body. At the level of professional responsibility, it felt inappropriate for a male staff member to be intimately involved with a female student who was working through personal issues at Inner Visions. And this particular student had a pattern of being involved in forbidden relationships, which is why it became a student issue for Gemmia and an administrative issue for me.

We were beginning a class weekend, where the student in question would be present. It was customary for students to bring their current issues and challenges to the floor for coaching. I discussed with the faculty how to handle this particular student if the issue was brought to the floor. We decided that we should not wait. We should call her out and deal with it in order to establish parameters for the entire student body. Little did we know that there was something bigger than we knew in store for us.

I called the student to the floor, asking how her month had been and what she was moving through now. She must have assumed that I already knew. I always told the students to assume that if I asked the question, I already knew the answer. It was an outgrowth of my training in law. It is a rule among attorneys never to ask a question unless you know the answer. Unwittingly, I was about to break that cardinal rule.

"So what's up for you, my dear?"

"Well, I moved."

"Great! Is there more?"

"Yes. I think I am physically and sexually attracted to my landlord."

Okay, that wasn't so bad. That was expected.

"Really. Tell me more."

"Well, I am attracted to him."

"What does that mean?"

"It means that we are having a sexual relationship and I want more."

With that, the bottom fell out of my planned line of inquiry. The students gave a collective gasp that sucked all of the oxygen out of the room. I glanced at the faculty. They all sat stone-faced, Gemmia among them. I continued. I had to. It was part of the process.

"So you are having a sexual relationship with your landlord and you want more. If that is true, why are you calling him your landlord? Isn't he more than that for you?"

"Yes."

"What meaning does this relationship hold for you?"

I could feel the heat and horror emanating from the student and the cold panic emanating from the faculty. The student said she knew it was wrong because of this man's relationship to her faculty advisor. She admitted that she had lied and that she was actually living in the man's house. I am not sure what else she said; I just knew that if I looked over at Gemmia, I would lose my mind. That didn't last long, however, because what happened next sent me into another level of horrification.

Another student stood up indicating that she had something to say. I acknowledged her, granting permission.

"I have had a relationship with Jimmy too."

She knew it was inappropriate, she said, and she warned the other student that they were both being used. I was speechless, utterly speechless. When the third student stood up, indicating that she too had been personally involved with Jimmy, the room erupted into total chaos. Each of the women was a student on Gemmia's roster. Each of them knew full well of Gemmia's relationship with Jimmy. The students were furious. The faculty were disgusted. With whom? I wasn't sure, but I had to restore order. I didn't dare look in Gemmia's direction.

This, I told them, was a matter of integrity. The integrity of the program and the faculty was in question. I accepted full responsibility for creating an environment where something like this could occur unbeknownst to me. I dealt with each student about her own integrity and her choice to engage in this behavior.

We looked at their pasts and their patterns. For one, it was the thrill of sneaking around. For another, it was payback to a sister who had stolen a boyfriend. For the other, it was just stupid, mindless gratification.

Once I had dealt with the students, I turned my attention to Gemmia. She was sitting perfectly poised as if none of it had anything to do with her. I called her to the microphone in the center of the floor. Obediently, she came. I asked her forgiveness for having aired this in such an impersonal way. I explained that one of the hazards of our working together was that I was first her immediate supervisor and then her mother. She said that she understood. I told her that the mother in me wanted to run and put my arms around her, but that I needed to address the integrity of the program and the needs of our students. She acknowledged that she understood and said she would and did forgive me. This woman was a master, and as proud as I was of her, my mother's heart ached for her.

I had to ask Gemmia the hard questions. I had to treat her as if she were a student in the program, who had created an experience that was up for healing. I just had to go there. I knew and so did she. This was what the work of Inner Visions was all about.

"So what does this represent for you, my love? Why are you having this experience?"

"It's about my false pride. The relationship is over, I know that. In one sense, what he does has nothing to do with me. In another sense, for this to come out this way tells me that I did not make myself or my relationship with him clear. It wasn't clear to me, to him, or anyone else. I was too proud to say, I am done with him."

"Is there more?"

"Yes. This is also about betrayal. In some ways, I have always been betrayed by the people I love. Well, obviously this man has betrayed me. I asked him about this woman and he lied. My father betrayed me by leaving and never looking back. My brother has betrayed me, my sister has betrayed me, and my mother has betrayed me."

"What can you share with me about feeling and being betrayed by me?"

By now everyone in the room was crying. I think they were crying at the sheer magnitude of Gemmia's presence. She wasn't bowed. She didn't cower. Her spine was erect. She held my gaze. Her voice was strong and clear as she prepared to take her hero down. All the faculty members were standing with their hands projected outward in front of them. Some were directed at me, others at Gemmia. They were holding the space, sending us love. I could feel it. I needed every ounce of it.

"One of the reasons I didn't end the relationship was because I was too proud. I didn't want to be like all the other women I know, women who allowed themselves to be used, dishonored, and disrespected by men. I lied to myself, telling myself I was different. I'm not different. So, I guess I have been betrayed because I betrayed myself."

Just as Gemmia was an excellent teacher, she was an excellent student. Gemmia had learned all of the lessons I had taught her, the good ones and the not-so-good ones. The magnificent news was that she knew how to apply spiritual principles to herself for her own healing. She was not a victim. The bad news was that we were not finished. There was more she needed to say and more I needed to hear.

"Can you tell me where or how you learned to betray yourself?"

"From my mother. My mother taught me to lie to myself, to deny my true feelings, and to always keep a happy face. My mother was the first person to betray me. She lied to me about my father. She lied to me about so many things, I can't even count them any more. And, for some reason, most of the lies she told me involved a man."

I could not move and I dared not breathe.

"Don't get me wrong. My mother is a good person, a really good person; but there are things that I heard and saw as a child that felt like betrayal. She put men, and people, and her work ahead of me, my brother, and my sister."

Now Gemmia was crying. That was a good sign. It meant that the energy in her body was moving. I knew better than to cry or move energy or move one fiber of my being. I was sitting on a stool 20 inches off the floor. It was too far for me to fall.

"Intellectually, I really do understand that is what you—I mean my mother—had to do. She has a very high calling in her life. But as a child, I didn't know that shit. I just knew that my mommy had important things to do, and that meant I would be left with someone or alone and scared. Intellectually, I knew she loved me, but it still felt like betrayal."

I could barely get the words out of my mouth.

"Is there more?"

"I helped my mother build this place. I put all of my time, energy, and resources into creating this dream, her dream. Then one day, I heard her thank all the people involved. She thanked the faculty and her friends. She called them by name. Then, she said, I would especially like to thank my husband, for without him, none of this would have been possible. It was like a knife in my heart. I thought to myself. Either she is crazy, or I have just been royally f——d! He didn't do a damn thing but take her money, use her name, benefit from all of my hard work, and walk away with her looking like a fool—and she thanks him publicly. Me she ignores. That, I believe, was the ultimate betrayal. That, I believe, is what has led to this. It is time for all of this shit to get cleaned up. It doesn't feel good, but it is time."

I don't think I had ever heard Gemmia swear, not like this, anyway. I'm not sure what happened next, who said what to whom, but I know that it was healing. I know that Gemmia and I spoke words of forgiveness. She forgave herself first, then her mother, then the man, then the students. She reminded them that we are all human, and that being so makes us good at teaching what we need to learn. She told the three students involved that she loved them and that they would be held accountable for their choices by something higher than her or me. She asked them to seriously consider their patterns and advised them to work toward healing. The woman was a master, pure and simple.

The next few days were awkward on all levels. As a faculty member, I had to repair the breach of safety and deal with the students. As an administrator, I had to deal with the possibility of sexual harassment charge against a member of my staff, which jeopardized the integrity of the program. As a mother, I had to find a way to support my child. As a woman, I had to heal. I talked to my godfather, my best friend, and the faculty and staff. I hired a management consultant to come in and govern the administrative part of the process. The stench of the entire ordeal hung in the air like a cloud.

Because of the enmeshed relationships between myself and Gemmia, Gemmia and Jimmy, and Jimmy and me, I had to protect myself and the organization from potential liabilities on a number of fronts. When the meetings and testings and conference calls were complete, it was recommended that Jimmy not be terminated. Instead, he was placed on 60 days of probation and ordered into psychological counseling. Each of the students was reassigned to another faculty member. Gemmia and I continued to come to the office each day in an attempt to address all of the issues, the professional as well as the personal.

When we finally got around to talking about what had happened, it started out as two coaches talking about a nasty situation. It ended up as a daughter sharing her most intimate feelings with her mother. She said she didn't blame me, although I blamed myself. Why hadn't she ever talked to me about any of this?

She was working through it. The feelings were too intense. She was confused. So much had changed. I wasn't that person any more. She hadn't known the depths of her anger. The conversation lasted for hours and then for days. She was, in so many ways, much stronger than I. She was, in every way, so much clearer than I was at the time. She reminded me of everything I had taught her, told her, shown her. It was a challenge that we would get through together. Each night, we would go to our separate homes and then spend hours on the telephone until one or both of us broke down. Each call ended with "I love you" and "I'll see you tomorrow."

Jimmy dismissed Gemmia and her concerns, telling her that they were no longer together and what he did in his personal life was none of her business. Bringing students into his home in front of Oluwa and Niamoja *was* her business. Threatening the viability of her mother's lifelong vision was her business. Dishonoring her and her mother among the students was her business. He didn't see it that way.

With me, Jimmy was cold and malicious. I asked him to take off his administrative-assistant hat for a minute and address his behavior on a personal level. He had lived in my house for more than 15 years, I loved and treated him like a son, I had bought the house he now lived in and the car he drove. How did he justify his behavior?

His tirade began. It was none of my business pure and simple. We didn't have a relationship. We never did things together like a mother and son. The car and the house could have come from anyone. As far as Inner Visions was concerned, it was a job and I was his boss. He didn't know it was necessary to report to his boss about what he did in his personal life.

For a moment, I entertained the notion of feeling sorry for him and making excuses for him. After all, he was my granddaughter's father, he had grown up without a mother and with an emotionally unavailable father, and he said he felt that he had never had a real family. We were it. After five minutes of that train of thought, I slapped myself back into reality. This man was a detriment to my well-being. How had I missed that? I had made excuses for him, just as I had with my father, brother, my husband, and every other man I had ever been involved with.

My friend Shaheerah reminded me that there comes a point where a person's psycho-social history is of little or no consequence. There comes a moment when you simply have to say no to their behavior, their attitude, and whatever else it is that they do that causes you harm. I accepted Jimmy's presence in my home because of his relationship with Gemmia. I also realized that any mother worth her weight in salt would have never allowed her daughter to live with a man in her house for years without being very clear about their relationship. He lived with us for his convenience, not from his commitment. I had failed myself and my daughter miserably.

Gemmia decided to take a few weeks off to clear her head. She was going on a 40-day pray-and-fast vigil. I left her alone as she requested. I would respond to her calls, but I did not initiate any. I had my own multiple madnesses to deal with: the incomplete divorce process, the IRS payments, my feelings of guilt and shame about how absent I had been from my and my daughter's lives, and what I needed to do to clean it up.

One of the students moved out of Jimmy's house almost immediately. The others were focusing on healing from their participation in the betrayal. The faculty and I did our best to maintain a spiritual, healing mode. Several of us put ourselves in therapy. I did my best to keep working and bringing money into the organization. The organizational consultant continued to work with us.

When Gemmia came back to work, she looked great and said she felt clear. She had lost some weight and cut her locks. She was ready to get back in the saddle, to continue moving the program forward. She was an inspiration to us all.

Ultimately, Jimmy failed to meet the terms of his work probation and was terminated for cause. Then I realized how long I had tolerated unnecessary crap in my life. With his departure, the stench lifted. It was very, very sad and eye-opening. For most of her life, Niamoja had seen her father every day. Although visitation had been negotiated, it was a shift, and Gemmia was doing her best to occupy her daughter's time and her thoughts to camouflage the change. Hence, the mommy-daughter activities began. Those two, Gemmia and Niamoja, became inseparable. Although the circumstances that created it were tragic, it was a beautiful thing to watch. Niamoja had a chair and a desk in her mother's office. After school each day, they sat and did homework together. Then, they would go home for the private activities— baking days, movie nights.

When we had late nights at the office, both Niamoja and Oluwa were there, along with the children and grandchildren of the other staff. Gemmia made a special children's corner that included books, games, a small television, and, of course, snacks. The children kept themselves occupied while we went about the business of rebuilding the insides of our organization.

I was amazed and pleased at the resourcefulness of this group of dedicated women. We loved each other, and we created a safe, loving environment for the children. Every now and then, my husband would stop by to see Oluwa, but we barely spoke. It felt surreal as Gemmia and I both settled into to being single mothers.

The Institute was running smoothly but it brought in very little income that first year. I did as many speaking engagements as I could, but my lack of public appearances was showing up in my royalties. They were down more than 75 percent, not enough to cover the cost of running the program. Once again, I began to eliminate staff positions. Once again, they refused to leave. Gemmia and I both took a cut in salary. Thank goodness she had encouraged me to nest a little bit on the side for emergencies. We were barely making payroll, and the payments to the IRS were out of the question.

Just when we thought we had resolved the issues that threatened the organization, the financial grip grew even tighter. My business manager was concerned that Gemmia and I did not have health coverage, and he insisted that he would get us covered even if it meant I had to cut another position. He surrendered half of his own salary to pay the monthly fees. We were all committed to Inner Visions and the programs we had created. We would do whatever was necessary to keep it afloat. We worked out a new deal with the IRS, which meant we were struggling, but we had faith. That is, until we were all blindsided by a blow that had nothing to do with money. It had to do with me. And it was all about Gemmia.

If rain doesn't fall, corn doesn't grow.

— Yoruba Proverb

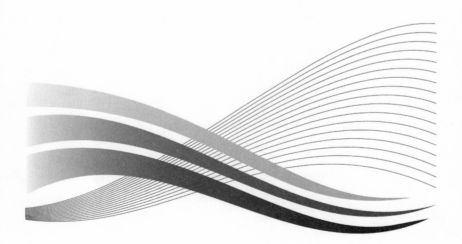

CHAPTER 13

THINGS FALL APART

When things start to fall apart, they fall apart fast. The downward spiral feels like it happens overnight, even if it takes years.

In late summer 2002, Gemmia discovered a huge lump on her side. It didn't hurt, but she was concerned. Her doctor said that the blood tests were inconclusive and ordered more.

At that same time, my publisher requested my overdue manuscript. I had been writing, but with all of the upheaval in my life, the ideas simply weren't flowing. For some strange reason, my creative process never seems to line up with my contractual due dates. I decided to send Oluwa and my brother's son to summer camp so I could have space and time alone to finish my manuscript.

I spent days typing things that made no sense, because I couldn't settle my mind down. When Gemmia went to the gynecologist, they found a large mass but couldn't determine if it was on her ovary or her uterus. They sent her for a sonogram. I promised to meet her at the clinic, but got turned around in downtown Washington and couldn't find the place. By the time I arrived, she was heading home. I could hear it in her voice—either she was very upset with me or she really didn't feel well. In either case, the report had not been good. The mass was so large they couldn't see it on the screen. They couldn't tell if it was a tumor or a cyst. She would need an MRI.

She was going home to lie down. No, she didn't need anything. Niamoja was with Muhsinah, who had become her next-door neighbor. The MRI was scheduled for the following week.

‡‡‡

I had just boarded an Amtrak train on my way to New York City to join Tom Joyner and his morning crew, who were hosting a commemoration of the World Trade Center tragedy. For once in my life, I wasn't late for the train. I had just sat down when my cell phone rang. It was Erika, Gemmia's best friend. Gemmia seemed to be in a great deal of pain. When Erika gave Gemmia the telephone, she didn't sound good, but she said she thought it might be gas. She said she would be okay and I should go to New York.

Something just didn't feel right to me. I had 11 minutes before the train left. I debated for a few minutes and then called Muhsinah. She said she had just walked in and would go next door and check on her. There were seven minutes left. I called Gemmia's house. Almasi answered the telephone.

"What are you doing there?"

"Gemmia called me and said she wasn't feeling well."

"Why would she call you and tell me she is okay? How is she?"

"I'm not sure, but she seems to be in a great deal of pain."

"Okay. I'm coming."

"She doesn't want you to come. I'm making her some tea right now. If it's gas, it should move out. You go. We'll be fine."

I had three minutes before the train left the station. Tom was expecting me; he had announced that I would be there. The last thing I needed was to be a no-show at a major national event—but you know what? Life happens. I called Erika.

"What's going on?"

"Akmal is here. He is with her now."

Akmal was a close personal friend and a traditional Chinese medical doctor and acupuncturist. Gemmia had been seeing him since she first found the lump. If Gemmia had called Almasi and Akmal, she must be in a pretty bad way.

"Do I need to come?"

"Well, if it were my daughter, I would be here."

I jumped off the train with one minute to spare. Speeding back to Gemmia's house, I called my doctor friend of 15 years, Dr. Carol

Mussenden, one of the best African American female OB/GYN doctors in the city. She encouraged me to bring Gemmia to her affiliated hospital in Virgina. I was to call her when I arrived. I was closer to Virginia than I was to Gemmia's house, so I called and told Akmal to bring her there.

I arrived first and waited. When Gemmia came through the door, she was doubled over in pain and barely able to walk. She couldn't sit down and she couldn't lie down. The pain was just that severe. Medical people! Why do they have to ask so many stupid questions before they decide to help you? No, she wasn't pregnant. No, she didn't use drugs. No. No. No. She didn't drink. She didn't smoke. She didn't even own a Tylenol. Please can you give her something for the pain? That meant they had to start an IV. That meant giving her a needle. Gemmia had a serious needle phobia. She hated them! But today, she was at least willing. Of course she got the nurse who poked and prodded trying to find a vein. I coached her to breathe and look away. When she started to scream, I screamed. That meant that Gemmia had to be stuck again.

It took hours for them to take her to get an MRI. When they did, the room was freezing and the technician was clearly annoyed. He needed Gemmia to lay flat but she couldn't. It was too painful. I called Dr. Mussenden. She ordered another dose of the lovely pain meds, and everything went smoothly after that. Two agonizing hours later, the doctor on call looked at the film, then looked at us.

"We are going to have to admit her."

"Why?"

"You should wait and talk to your doctor."

"Why?"

"The nurse will be right over to give you her room assignment."

"Can you please tell me what is going on? I am her mother."

Gemmia was in and out of consciousness. When the nurse finally showed up, I asked her what meds she was on. She looked at the chart and told me morphine. Morphine! Why was she on morphine? This woman didn't own an aspirin.

By the time they rolled Gemmia into the hospital room, she was out cold. I had left Muhsinah and Akmal downstairs, promising to retrieve them as soon as I knew where we were going. Gemmia was coming around just as Dr. Mussenden arrived. They kissed and hugged. Dr. Mussenden told Gemmia that she wanted her to rest for the night and she would order some tests in the morning. She motioned me out of the room.

"This does not look good, but she is young and strong."

"What is it?"

"We're not even sure. There is a mass and it is large. What we cannot determine is its origin. We can't tell if it is growing onto the uterus or emanating from the uterus or some other organ. Her blood work indicates that there a carcinoma present, but we can't determine its exact origins."

"What does that mean?"

"It means we still have a long way to go."

My heart was racing and my head was spinning. I was ready to pass out right there in the hallway. Dr. Mussenden must have noticed me swooning.

"Now, you calm down, or you will end up in the bed right next to her."

"I will calm down when someone can tell me that my child is going to be all right."

"Well, what I know is that all things are possible with God. She will probably sleep through the night. I'm ordering a battery of tests for the morning. I also have to bring in an oncologist so that we can get this thing nailed down. Don't worry. I will make sure she is taken care of."

I went back into the room. Gemmia was still asleep. I stroked her head and kissed her face. I could feel the ocean of fearful tears rising in my body. I am not sure if I said it aloud or silently, but the words were very clear: *God, please don't let my child die.* Please! I left to find the elevator. I had to find Muhsinah and Akmal. I pressed the elevator button at least 50 times before the door opened. As I was about to step in, Muhsinah stepped out. I took one look at her and collapsed into her arms. We sat on the window ledge as I told her the doctor's report. It was cancer. A tumor. When the elevator bell rang again, Akmal emerged. Muhsinah relayed the facts. He felt sure that once we knew where it was located, we would know what to do.

Before she left, Dr. Mussenden again told me that Gemmia would probably sleep through the night. I should go home and get some rest. I had mixed feelings about leaving her alone in the hospital, but Akmal said they had given her so much morphine, she didn't know where she was. At 2:45 A.M., we all left the hospital. When I arrived home, I told my housekeeper what was going on and asked if he could stay to get Oluwa off to school. Erika offered to make sure that Niamoja got off to school. We decided it would be best to say that mommy had to stay in the hospital to have some tests. I took a shower, lay down, and headed back at 5:30 A.M. I wanted to be there when she woke up.

Hospital days start very early. By the time I arrived at 7:10 A.M., they had already started Gemmia's blood work. I didn't want to give her details, but I did let her know that either the ovaries or the uterus were involved. She did not want surgery. She wanted to have more children—two boys. How had this happened? What did they want to do to her? I had no answers.

By noon, we had been through every department in the hospital and had seen no fewer than six different doctors. By 6 P.M., we both had questions and no one was giving us any information. It was 8:30 P.M. when Dr. Mussenden came into the room. She pulled up a chair and told me to sit down. I crawled into the bed with Gemmia and held her in my arms.

The tumor was growing from her colon. It had covered one of her ovaries. There was a good chance she would lose them both, and possibly the uterus too. Both Gemmia and I moaned a deep "Oh my God!" They needed to run more tests, Dr. Mussenden went on. We should know about the surgery in the next day or so. Once that was done, Gemmia would probably need chemotherapy, but no radiation. She had seen worse cases, so we were not to lose faith or hope. This was a great hospital, and she was calling in the best people she knew. Did we have any questions? We were both stunned into silence. We were just grateful she was there. She said she would see us in the morning.

I called Almasi first. She wouldn't overreact and could get the word out to the team quickly. When I called Erika, she fell apart. I called my husband and told him I would need his help with Oluwa. He was getting ready to be testy until I told him why. He said he had a few meetings but he would work it out. I was not to worry. We were always good together in a crisis. Next, I contacted Damon and Nisa. Once all the appropriate people had been notified, I turned to face Gemmia. She looked ashen.

"What are you thinking?

"I am just wondering if I am going to die."

"Wrong thought. A better thought is *I will not die*. Hold on to that thought."

"Are you coaching me?"

"No. I mean yes. I don't know."

"Well, good; coach me, and come here and kiss me."

I'm not sure who cried first but we both did. We cried for a very long time. We were crying when the nurse came in to give Gemmia her pain medication. Crying when she came back to take her temperature. Gemmia cried until she vomited. I stopped crying so that I could clean her up. Once we stopped crying, we both vowed to never do that again. Gemmia got very quiet.

"What are you thinking?"

"I am just thinking about what am I going to tell Niamoja."

With that, we both burst into tears again.

The next four days were torture. Every doctor had a different opinion. One thought her lungs were involved; another thought that the cancer had originated in her ovaries and spread to the colon. Some doctors were very nice and helpful, answering all of our questions. Others, well, they were doctors. They spoke a language that we did not understand. Each day, different members of the team came to stay with Gemmia so that I could go home for a few hours. Gemmia spoke to Niamoja every day, assuring her that everything was okay but that she had to have an operation. It wasn't a test, it was something bigger, but she would be home real soon.

The issue with the surgery was whether to remove the entire colon, which meant that Gemmia would have a bag on the outside of her body to catch her fecal matter, or to remove just the affected part of the colon along with the ovaries. Gemmia did not want a bag. She was too young. She was really distressed about losing her ovaries, but all of our energy practitioners, Ebun, Yawfah, and AdaRa, assured her that as long as she had her uterus, she could have children. Gemmia no longer seemed to be worried about dying. Rather, she was concerned about how she was going to live. I taught her everything I new about EFT and we did it together everyday, affirming that she would live without being specific about how or where.

We met the surgeon the day before the surgery. He was lovely. Gemmia told him exactly what she wanted and what she did not want. He promised to do his best, but also assured her that he was going to do whatever it took to make sure she would survive and have a normal life, even if that meant she had to wear a colostomy bag. On his way out of the room, I followed him. I grabbed his hand and told him who Gemmia was for me. She was not only my daughter, she was my best friend. I told him that I was holding him personally responsible for her and that he better not screw this up. He told me he would do his best. I yanked his arm to stop his stride. I looked him dead in the eyes and said:

"Your best is not good enough. I want you to pretend that you are performing that surgery on your own mother or daughter or someone who means the world to you. I don't want your best! I want your God-given, unfailing excellence. Are we clear?"

He stared at me for a few seconds before he responded.

"I wish I had had a mother like you. Yes, we are clear. I will give her everything I have."

Seventeen of us followed the gurney into the surgical suite. When the doors of the operating room swung shut, I fell to my knees. Two nurses helped me up and out to the waiting room. We didn't hear anything for two hours. Then Dr. Mussenden came out to report that so far, they had removed the tumor, her ovaries, and her appendix. They were waiting for the pathology report to decide the next step. I knew I had to pray. I needed to tap into the GPS, God's Protective System so that I would not lose my mind. That's the good thing about having a GPS, when you are totally lost, it can and will point you in the right direction. If you can get still enough, long enough to ask for clarity and direction, your internal GPS will kick in, if only to keep you calm enough long enough to find your way.

Another two and a half hours passed. They had to remove several inches of her colon. There were some seedlings in her stomach. The chemotherapy should take care of them. They would bring her into the recovery room in a few minutes. I had just experienced the longest four and half hours of my life and my GPS had guided me through the process.

Gemmia was eating solid foods within three days. Her blood work looked good. She stayed in the hospital for a week, and when she left, I took her home to my house. There is nothing like sleeping in your mother's bed when you don't feel good. But Gemmia had so many questions that the doctors could not answer. "Why?" "When did it start?" "How could this happen to a semi-vegetarian?" "Did she still have cancer?" "Was she going to be all right?"

Armed with Gemmia's official diagnosis—Familial Adenomatous Polyposis, a rare form of colon cancer that is hereditary, though we couldn't find any cases of the disease in her family history—I started scouring the Internet. Bad move! The information overload quickly left me overwhelmed. I started to share what I found with Gemmia, but she was too weak and, frankly, too frightened to care. She needed a recovery plan now. More than that, she needed to be in her own space. After a week in my house and my bed, I took Gemmia home. Niamoja was delighted. She liked my house, but she missed her room and all of her toys.

Gemmia had been home about a week when she shared her recovery plan with me. She did not want chemotherapy. She wanted to try some natural methods first. And that is exactly what we did. We started with the acupuncturist and hyperbaric oxygen therapy. Acupuncture, one of the main forms of treatment in traditional Chinese medicine, involves the use of thin needles that are inserted in the body at specific points to adjust the body's energy flow. It was a real challenge for someone who was so afraid of needles! The oxygen therapy, designed to increase oxygen saturation in tissues where the saturation levels are too low due to illness or injury, was easier. Gemmia would sit in an oxygen chamber for 30 minutes, twice a week. It gave her a lot of energy, and we hoped it would destroy any remaining cancer cells.

For the first three weeks, I did my best to get Gemmia to all of her appointments. Viviana and Muhsinah lived close enough to check on her when I was running errands or trying to write. Ebun, and Yawfah gave us a juicing protocol, which meant that each day, one of us had to prepare fresh fruit and vegetable juices for her. I did all of the shopping and the bill paying. The coffers at Inner Visions were all but dry. Almasi and Helen were the only staff left, and they did their best to keep everything afloat. The rest of the staff had been terminated, and the faculty taught for almost nothing. Because most natural treatments are not covered by health-care benefits, Gemmia and I were both draining our savings accounts. Hers dried up first. I cashed in all of my investments and used the money to keep her household and mine above water.

The next three months dragged on forever. I watched Gemmia go up and down, from feeling great to hardly being able to get out of the bed. I was running back and forth between her house and my house almost daily. I asked another staff member from Inner Visions Rev. John and Muhsinah to support me in making her daily juice, because I was once again late in delivering my manuscript. When I was at Gemmia's house, I could not write. When I was home, I didn't write. When I wasn't on the computer researching some new treatment, I was on the telephone talking to someone about the same thing. Gemmia didn't want to hear anything about other forms of treatment, but I needed to know.

I let my housekeeper go to save money. That meant that I had to be home when Oluwa arrived from school. Most days I would send him off, go to Gemmia's, and spend the day with her. On other days, as soon as he got home, we would go to Gemmia's together. He and Niamoja did their homework with Gemmia's help while I juiced and prepared her meals. This went on for weeks.

One day Gemmia called me and told me I didn't need to come over, she was going out. Out where? Just out, I have some things to do. I thought it was the beginning of her full recovery. The next day, before I could leave my house, Gemmia arrived. She looked good and she seemed to have a lot of energy. I was both shocked and pleasantly surprised. We spent a lovely morning together chatting before she dropped the bombshell. She had decided to begin chemotherapy. Her recent blood test indicated that she still had cancer in her body. She wanted to knock it out because she was moving.

Moving where? She was selling her house and moving to Los Angeles. She wanted to study under Reverend Michael Beckwith and start her own business. If she did the chemo here, she could get the cancer under control, and she would find a doctor when she got to Los Angeles. She needed and wanted my support. "Well, of course, you have it," I told her. I just didn't understand why now.

Gemmia told me that she had been thinking about it for a while, but she didn't want to take Niamoja away from her father. She also didn't think I would support her, because I needed her at Inner Visions. Her health challenge helped her to figure out that at 30 years old, she could no longer live my vision. She needed to pursue her own. She was a certified aroma therapist and wanted to continue her studies and start a product line. She wanted to complete the ministerial studies she had begun at age 19. She was ready to put on her big girl panties and move away from Mommy.

I knew better than to ask one single question about anything other than the chemo. Was she sure? She had spoken to her doctor and she was very sure. She was going to start the following week. She would receive treatment twice a week for six weeks, and then they would do another CAT scan and more blood work. She would not go bald. It was her intention to do one round of chemo and then prepare to move. She asked if I would go to chemo with her. I told her I would be honored.

We took a special blanket in a special bag, lots of snacks, and a few things to read. The room was filled with men and women, old and young, some bald, others not, all sitting in chairs, reading, napping, or chatting with their escorts. It was nothing like I had imagined. The nurses were funny as heck, and not one of them blinked when I asked if I could pray over the medicine before they administered it.

After the second visit, each nurse knew to hand me the bag of medication before they hung it on the pole and started the IV on Gemmia. It took four visits before she experienced even the slightest nausea. By her sixth visit, she felt tired the day of the treatment and great the day after. By the fourth week of treatment, we were going out to lunch afterwards. One day we treated ourselves to a stroll through Saks Fifth Avenue, right down the street from the doctor's office. By the time she finished treatment, she was living on her own again, coming into the Inner Visions office once or twice a week. She even taught her class one weekend. She still needed a lot of rest, but it seemed as if she had turned the corner. According to the doctor, her white cell count was only six points above normal, and the CAT scan indicated that there were no abnormal cells in her abdominal area. We were not out of the woods, but she didn't need to see him for another three months.

She immediately got busy working on her product line and studying for advanced certification as an aroma therapist. She put her house on the market and made plans to give away or sell most of her belongings. She started gathering boxes and packing. She was alive again. She didn't want to wait until June to move. She was thinking more like January. The only question was what to do with Niamoja, who would be in the middle of a school year. I suggested that instead of selling the house, she could rent it out; that way she would have an income. She didn't like that idea at all. She needed the money to buy an apartment in L.A. She wanted her own place as soon as possible. Being the wise mother, I decided to keep my mouth shut; no more suggestions from me. But Gemmia mistook my silence for something else, which took us down a road we had never traveled.

We must learn not to give up when requirements
are not met or when commitments are broken.
To do so is a refusal to allow mistakes to be corrected
and a demonstration of an unwillingness to forgive
yourself or anyone else who needs forgiveness.

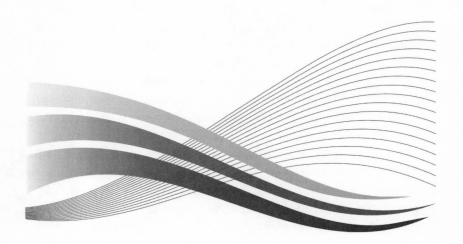

CHAPTER 14

TRUTH AND CONSEQUENCES

Dealing with Gemmia's illness opened up a new can of deadly worms in my heart and mind. They were worms of guilt and fear; worms of failure and helplessness. There was nothing I could do about the fact that my child had cancer. There was nothing I could do about the way she was choosing to address the cancer. And there was absolutely nothing I could do about the fact that she wanted to move to the other side of the country and take my grandchild with her.

The only thing I could do was Tap and create affirmations to convince myself that things were exactly as they needed to be. On some days, the doubt and fear were so strong, by the time I finished my EFT practice my body was sore. On other days, I Tapped so hard, I expected to start bleeding. I didn't and I always felt better.

On some level, I was really okay with the fact that she wanted to move. Gemmia was a brilliant and talented young woman; she would do well wherever she was. As much as I dislike L.A., I was really okay with the idea of traveling there two or three times a year, and she made it perfectly clear that she planned to come to Maryland to teach her classes and participate in the workshops. I was thrilled that she would be studying with Reverend Michael and that she would be a part of his church, a large, loving, diverse community. Between all of the classes and activities at the church, and with the help of Rev. Michael his wife Rickie, Ms. Alice, Rev. Michael's mother and his brother Akili, I knew that she would be well supported and protected.

My challenge was different. My challenge was about the statement she made about why she was moving to L.A. It had a very unsettling ring to it: "I have been living your vision, not mine." As gently as I could, I tried to get more information. Did she feel trapped? Did she not want to participate in Inner Visions? Had I forced her to become part of my vision and ministry? There were times when she would respond in a very clear and honest manner. At other times, she seemed downright hostile and said I was trying to talk her out of her move. The information I did get from her was astounding.

Gemmia knew that I had done the best I could as a mother, which meant that she didn't hold things against me. She knew I was no longer that frightened and confused young woman, chasing men and money to her own detriment and the detriment of everyone around her. But she had deeply mixed feelings about the way I had raised her, and she was angry over all she felt she had missed as a child. What the child heard, saw, and made up often had very little to do with what was really going on. During Gemmia's recovery, we spent time telling stories and remembering the good old bad days. Gemmia said that she was very, very proud of me and what I had accomplished in my life, with very little help from anyone. She reminded me that she was there, she was involved, and she knew everything, from her perspective. It was the things that she saw and felt that drew her into my vision called Inner Visions.

When I first started Inner Visions back in Philadelphia, it was Gemmia and Nisa who helped me fold and mail a one-page newsletter. She remembered when I had to decide between buying stamps to mail the newsletter and buying food for dinner. She remembered my first keynote address and my first media interview. She remembered how excited we all were and the sacrifices she made to support me. There were many things that Gemmia admitted she hadn't told me, and there were things she hadn't asked me for, because she didn't want to be a burden. No, she didn't feel trapped at Inner Visions. It was also a part of her dream; it simply wasn't all of her dream. She was proud to be a part of something built from the ground up and that now had a national reach and reputation. Everything she did, everything she gave, she had given willingly. All these things we had talked about many times. Many difficult memories and hard feelings had already come to light when we dealt with Jimmy's misconduct in the school and the issues that that raised between us. But now there were other revelations that literally took my breath away.

Gemmia talked about betrayal. The most serious was my failure to tell her who her real father was, and the way I finally did tell her. Gemmia's father, my first husband, left New York when she was three years old. I didn't hear from him for almost ten years. His mother was always around, but I never explained to my children how she was related to them. When Gemmia's father returned to New York, he wanted to see his daughter. According to Gemmia, one day when she was about 12, she saw this man in our house. When she asked me who he was, she remembered me saying, "That is your father, your real father." Then he didn't come around any more. I never said another word to her about it, and she was afraid to ask. Of course, I didn't recall it happening that way, but that didn't matter. I had lied to her about her father, and he had been absent from her life with no explanation. Now she wanted to have a relationship with her father and realized that she didn't need my permission to do so.

She was perfectly right. Like every parent, I tried to protect my children. I wanted the best for them. When a man showed up who was willing to take on a ready-made family, I slipped into a happily-ever-after fantasy. Now I knew it was wrong. Back then, I was young and stupid and emotionally immature. The worst of it was the repetition of the pattern with which I had been raised, immersed in lies and other people's fantasies. Talking to Gemmia made it perfectly clear that I had unknowingly perpetuated the same pathology that I grew up in. I had created a web of lies. I knew how much it had hurt me, and I had vowed I would never do that to my children. Now I realized that I had failed miserably at keeping that promise to myself.

As the middle child, Gemmia said, she always felt ignored and dismissed. Damon and Nisa were very strong personalities. They demanded my attention. They were disobedient and acted out in ways that she did not. She thought that if she were good in school, obedient, and helpful, I would see her. When I created Inner Visions, she found a way to get and keep my attention in a way that her brother and sister could not. Gemmia never felt important in my life until we started building Inner Visions together.

For my part, I had no idea she was performing to get my attention. I assumed that it was who she was. She was wise beyond her years and inherently brilliant. Listening to her version of her life, though, I could see the dysfunction that I had perpetuated. I had never acknowledged her, affirmed her, or praised her enough. Of course, I had rarely been praised or acknowledged as a child.

As I listened to her, I realized that Gemmia's story was my story. I had visited upon her just what I had endured, minus the physical violence. The thought of it made me sick to my stomach. How was this possible? How could I have been so blind? *So stupid?* I thought that I had shifted my patterns enough to spare my children my tragedy. According to Gemmia, I had been a carbon copy of the people who raised me.

The truth of what she said left a gaping hole in my heart. More important, it left me feeling as if my work in the world had all been a farce. I was a fake! A phony! I was selling a bill of goods, teaching things that I was not doing in my own life. I didn't think I would ever be able to stand in front of an audience and open my mouth with any sense of legitimacy again.

If what Gemmia said was true, then it stood to reason that much of what my husband had said to me was also true. He often accused me of not practicing what I was preaching. He was very good at pointing out to me when I had breached integrity or where I was not being loving. Of course, most of what he was telling me focused on his needs and what he thought I was not doing for him. Yet in the vortex of criticism and rejection from those I loved, his words and Gemmia's collided and took on the same meaning. I was not who I held myself out to be. And if I wasn't, *just who the hell was I?*

With these thoughts swirling in my mind, I concluded that my husband had not destroyed my marriage. I had. Perhaps he had been the voice of reason. Maybe the things he told me about myself were true. He always complained that I made everything a priority over him. He often challenged me about only seeing things my way. He said that I was manipulative and dishonest. According to Gemmia, some of that was true. I had discounted and dismissed the only man I ever really loved, and now he was leaving my life. I often wondered why I kept being guided to *be still* and let him *take the lead.* Maybe that was God's way of keeping me on hold, because God knew that the day would come when I would have these conversations with Gemmia and come to my senses. *Oh my God! What if it was me all along? My fault! My bad! What had I done?*

With all of these storms raging in my mind, I was attempting to write a book. A book about how people needed to clear their minds and hearts of their personal lies. It was the book that I needed to read. A book in which I thought I could share the truth as I was learning it moment by moment. Unfortunately, I couldn't get the words onto the paper. When I did, they were a jumbled rambling. Instead of seeing that it was a function of the emotional turmoil I was experiencing, I fell into a deep well of shame.

Rather than staying hopeless, guilty, and angry at myself, I decided it was all God's fault. If I was so messed up, if I had done such damage to the people I loved, why had I been guided to serve in the world? Why had I been raised to a position of prominence only to be torn down? Most of my money was gone. I had been publicly disgraced by losing two television shows. My marriage was in shambles. I concluded that somehow, somewhere along the way, I had missed the mark. The voice I had accepted as Divine Guidance was actually the voice of my ego leading me right into destruction. I was being punished by God for not being able to tell the difference between the voice of God and the voices of my own self-made distortions.

I decided that I was being punished for all the bad choices and poor decisions of my youth. I had lied, stolen money from the government, had three abortions and slept with a married man. I had failed to honor commitments, been late for almost everything I ever did, was in conflict about being Christian and Yoruba at the same time, and I had not been to church in years. Maybe I had used people to get want I wanted and needed. Maybe I had inflicted immeasurable harm on my children. Maybe I had made a mistake by taking my grandson away from Nisa. My only son had gone totally astray as a result of what I did and did not give him as a mother. This was all God's fault! Not mine!

God bless Ken Kizer and Steve Hardison. These two men stood with me through the tornado of turmoil that I was creating in my own mind. Ken told me that it was a natural, normal reaction to the events of the past seven months. He assured me that I had not been a fake or a phony. He was willing to be a living testimonial to the power and veracity of what I taught in the world. The guilt, well, that was another story. He knew that guilt was my Achilles heel. It was in my DNA. He said that everything that Gemmia shared was a function of her own soul-searching in the midst of a life-threatening experience. That too, he said, was normal. What she felt and what she thought was none of my business, unless I had held a conscious intention to hurt or harm her.

Ken reminded me that like everyone else, Gemmia's soul had chosen its mother. It just happened to be me. She, like me and everyone else, had chosen, at the soul level, to be born into the circumstances of her life for the purpose of growing, learning, and healing. He felt that we were a great team. We had done great work together. Now our relationship and the circumstances of our lives were changing. It was hard. It was frightening. And he was sure that we would both land on our feet.

There can be no change without chaos. All real, lasting change comes as a result of trembling at the foundational level of what exists. Change was a good thing, and I didn't need to beat myself down because of the past. It was every single one of those circumstances that had led to the change that we were both experiencing, and it was all good. I spent many hours talking to Ken and working myself back to a state of balance.

Steve and I talked about my marriage. He was not at all in agreement that everything was my fault. Of course, I knew that it takes two people to make a marriage, and I did realize that people come together based on the needs of their souls and their spiritual curriculum. I could acknowledge with Steve that the problems did not come from within the marriage itself. Instead, they came from within both of us. I went all the way back to my experience in Africa, to not really knowing the man I was marrying, and recognized that I saw him from a place of wounding and need rather than choice.

Loving him as I did had almost nothing to do with him. It was about having more of what I had always known. In my mind, if I could get him to love and accept me, it would somehow mean that my father really did love and accept me. The world-renowned author, teacher, and speaker had not married the man she loved. The 13-year-old, lost, confused, ugly, bad girl had married the man she thought she could never have—her father.

Once again, Gemmia was my teacher. I was being healed as a result of her illness. I was getting more from her than I had ever given to her. According to both Ken and Steve, when parents are conscious and open, that is the way it should be. Children bring to life the subconscious issues of the parents. How parents deal with their children creates a direct line to the things they need to heal within themselves. This led me to another question, one I dreaded asking, but had to ask. It had been looming in my mind since that first day at the hospital when Dr. Mussenden revealed the nature of Gemmia's illness. I had tried to hide it in the back of my mind, but it kept inching forward. Now, with these two men holding me so closely to the truth, I just needed to know, how was I responsible for Gemmia having cancer? What, if any, role did I play in her illness? I needed to know. Unfortunately, neither Ken nor Steve could tell me the answer.

Even though there is a
part of me holding on to the belief
that I am now, have always been,
and will always be unworthy,
I am still willing to love and accept myself.

CHAPTER 15

THE UPWARD DOWNWARD SPIRAL

Gemmia was doing great! It had been six months since her surgery and almost three months since her chemo ended. She felt good and she looked even better. She was busy packing, preparing to sell her house, and working on her product line. She had four staple fragrances, with three products each: shower gel, hand soap, and body oil. She often used the Inner Visions faculty and student body as her guinea pigs. We didn't mind. Her products were wonderful. She came to the office less frequently, but she continued to teach her classes at the Institute.

The day she called to tell me she was sick, I did my best not to panic. She assured me that it was not the cancer. She had eaten some Chinese food, and it upset her stomach. Could I pick up Niamoja from school? By the time I got to her house, she was sweating bullets and in terrible pain. I had to fight the flashbacks in my mind. I told her that I was going home to pick up Oluwa and I would be back. If she wasn't better by then, we were going to the hospital.

Two hours later, when I returned, she was weak and vomiting but would not leave the house until I promised her that I would not, under any circumstances, leave her in the hospital. I promised but my fingers were crossed. It turned out it was food poisoning. That would pass, but her blood test showed there was something else going on. The ER doctor recommended that she go back to her oncologist. My heart sank. It just couldn't be happening again!

It took ten days before we could get her to the doctor. The food poisoning really took her down a long and winding road. It was, however, nothing like the one we were about to get on. The cancer was active again, and the CAT scan showed a small growth in her abdomen. He wanted to do another round of chemo, eight weeks, two different medications this time. "Let's kick this thing in the butt," he said. We started the following week, but this time it wasn't so pleasant. I prayed over everything she used: the sheets, the towels, the blankets, and of course, the medication. By the time we got to the parking lot in the basement of the building, she was heaving. She never vomited, just dry heaves. I would stay to make sure she and Niamoja had dinner. Then I would drive home, help Oluwa with his homework, and write for a few hours before I went to bed. Gemmia was usually able to get up the day after the treatment, but it took her two days to really get back on her feet. By then, it was time to go back for the next treatment. Her hair was not falling out, but she was dropping weight rapidly. And she was regressing emotionally.

At first, I acted like I didn't notice it. But then, it became obvious to others. Any time I went near her, she would turn away. If I tried to touch her, she would block my hand. Then she started to raise her voice at me. One day she told me I was crazy. Another time she told me I was a pain in her ass. I knew she was feeling like crap, but I was dismayed. Often I had to excuse myself and go home. Before I was ten minutes down the road, she would call me. "Mommy, are you coming back?" Gemmia had never called me Mommy, not even as a child. She called me Mumzie or Ma or Yeye. Not even as a child did she call me Mommy. Many times, I would turn around, go back to her house, and sit with her until she went to sleep. But that was a problem too. One of her medications kept her awake. The doctor prescribed a sleeping medication that made her hallucinate. She would call me at 3 or 4 A.M. and ask me to come right away because there were people in her bedroom. Sometimes I went. Other times, I would calm her down and stay on the telephone with her until daybreak.

Yawfah had her on a strict juice regimen to counteract the effects of the chemo. "We have to boost her immune system and protect her liver" was the mantra. This required 24 ounces of carrot juice three times a day, 4 ounces of wheat grass juice twice a day, and a combination of vegetable and fruit juices throughout the day. But by the fourth week of chemo round two, things were not looking good. Gemmia rarely got out of bed anymore. She weighed about 100 pounds, which was 44 pounds less than her normal weight. She was starting to have pain again, and she rarely slept at night. By now, I was also noticing a change in Niamoja. She spent most of her time in her room with the door closed. When I knocked, there were times she didn't answer. Gemmia said she was angry because she couldn't sleep in Mommy's bed. But because Gemmia wasn't sleeping and because Niamoja slept like a wild banshee, Gemmia had sent her to sleep in her own room. Niamoja could hold a grudge for weeks if she was upset about something. It was difficult for her to see how much her mommy had changed. It was hard for me and I wasn't a child.

The one thing Gemmia would do every week as usual was braid Niamoja's hair. Gemmia was a master braider, and Niamoja had five pounds of hair on her head. They would get in the shower together where Gemmia would wash her hair. Then, they would get out naked and soaking wet, run around the bedroom for a while, and then the ritual began. Gemmia would blow dry Niamoja's hair while they watched cartoons or a movie they had already seen 20 times. The process usually took about four hours. It was an amazing thing to watch. So, I was quite alarmed when Gemmia asked me to wash and braid Niamoja's hair. She was too weak, she said, to blow dry it. If I washed it, she would try to braid it. Of course I didn't mind, but I was very, very alarmed.

A friend in New York—Susan Taylor—suggested that I take Gemmia to a naturopath, acupuncturist, and Chinese herbal master in New York who had great success with all sorts of cancers. He had a three- to four-month waiting list, but she got us an appointment. By then, I think Gemmia felt so poorly she would have done almost anything. Dr. Nyuen was great, very gentle. Gemmia made her usual objections to the needles, and he promised not to hurt her. By the time we left, I had spent over $1,000 for the treatment and three weeks' worth of herbs. He made her promise to come back in three weeks.

By that time, though, Gemmia could barely walk. Things were really getting bad. She was now down to 95 pounds. She rarely got more than two hours of sleep a night. The only thing she could keep down was oatmeal, and that made her furious. Gemmia loved to eat, and she was fed up with the juices. No matter what I said, she would argue with me. It got to be so tense between us that Yawfah offered to come up and give me a break. Gemmia loved Yawfah, and Yawfah didn't take no mess!

I was both relieved and jealous at the way Gemmia responded to Yawfah. Then again, Yawfah knew how to do things about which I knew nothing. She would massage Gemmia until she went to sleep. Because all she had to do was provide care, she answered her every beck and call. In fact, she gave Gemmia a bell so that whenever she needed something, all she needed to do was ring. She said that yelling throughout the house disturbed the energy. She stayed for ten days and when she left, Gemmia cried. It was clear that whatever was going on with her and the cancer had something to do with me. Or at least that was the way it felt.

I hadn't received one of those 3 A.M. calls in a while. When I did, I knew that something must be wrong. She was crying her heart out. "What's wrong, sweetie? Tell me what is the matter." She couldn't speak. I told her to hang up. I would get dressed and come over. I would call her from my cell phone when I got in the car. I scooped up the sleeping dead weight of Oluwa, put him in the car, and tore off like a lunatic. On the phone again, I got a few words out of her about being tired and scared. She told me that she had told Niamoja about menstruation. She was nine and she needed to know. Then she told me that she could not see her life beyond age 30. She felt like her life had come to an end, and she felt incomplete.

Then she asked me a very strange question. She asked me if I had wanted her when I was pregnant. *Oh my Lord!* I told her the story about the Bellevue abortion clinic and how Nett had stopped me from doing what I planned. I told her that I wanted her, but I did not know if I could provide for her. I told her that her father was in jail then and I was scared to even try to raise two children alone. I also told her that she might have an *in vitro* memory of not being wanted because I had spent so much time contemplating the abortion. She said she understood and thought that might be the reason she could not see a vision for her life beyond age 30. She said she tried but, she just couldn't see it.

By the time I reached her front door, she had started crying again. I ran into her room, scooped her up in my arms, and held her as tight as I could. When she could catch her breath, she asked me:

"Am I going to die?"

"Do you want to die? Are you ready to die?"

"No, but I can't see how this is going to get any better."

"What do you mean?"

"Look at this." It was then she showed me the opening in her navel. There was a small white mass. It looked like an oozing blemish.

"How long has that been there?"

"About a week."

"Does it hurt?"

"No."

"Did you tell the doctor?"

"No."

"Well, before we start making plans for the funeral, let's ask him what it is."

"You are so silly."

"I learned it from you."

We curled up in the bed and rocked each other. I knew then. I knew in that moment, but I could not allow myself to even think it. I was her mom. As long as she affirmed life, I would affirm it with her and for her. *No more thoughts!* I held her tighter. *No more f——g thoughts!*

"Mumzie."

"Yeah, sweetie."

"You are squeezing the life out of me right now."

"Oh Lord! I am so sorry." And we both laughed a very tearful laugh.

Three seconds later I jumped up, startling both of us.

"What's the matter?" she asked as I disentangled myself and scrambled to my feet.

"I left Oluwa in the car."

Self-pity in its early stages
is as snug as a feather mattress.
Only when it hardens
does it become uncomfortable.

— Maya Angelou

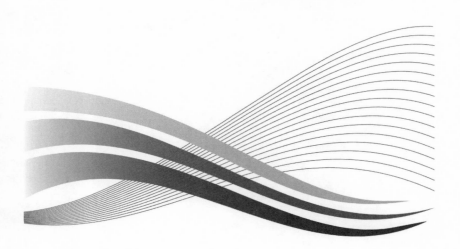

CHAPTER 16

UNFINISHED BUSINESS

How as a mother do you watch your child die? How do you make sense of it? You don't. You go through every day, day after day with a huge wad of despair in your throat. At times you want to gag. At other times, you try to swallow it; but you can't. Instead, you put your face in a pleasant position and you keep it there, no matter what you see or hear. When people ask you how you are, you lie and babble something ridiculous that even you don't believe. When people ask you how she is doing, you just say that you are hoping for the best. In your weak moments, you call your best friend who has enough sense to just listen to you cry without making any false promises. Then, if she is like my best friend, she will pray for you. When you're a mother whose child is dying, you listen to the prayer and hope with all of your heart that you can believe it. You muster up every fiber of faith you have left to force yourself to believe it. If you don't, and the wad of despair in your throat becomes too much to bear, then you do your best to pray for yourself. It is not, however, a real prayer. It is a begging, pleading, angry prayer that you don't even believe yourself. I was losing it fast but my face stayed pleasant.

‡✛‡

Yawfah came up from Atlanta for another ten-day stint. Lydia came down from New York to support me with Oluwa. Almasi and Helen told me not to come into the office. Everything seemed to be moving in slow motion, and I felt totally alone. I must admit, when I called to ask my estranged husband for support with Oluwa he usually came. The energy between us had become pleasantly unpleasant. We never came within three feet of one another. We never looked each other in the eye any more. And we never talked about anything of substance.

One evening after he had stayed with Oluwa, I asked him a question—I don't even remember what it was—and he blew up.

"You know, one of the reasons it was so difficult to be with you was the drama. You always have some kind of drama going on in your life."

"Excuse me?"

"I want to live in peace, and you don't seem to know how to do that."

"I'm not sure what you mean by drama."

"Well, you wouldn't know about it because you create it all the time."

"Are you talking about Gemmia being sick? Is that drama? Or are you talking about the fact that I have spent every dime I have taking care of her household and this one? Is that drama? Why not tell me what you are talking about?"

"Why didn't you tell someone where you were going? Why would you just disappear like that?"

Now I knew what he was talking about. The week before, I had become so unfocused that I could barely find my way home. My mind was racing. I was awake for two or three days at a stretch. One morning, I was praying and I heard, "Go to the ocean. Take a bag and leave." So I did. I took my Bible and two nightgowns and I drove to Ocean City, Maryland. I stayed in the hotel room for three days, sleeping and reading scriptures. In the day, I would walk on the beach. At night I would read. I thought about calling home, but since I knew Gemmia and Oluwa were being cared for, I opted to remain in silence. When I returned, I went directly to Gemmia's house. She told me that she thought I was off with him so she had called him.

"Are you upset that I went away without saying anything?"

"You had everybody worried. I thought something had happened to you."

I told him how it happened and that I really felt guided to be in silence. It didn't seem to matter. He rolled his eyes, got in the car, and tore off down the driveway.

On a warm Sunday afternoon about two weeks later, Yawfah was with Gemmia and I was home, piddling around the house. I had just made some iced tea, and I was sitting on the deck outside the bedroom thinking about not thinking. When I looked up and saw him, I was pleasantly surprised. A part of me wanted to tell him that it was no longer appropriate for him to show up without calling. I shooed that part of me away and decided that I would simply be nice. I gave him an update on Gemmia. He seemed concerned but had nothing to offer other than positive platitudes. Then he told me that he was going to move forward with the divorce. Nothing in my body shifted or moved, so I listened.

"Isn't that what you want?"

"It isn't, but at this point the ball is in your court."

"No, you filed the papers." So he had received them after all.

"I never completed the paperwork. I was angry and I started it, but I was told to be still and let you take the lead."

"You never told me that."

"You never asked about it."

"I don't understand why you want to be married to me. I just don't."

"Well, if you don't understand, there is nothing I can say that will help you understand."

"You know, your mouth has always been an issue."

"Please forgive me. Right now, I am too exhausted to fight with you. I am facing the possibility of losing my child. Fighting for a man who doesn't even like me is not an option."

"I love you, Iyanla. I just don't think we were meant to be together as husband and wife."

Maybe he was right. Or maybe he was covertly trying to get me to say something that would make him feel better. I didn't know, and at that point, on that day, I really didn't care.

"What do you think? Do you think we can ever be together?"

"That has been my dream since I was 13-years-old. I have loved you all of my life. I thought that when I closed my eyes for the last time, I would be looking in your face. Right now, I don't have the strength to fight for you or with you. This just isn't the time."

"It will never be the right time. I started to do this long ago, way back when you were on *Oprah,* but I knew that wasn't the right time. Then you had your show, and that wasn't the right time. So I guess there will never be a good time for something like this."

After he left, I kept sipping my tea with no response whatsoever anywhere in my body. *Done!*

‡‡‡

Gemmia's deteriorating condition was just one of the large problems looming over my head. I had fallen out of compliance with my IRS payment arrangements. There simply was no money to pay them. I was down to one staff member. Almasi and I were scraping by on whatever came in from the sales of my books and tapes. We did our best to keep the faculty paid so that we could continue the Institute classes. We were three months behind on the rent for the Inner Visions Center, and to the tune of $5,700 per month, the landlord was getting a bit aggressive. The other challenge was my publisher. They wanted me to deliver my manuscript, or they were going to cancel my contract and sue for the advanced they had paid. "When it rains, it pours" took on an entirely new meaning in my life. So did "God never gives you more than you can handle."

Thank God for good accountants! Mine was a former IRS investigator. He knew the ins and outs of the bureau. He contacted the right people and provided the right information, and they agreed to give me a year of grace. Somehow, we were able to send the landlord one month's rent. That calmed him down, but not for long. The truth is that he wanted us out. The neighborhood had changed drastically and he could get much more for the building than what we were paying. I turned the matter over to the prayer team and told them they needed to pray for him to be amicable.

There was absolutely nothing I could do about the book. I had produced over 600 pages and still had nothing that was worthy of being published. It felt like I was about to end my publishing career. Everything that I had worked for was about to go up in smoke, and for some reason, I could not get upset. I had done all I could do, and I was doing the best I could.

I was amazed at the cost of fresh fruits and vegetables. No wonder poor people have bad health. Gemmia needed about 40 pounds of carrots a week to keep her supplied with fresh juice. In addition to that, Yawfah wanted everything to be organic so that we would know we were not putting any unknown chemicals into her body. Six pounds of grapes is one thing. Six pounds of organic grapes takes the cost up by about $8. It had been a long time since I had counted pennies, cashed in bottles, or borrowed money from anyone. Everything I had saved was gone. Everything Gemmia had was long gone. In fact, one day when she was feeling pretty good, she took herself down to the County Court and filed for child support. She told me that in her entire life, Jimmy had never given her money. He had purchased a few things here and there, but he had never put cash money in her hands, and she was sick of it. Wow! Another family pattern. My children's fathers had never made a financial contribution to their lives. After several weeks of Jimmy missing court dates, she was awarded $150 per month. He was to pay it directly to her. *What a victory!*

In the midst of her illness, the victory of her awarded child support was short lived, because Jimmy had told her to deposit the check on one date and she deposited it earlier. His tirade over this mistake left her drained and depleted.

I, on the other hand, had no such luck. I had friends who had money. I just couldn't bring myself to ask them for any. I knew people who had money. I wouldn't even entertain the thought of asking them. I had helped so many people, invested in so many others. Now that I needed help, I had nowhere to go. But I had a community of people who loved and supported me. They didn't have money, but they gave what they had—their time and a few carrots here and there. So I focused on the blessings I did have. I had to stay positive because it seemed that Gemmia had become hypersensitive to me and everything about me.

She was telling people that I was going crazy. She told them that I would go out and stay for hours and come back like nothing had ever happened. What she didn't know, though the others did, was that there were many days when I would get lost, literally. I was so physically exhausted and emotionally drained that I would lose my way going home. One night, I drove past my exit off the Beltway. It took me a tearful hour to get my bearings. I also heard that Gemmia was furious about what was going on at Inner Visions. She had worked for the last 12 years of her life, given everything she had to build that place, and she said I was running it into the ground. That is what she said about me behind my back. What she said to my face was quite often worse.

When Gemmia told me that she had called her father, I was really happy for her. She told me that he was going to fix the cabinets in her kitchen and do some other work to get the house ready for sale. He was a master carpenter, so I was sure that would save her some money. Then she told me that she had to buy the supplies for him. That sent ice water rushing through my veins, though I didn't say a word. This man who had never given me or her one single penny was asking her to buy his supplies? This man who had disappeared for almost ten years wanted his daughter to buy his supplies? This man who had remarried and had a son the same age as Niamoja wanted his only daughter, his eldest child, to buy his supplies? It was a disgrace! I thought it but I didn't say it. The worst part was that Gemmia was okay with it.

He told her he would come on Saturday to pick up the money. When she told him she didn't have it, he said she should call when she was ready. I was livid but I didn't say a word.

One Sunday, he did come by to take her to church with him. The service lasted from 10 A.M. until 3 P.M. Afterwards, they stayed for a lunch of traditional church food: fried chicken, mac and cheese, and cakes and pies. She arrived home after 5 P.M. starving. Was he crazy? Did he realize that this woman was fighting cancer? How could he keep her out all day and not make sure she had something she could eat? She was just glad to spend time with her father. I could see very clearly that I had taught my daughter to accept the worst of all treatment from men. I had taught her that crumbs were tasty treats and that she should rejoice when they were being offered. I was furious with him. I was outraged with myself!

I talked to Yawfah about it. She agreed with me but said that it was something Gemmia needed to do. She needed to know that her father wanted to be in her life. In fact, Yawfah also agreed with me that on most days Gemmia was reliving her life at age 13. At that age, she wasn't angry with her father, she was in a total rage at her mother. I knew that also. Yawfah said they had talked a lot about her feelings and Gemmia was still an avid journal writer. Yawfah had her on a program of journal writing three times a day to express what she was feeling. Then we talked about something else I already knew and had been avoiding.

Any spiritual healer on the planet would probably tell you that at the root of all cancer is a seed of anger. When anger festers, it promotes cancer in the physical body. Some people bring the anger into this life with them. Others experience anger throughout their lives and stuff it down. This does not mean they don't feel anger. It means that they deflect it. They camouflage it. Yes, I did know that Gemmia was angry. I also knew most of the anger she felt was directed toward me. Now that her resistance was so low, she was emotionally vulnerable and her true feelings were rising to the surface. Gemmia mentioned that she had not heard from her father in a few weeks. I could feel the sadness attached to her observation. I asked if I could help. She said no and we left it at that.

But, thinking about what Yawfah had said and remembering my experiences with Gemmia's father, I felt a little motherly intervention was required. I called her father and left him a message. I thought the message was very clear and direct, delivered with care and concern. I told him that Gemmia was in a very vulnerable place right now and that she needed to know that she could trust him. I suggested that he should stay in closer touch with her, and if he made any promises, he should keep them, because she didn't need any further disappointments. I concluded by saying that I was at home and if he needed clarity, he should call me. Fifteen minutes later, Gemmia called instead.

"I know you don't mean any harm and I know you think you are being helpful but I really need you to stay out of my business."

I knew I had to tread very lightly.

"Okay, but can you tell me what you are talking about?"

"I'm talking about you telling my father that I don't trust him."

"That is not what I said, Gemmia."

"I want to know why you think you had to say anything at all. I am a grown woman, and thanks to you, I know how to take care of myself."

"Can I explain what I said?"

"Go ahead."

I told her about the message I left and why I had left it. I didn't want her to be disappointed. I told her that I had asked him to call me. I wasn't clear about why he had called her and given her inaccurate information to boot.

"If I need you to do something for me, I will call. If I need you to say something for me, I will let you know. This is none of your business."

By this point, she was crying.

"Gemmia, please forgive me. I do apologize, and you are absolutely right. Your relationship with your father is none of my business. I guess I just wanted him to know how important this is for you."

"How do you know what is important to me? You never ask me. You just run around doing whatever you want because you think it is important. This is none of your business, and you need to stay out of it."

Can I tell you that my heart was broken? Can I tell you that the pain and remorse I felt in that moment was like going through 80 hours of labor and giving birth to triplets all at the same time? Here I was running up and down the road like a maniac, giving every fiber of my being, every ounce of my life, and this was how she spoke to me. What had I done that was so bad?

Then Gemmia's friend Erika called. Apparently, she was with Gemmia and had heard what Gemmia said to me. She wanted to know if I was all right. No, I wasn't, and chances were that I never would be. Erika said she thought Gemmia was just being protective of the relationship with her father. Then she drove the stake deeper into my heart.

"You know she blames you for him not being in her life. And she is very angry about the way you told her about him."

"We have already had that conversation. Why is that up again?"

"I don't know, but right now, I think it is best for you to stay away from him and from her."

"What do you mean, stay away from her?"

"I don't think she wants to see you right now."

"That's crazy. Is that what she said?"

"Well, kinda."

"What do you mean, kinda? Did she say that or not?"

"I know it's hard for you right now. It is hard for both of you. That is what she said. But you know how she is right now. She will probably change her mind tomorrow."

"Thanks, Erika. Thanks for calling."

✠✠✠

I didn't hear from Gemmia for 11 days. I thought I was losing my mind. Yawfah talked to her at least three or four times a day. According to Yawfah, Gemmia was very remorseful; she knew I was hurt, but she was also angry. All of this, according to Yawfah, was normal. It was the disease. It was the medication. It was the healing process. I just needed to hold on and not take it personally.

Instead, I called Gemmia's father again. I asked him why he hadn't called me. I told him that Gemmia did not want to see me and that she was home alone. I told him that this would be a good time for him to step up and be there for her. I found out from Gemmia later that he never called her back. He never called me either.

When Gemmia did call, she told me that the growth in her navel was a tumor. It was getting bigger. She had been to the doctor. The doctor didn't want to operate yet. Instead, he wanted her to do another six weeks of chemo. She was going to do it because she wanted to be in L.A. by January 15.

She was starting next week. I asked if she wanted me to go with her. She asked me if I had the time. We never talked about her father again. The kitchen cabinets were never repaired.

Sometimes when you fall down, you just have to lie still, and hope that no one runs over you. If they don't and you lay there long enough, taking care to be very still, breathing slowly, refusing to whine, God will lift you and perform a soul surgery.

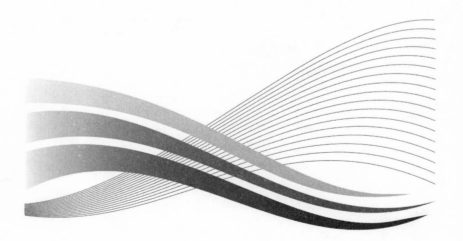

CHAPTER 17

LIFE AND DEATH

The tension between Gemmia and me had eased somewhat, but she was quiet and distant. I couldn't tell if it was the result of our blow-up or if she was feeling just that awful. Although she denied it, her weight still seemed to be dropping. As she dropped weight, the tumor seemed to be growing larger. It was now the size of a walnut and protruding through her navel. She was in good spirits, though. Her bedroom and living room were filled with the boxes she had packed. She had a yard sale and got rid of the things she did not want, including clothes and shoes. I sure wished we wore the same size shoe. We didn't, but Danni and Yawfah made out like fat rats!

We were on our way out the door to what we hoped would be her last round of chemotherapy when the telephone rang. It was my friend Susan from New York calling to check in on Gemmia. She had gotten a call from Dr. Nyuen, the acupuncturist. He was very concerned that she had not returned for additional treatments. I explained that Gemmia could not stand the needles. My friend said she would let him know.

Chemo that day wasn't bad at all. Praying as I usually did, I asked for her suffering to end and that she be filled with the Spirit of wholeness and wellness. One of the nurses asked me to pray aloud, but Gemmia said it would embarrass her. We got through the treatment and made it home without incident. Yawfah was coming in later that day, and her arrival always lifted Gemmia's spirits.

The next morning, while the three of us were sipping tea, Susan called again. She said that Dr. Nyuen insisted that I bring

Gemmia in as soon as possible. He was afraid that if we did not continue her treatment, treatment other than chemo, we would lose her. Susan asked me to try to convince Gemmia that it would be best for her to go.

I went into the bathroom, where I could talk. Then I revealed the real issue. I didn't have the money to get Gemmia to New York or to pay for the treatment. Before I could stop myself, the nightmare of my financial reality spilled out. I didn't have time to be ashamed. Susan listened silently before she responded, "If you can convince her to come, I will take care of it. I have seen what this man can do and he is good."

I motioned Yawfah aside and told her what my friend had said and what she wanted us to do. Yawfah was all for it. Transportation was our biggest concern, as Gemmia might have been too weak to take the long drive. We were also worried about taking her on an airplane, although the flight was only 45 minutes. We decided to let Gemmia decide, once she had agreed to go. Yawfah sent me to the store for more grapes. She would talk to Gemmia.

By the time I returned, the deal was done. Bright and early the next morning, Susan sent a limo and a driver to Gemmia's home. He was to take us to New York. Gemmia, Yawfah, Lydia, and I piled into the car as if we were going to a ball. When we arrived at the doctor's office, all of her treatments and her herbal teas had been paid for. In order to make sure she kept up her treatments, we had been provided with a suite in a private hotel. It was a blessing beyond anything I could have imagined.

We decided that Lydia and I would return to Maryland to take care of the children and Yawfah would stay in New York with Gemmia. I talked to them twice a day, once before they went to treatments and once when they returned. The good news is that the acupuncture treatments helped Gemmia sleep. The bad news is that the pain woke her up. The nights were really rough on Gemmia, on Yawfah, and on me. By the third day, I could not stop crying. I felt awful for leaving Gemmia in New York. Sure, she loved Yawfah, and Yawfah comforted her in ways Gemmia would not allow me to, but I was her mother. I felt I should be with her.

By the fifth day, Gemmia couldn't keep anything in her stomach, and Dr. Nyuen said she was dehydrated. He suggested that we take her home for the weekend, take her to her oncologist, ask him to give her IV fluids, and bring her back on Monday.

Danni bought two plane tickets because I barely had gas money to get to the airport. I realized on the way there that my entire body was trembling and I could not make it stop. It didn't help that once I arrived at the airport, the police officers kept chasing me away from the pick-up area. It was a cold December day, and I did not want Gemmia to spend one minute longer than necessary out of doors. I saw Yawfah first. She was pretty hard to miss in her huge, beautiful gele head wrap. At first I didn't see Gemmia. Then I noticed the airport escort pushing a wheelchair. In the wheelchair was my Gemmia, *my precious jewel*. Her skeletal frame was swallowed up by her ski jacket. Her face was so small and sunken, her knit cap almost covered her eyes. *This could not be the woman I left in New York five days ago!* When she saw me, she smiled and attempted to wave her hand. I fell to my knees, put my head in her lap and wept. Once again, I knew. I knew but I could not, would not accept it. I just wouldn't!

We took her directly to the hospital. Her oncologist had called and given the orders for her to be placed on an IV. But she was in terrible pain, and the doctor had forgotten to leave orders for pain medication. I called Dr. Mussenden. After about two hours of agony, Gemmia was resting peacefully. I, on the other hand, was losing my mind. As she slept, I inspected her body. What I saw has been etched into my mind, and I am sure it will remain there until I take my last breath.

The tumor had tripled in size and was now hanging out of her body. She looked like a skeleton with a thin layer of flesh, beautiful brown sagging flesh. Every bone in her body protruded through her flesh; every rib, every vertebra, her knuckle joints—every single bone was exposing itself through her skin. The final straw was that she was wearing a diaper. There was nothing Yawfah could say about it other than Gemmia didn't always have the strength to make it into the bathroom. Yawfah and I just stared and hung onto one another. We didn't realize that Gemmia had opened her eyes and was staring at us staring at her.

"Are you two doing some kind of spell, or are you in deep meditation?"

Walking was out of the question, so I carried her in my arms to the car. As I was lowering her into the seat, I banged her head on the roof of the car. Gemmia said she would never let me forget it. Over the course of the next week, she did not. I had to carry her to the car again on Monday morning to take her to the doctor's office. He told me that he was going to stop her treatments. He suggested that I find hospice care for her. My body somehow found itself plastered to the wall outside of the office while he went back into the room and told Gemmia. I wheeled her out of his office, down to the car, where I made sure not to hit her head. She remained silent all the way home. I carried her upstairs and put her in the bed. The moment her butt cheeks hit the sheets she said:

"That m—— f——! He pumped my body full of that s——, and now he wants to discard me. He really thinks I am going to die, but I refuse to do that! I refuse to leave my daughter, and I refuse to let this thing win!"

Her voice was so strong I almost believed her. She reached for the telephone and called Yawfah. They talked for hours, creating a plan of action. When she hung up, she told me that Yawfah was glad she wasn't going to do any more chemo. She gave me the list of things that Yawfah had prescribed and asked me to run her a bath. Bathing was one of the things she did every day, three or four times a day, because the warm water helped her muscles. I did as I was told. I ran the bath and then carried her into the bathroom. She put herself in the tub, and that was a good sign. Now, all I needed to do was find the money to purchase all of the new things she was going to need.

I continue to be amazed at how God will let you know what you need to know, exactly when you need to know it. I had completely forgotten about the grandchildren's college fund. I called my broker. I still had $12,000 in the fund. Great! He could overnight it to me since he understood the need. Fantastic!

That would enable me to pay the faculty for Christmas and keep Gemmia supplied with carrots, grapes, wheat grass, and all of the new tidbits she needed. In the meantime, however, I couldn't buy a mosquito a hair net! What was I going to do? Swallow my pride and make some calls. I did. One person had it to give a week before Christmas. Vanessa told me to come and pick up a check for $10,000. I cried all the way there, all the way to the bank, and all the way to the supermarket.

Almasi had the brilliant idea to let the students get involved. This was not the time to hold back. They knew Gemmia. They loved her. Instead of buying her Christmas gifts, they could contribute grapes, carrots, and vegetables. The e-mail went out and the calls started pouring in. This meant that I could pay the telephone bills, Gemmia's and mine; the light bills, hers and mine. It also meant that I could cover both of our car payments and still have enough left over for at least three days of veggies. God is so good!

Christmas was just five days away, and Gemmia insisted that we plan to do everything as we usually did. Lydia and the children put the lights up on the house. I planned the menu with Nisa and Gemmia's help. We would get the tree, as normal, on Christmas Eve. For presents, we would scour Target and get what we could for the children.

It was all planned. Then something happened so quickly, it caught me off guard. I heard Gemmia screaming. The pain meds were not working. She couldn't lie down and she couldn't sit up. Her back was too tender to touch. I called the doctor. He would meet us at the hospital. She was dehydrated again. He wanted me to start her on a regimen of Ensure so that she would get some more nutrients. Yawfah wasn't pleased about putting chemicals in her body, but we needed to keep her nourished. She was still working off the effect of the chemo meds.

She stayed in the hospital for three days. During that time, Dr. Mussenden came to visit her. When she left the hospital, she called me. She wanted to know if Gemmia had spoken to Niamoja. She didn't think Gemmia had. She knew that Gemmia was fighting and that anything was possible, but she also wanted me to know that things did not look good at all. "I am her mother and I will not hear that! This thing could turn around any minute." Dr. Mussenden agreed with me and said she would check in later in the week.

It is so good to know people, a variety of people who do different things. Judith's ex-husband was an old-fashioned medical doctor. He still believed in house calls. He would come to the house and give Gemmia everything that she needed, including vitamin shots. Was that safe? Absolutely! In fact, I should have some also because the stress wasn't good for me. When he arrived, he started Gemmia on an IV of all sorts of goodies. He also told me about a clinic in Mexico that offered a nontraditional cancer treatment using vitamins. He had a friend...he would give him a call...was her liver involved...what was her last blood count...don't worry about the tumor. The next voice I heard was Gemmia's. She had walked to the bedroom door to ask for help to use the bathroom. She saw us talking. "I hope you are not down there making arrangements for me to do anything else. I am in charge of my own healing. Why do you always have to be sneaking around behind my back?" She stumbled back into the bedroom. She was mad at me again.

I called Almasi, who came over immediately because Gemmia would not allow me into her bedroom. Gemmia had calmed down by the next morning, in part because she needed me to help her, in part because she had written me a letter. It was a three-page letter thanking me for everything I had done for her. That was the good part. Then she blasted me for everything she could think of. She ended the letter by writing that if she was going to heal, she was going to heal on her own terms and God's terms. She wrote that most people get sick and then find God. She had found God and then got sick. She didn't understand why she, the good kid, was having this test of faith, but she would survive it. She could not heal for me or Niamoja or anyone else. She needed to heal for herself so that she could follow her vision—not my vision, but her own. She ended the letter by asking me to honor her choices and to stop making plans for her life.

I was too tired to be angry. I gave the letter to Almasi to read. Then I folded it up and threw it somewhere. By the time I woke up the next morning, my eyes were swollen, my head ached, my nose was running, and my ears were ringing. Despite the doctor's insistance that we both get vitamin shots, I had a rip-roaring cold. Great! Just great! How was I going to be near Gemmia coughing like a lunatic?

Gemmia didn't get up the next morning. She allowed herself to be supported by the diaper. Nisa put her in the tub and tidied up her room while I, face covered with a bandana, made juice and oatmeal. I did my best to stay away from her throughout the day, even though she wasn't mad at me any more. I didn't want her to catch my cold. Once all of the kids were fed and went off Christmas shopping with Erika, I cleaned the house, made the evening juices, and flopped down at the kitchen table. I felt an incredible sadness and an even greater hopelessness. I called Rene, Ken's wife. She told me that I should not be alone. She was willing to drive up from Richmond, but I assured her that the kids would be back soon. I sat for a while longer before the inspiration hit me.

I called my husband. I had seen him when Gemmia was in the hospital. He was kind enough to pick up her medications when she was discharged. He seemed to have softened up a bit, so I decided to give it a shot.

"Are you busy today?"

"I'm just doing some Christmas shopping. How's Gemmia? What's up?"

"I need you. I need you to be here with me. I don't care if you sit in the living room and watch football, I just can't do this alone any more."

"I hear you."

We were both silent.

"Can you come?"

"I don't think I should do that."

"Okay. Can you tell me why?"

"I just don't think we need to be doing that."

"You know, you are still my husband and I am your wife. It has taken a lot for me to make this call. I really need you today, and Gemmia needs you too. This woman whom you hold out to be your daughter needs to know that you are here and so do I."

In that moment the tide had turned.

"You know what? I am not going to allow you to use the children to manipulate me into doing what you want. I just saw Gemmia. She knows I am there for her. This isn't about her, this is about you and the way you manipulate people. I am not the one. Not me! Not today!"

"You are right. This is about me. As I said, I need you today. How foolish of me to think that you would respond. Please forgive me. I will not trouble you any further."

When was I going to learn? I hung up the telephone and sat there until I heard Gemmia's bell.

To my surprise, he showed up the next day. He had made arrangements with Nisa to take the children to buy the Christmas tree. They were excited and delighted to see him. When the tree was up and lit, he told me he would stay with Gemmia so that I didn't infect her. He and Damon would take turns watching her throughout the night so that I could rest. It was 9 P.M.

When I awoke, it was 6:30 A.M. I ran upstairs to check on Gemmia. My husband had left, probably to go to work. Damon was asleep on the floor in Gemmia's bedroom. Gemmia was also on the floor. Her body was contorted, and it didn't look like she was breathing. Then I noticed the foul odor in the room. My screaming brought everyone in the household, including the children, to their feet.

"Call 911! Call 911!" I was rocking her in my arms. There were very slight convulsive waves moving through her body. I found the source of the odor. Gemmia had soiled herself, and it was all over the bed and the floor. "Why did I leave you alone? Please forgive me!"

Damon was beside himself. "Ma, Ma, I was right here and I didn't hear anything. Ma! I'm sorry!"

The next few hours are a blur. The ambulance did come. We did make it to the hospital. Her blood sugar had fallen. They cleaned her up. The nurse called the entire family into a room.

The cancer had spread into her liver and was moving up her spine. We should take her home and keep her comfortable. She was sorry. She was very, very sorry. Then we were all back at Gemmia's house. Somewhere along the way, my husband had reappeared. He had left his wallet and when he came back to get it, he saw the ambulance and followed it. Almasi had cleaned up the bedroom. Helen was sitting in the armchair praying. Muhsinah had also followed the ambulance. The children had not gone to school. They were fine.

Gemmia was heavily medicated and sleeping soundly. I was sitting at the side of her bed. Everyone else was downstairs. When I felt her, she felt cold. *Why is she so cold?* I called down to the team to come up and help me. I knew that there was something going on and I didn't like it. I asked Almasi and Muhsinah to rub Gemmia's hands. I got in the bed with her and put her feet on my belly. Helen was praying in her ears. Viviana and Judith were praying aloud and crying. Lydia was just praying. I kept rubbing her feet and her legs. We worked with her and on her for hours. Then, in her usual Gemmia way, she woke up and said:

"What are you people doing? What is going on? Will somebody help me go pee, please?"

We all started laughing, falling all over ourselves trying to get the portable potty that Nisa had brought the day before. When Gemmia was sitting firmly on the potty she looked around the room, shook her head, and called us a motley crew. Then she looked down and realized that her privates were exposed. To that she said, "Boy, talk about a lesson in humility."

She didn't remember anything about the morning. She didn't know that she had been in an ambulance or that she had gone to the hospital. I explained what had happened. I did not reveal what the nurse had said.

She said she was tired. She wanted to take a nap so that she could get up and wrap some presents. She asked me to stay with her. Everyone else left the room. I sat there for many hours, watching her, every now and again checking her feet and hands. They were warm.

Suddenly, I had an overwhelming urge to pray. So I did. I remember asking God to forgive me for anything I had done to cause harm to His child, my child. I asked Him to forgive me if I had called this affliction into her life. I asked Him to forgive me if I had abused her in any way, knowingly or unknowingly. I asked God to give me the strength to walk through His will, whatever it was to be. I asked Him not to take her away from me. At that point, I stopped. I asked for forgiveness and surrendered. *Whatever your will is, God, I accept it.* I could feel myself drifting. It felt as if I was being lifted, and I could not open my eyes. I wanted to speak but I could not. I wanted to pray, but somehow I knew I no longer needed to.

I felt as if I were standing in a very high place looking up. The sky was very close to me, and the air was very clear and clean. I could feel my heart racing, although I was not afraid. Then I saw Him. He was standing above me, in front of me. It was the Christ. It was Jesus. He looked to be 10 or 12 feet tall. His skin was dark, darker than mine, but I could not see His face. I am not even sure He had a face. He was dressed in a long flowing robe with a Kente cloth strip around His neck. I could hear myself thinking, *Iyanla, you have lost your mind. You are looking at a black Jesus in Kente cloth.* In that instant, He seemed to grow larger and come closer. In that instant my heart stopped racing. We stared at each other for a moment. I was amazed at what I was seeing and feeling.

Then I heard a voice. *Will you give her to me?* I was stunned. What did He mean? We stood in silence for what seemed like forever. The question was repeated, *Will you give her to me?* My heart started racing again. I could hear it in my ears. *Will you give her back?* There was silence.

I remembered my prayer. I wanted to cry but could not. I saw myself reach down and lift Gemmia in my arms, the way I had carried her many times before. I didn't know if she was asleep or dead. As I lifted her, I could see that she was naked, her arms dangling. I walked toward Him and lifted her up. Gently, the enormous figure reached down and took Gemmia from my arms. At the same time, I felt an incredible sense of peace. It was almost joyful. Holding her, looking at me, He walked or floated backwards, I am not sure which.

My eyes were affixed to His. I watched closely until I couldn't see them anymore. I stood looking into the emptiness. As if someone were whispering into my ear, I heard: *If she makes it through Christmas Day, she will make it.* Then I heard the children laughing in the hallway.

‡‡‡

Gemmia was still asleep, still warm. I was kissing her face when she awoke. With a strength and power I had not heard from her in several days, she greeted me with "Hey, Mumzie!" and sat up unassisted on the side of the bed. She seemed to be glowing. Her eyes were clear, not foggy like they had been earlier. She gave her body a huge stretch and tried to stand up.

"Oh my God! How do you feel?"

"I feel great but I really must pee." I reached for the Porta Potty. . "No, not that. I want to go to the real bathroom."

"Okay!" What the heck was going on here? I took Gemmia to the bathroom, left her there and ran downstairs, where the team was snacking and chatting.

"You have got to see this. You have got to come see Gemmia." I ran back upstairs. Her energy had given me energy. When we emerged from the bathroom, everyone greeted her.

"You guys are still here. Is it Christmas yet?"

"No, G, that's tomorrow. You still have some time."

"Good, I want to wrap my presents." She pulled away from me and headed toward the closet.

"Wait, the kids are still up. They will see. Let's wait."

"Okay." She flopped down on the bed. I was beside myself with joy. I called Niamoja.

"Nini, come here. Mommy is awake."

She was hesitant, first standing in the doorway, then backing up just a bit. I was so wrapped up in my own fear, I had forgotten how hard this must be for her. Gemmia knew just what to say:

"Nini, come here and give me a hug."

With that permission, Niamoja ran into the room and all but tackled her mother. They were interlocked like a human pretzel. Everyone in the room stared, smiled, and almost cried.

I called the other children in to see Gemmia so that they would know that she had recovered from the drama of the morning. While Gemmia hugged, kissed, and entertained the children, I called Yawfah. I told her Gemmia seemed to have turned the corner. I did not tell her about my vision. I told her that Gemmia had sat on the toilet and walked out of the bathroom unsupported. She was yelling, screaming, and, I suspect, jumping up and down.

Lovely strawberry Ensure and carrot juice for dinner. Yum! Tulani called to say that she was on her way down to spend Christmas with us. She hadn't seen Gemmia in a few weeks. I was excited. I wanted everyone to see that Gemmia was on the way back. Nisa had started Christmas dinner. I was glad that I did not have to cook. The team had left, so the house was pretty quiet. Damon stopped by to say he had to do a few drop-bys but he would be back to wrap gifts. I kept thanking God under my breath and checking on Gemmia. First she was reading, then she was in Niamoja's room, then she wanted to take a bath, then she was asleep, then I remembered, *if she makes it through Christmas Day, she will make it.*

I lift up my eyes to the hills—
where does my help come from?

Psalms 121:1 (NIV)

CHAPTER 18

BEYOND DEATH

I was not new to the experience of death. I knew she was gone. Viviana gave me her stethoscope to check for a heartbeat. What I heard was a hollow sound, as if I were listening to the inside of a tunnel. I laid Gemmia flat on the bed, and we all gathered around her to pray. I heard this ear-piercing scream. It was my own.

After we prayed, I washed Gemmia. Then we changed her clothes and covered her body, not her face. We tidied up the bedroom and played her favorite music. All of this we did before we called 911. All of this we did before anyone shed a tear. There were no tears until the undertaker came. Damon was the first one to break down.

I was determined that Gemmia was not going to the morgue. I did not want her body mutilated and probed. The fact that it was Christmas Day and no one wanted to be disturbed probably worked in our favor. We needed a death certificate in order to move her body from her home to the funeral home. When I called her doctor, I got his answering service. When the operator heard my name, she became severely star-struck. I explained what I needed. She started telling about her favorite book and how much I had helped her. I gave the telephone to Tulani and went back to sit with Gemmia.

Every 15 minutes or so, I relived the experience of Gemmia's organs shutting down. First, I would see the black curtain. Then, my head would get woozy and heavy. Then, one by one, I felt the organs go. After the second or third time it happened, I went into a daze and I didn't come out of it until we had placed Gemmia's casket in the ground, high on a hill, in the Garden of Faith at Harmony Memorial Cemetery.

I don't remember much else. I do remember that everything went smoothly. There was absolutely no drama. The team and my closest friends covered me like a human blanket. Everyone did something, which meant I needed to do nothing. We had a private funeral for family and close friends where we performed the traditional Yoruba burial rites. Following that, we had a public memorial where four ministers of different faiths spoke. Carl Big Heart, my friend and teacher brought greetings and songs from the Lakota Nation. Minister Louis Farrakhan sent a message from the Nation of Islam. The hosting mininster was Rev. Willie Williams of Union Temple Baptist Church. Rev. Michael Beckwith gave the message. His wife, Rickie Byars Beckwith, sang all of Gemmia's favorite songs. Tulani also sang a heart-piercing song. It was two words: "Thank You." She sang it in different octaves, different languages, and she sang it a cappella.

It was January 2004, and my life had changed in an unspeakable way. Lydia moved in with me because more often than not, I didn't know where I was. It was two weeks before I realized I had no clue where Niamoja had gone. Erika told me she was still with her father. "Is that where she wants to be? She should be with me, shouldn't she?" I called his home and got no answer.

I did my best to comfort Oluwa, and he kept telling me he was fine. *He was not fine!* Gemmia had practically raised him. Her death meant that he had lost his primary mother figure. He knew that I was his grandmother. He knew that Nisa was his mother. But he looked to Gemmia for everything. He had even said so at the funeral, where he spoke so eloquently that we gave him a standing ovation. He was a 12-year-old boy who probably didn't know how to show his emotions. I wasn't doing much better.

Lydia had taken over getting Oluwa to school and picking him up. As she said, I couldn't be loose in the streets without an escort. One day while she was out, I got in my car and drove off with no destination in mind. My house seemed eerily quiet. Everything seemed to be moving in slow motion. I wanted to get back into the world and get my life moving again. I went to my favorite bookstore in Annapolis, Maryland, a small Christian bookstore where everyone knew me. I walked in quietly and went directly to the Bible section, not that I needed another Bible. I collect them. I must have 50 different Bibles—different translations, colors, and sizes. I only use one. It is ragged.

I walked up and down the aisles that I knew so well. There was a new comparative Bible. Other than that, everything was just as I had seen it hundreds of times before. I was about to walk out of the store when one of the clerks called out to me.

"Good day, my sister. You look beautiful today."

He looked and sounded like an old-world Christian missionary. Tall. Thin. Pasty white. And enthusiastically joyful. He was new in this store.

"Well, thank you. I'm good today." I didn't bother to give him an explanation.

"Didn't find anything? That's okay, God is still good. Hey, can I give you something?" He jogged through the bookshelves over to the counter. "Here. I want you to have this. I love this and I read it all of the time. It's my favorite scripture."

When I looked down, I saw that he had given me a tract, a small pamphlet that many Christians give out when they are "winning souls" or recruiting for the church. It was Psalm 27—Gemmia's favorite Psalm. I thought my knees were going to buckle.

"Do you know that Psalm?"

"Yes, I do." I was debating whether I should tell him about Gemmia. Before I could decide, I turned the tract over, and then my knees did buckle. On the other side of the glossy white paper, there was a picture of Jesus, the same Jesus I had seen in Gemmia's bedroom. He was dressed in a long white robe, and He appeared to have a multicolored strip of Kente cloth draped around his neck. The clerk caught me as I fell forward.

The next thing I knew, I had a cup of tea in one hand and a soggy wad of tissues in the other. I told the new clerk and a familiar clerk the whole story about Gemmia's illness, the vision I had the night before she passed, and how crazy I felt, still believing that it wasn't real, that I had made it up in my grieving mind.

"Oh no, sister. You didn't make that up. Coming in here today and getting this is just confirmation. God wants you to know that she is safe in His arms. God always sends us a confirmation of His works."

"But a black Jesus? Come on now! You're a white guy—doesn't that sound strange to you?"

"Not really. I think the Lord appears to us in any way we will recognize. This here, this picture of him, this is the Christ. This around his neck, those are the flags of the world. He loves us all, sister. He will come to us all if we let Him."

I looked closer and they really were flags. Well, it looked like Kente cloth to me.

The next few days and weeks floated by slowly. I couldn't get in touch with Niamoja and that really bothered me. We were debating what to do about our offices because the landlord wanted us to pay all of the back rent or leave the premises. I was in the process of selling the building I had purchased because we could not afford the payments or the cost of the renovation. The landlord indicated that he understood about Gemmia's death and he had been patient; now we had to pay or leave. I couldn't leave our building and I couldn't stand to be in it. Gemmia had built that place from nothing. She had decorated every room, purchased every piece of furniture, every book, and every plant. This was where I felt her presence the strongest, and that was why I ached every time I walked through the doors.

It was the last week in January. The landlord wanted us out by February 1. We started packing, thinking we would move everything to a storage unit and hold classes in a hotel conference room. Almasi was doing the legwork, looking for another location. I pulled up in front of the building. I dreaded going in but couldn't bear to leave. I was resting my head on the steering wheel when I heard her voice.

Release the physicality. My head shot up and swiveled on my neck. I was looking around the car, expecting to see her. My heart was pounding. I think I said it aloud: "Gemmia?" Then I heard her again.

Release the physical. It doesn't mean anything. That's what I did. I released the physical to become One with spirit. It was the answer to my prayer.

My mind started racing, then it slowed down. I had a conversation with Gemmia in my mind.

Where are you, sweetie?

I am right here.

Are you okay? I mean . . .

I am wonderful. I am good. Now you must let it all go. Release every physical thing. It is not the building or this place that matters. It is the Spirit.

When I got inside the building, I told Lydia and Helen what had happened in the car. They didn't seem shocked or surprised. They were both teary-eyed, shaking their heads. We were still sitting there when Almasi showed up.

"You are not going to believe this," she said.

"Oh Lord, what is it now?"

She told us that she had found us a place. We could afford it, and it was available immediately. It was five minutes down the road from where we were now. In fact, in order to get to Gemmia's house, you had to drive right past it. We must have passed the building a million times over the years and never even noticed it. Almasi was excited to the point of jumping up and down. We sat her down and told her what had happened to me in the car. The room fell silent until, as if on cue, we all burst into tears. We were all crying in the same choir: "Thank you, God! Thank you, Gemmia."

Two months, two weeks, and four days had passed. Lydia gave me permission to go to the supermarket alone. I went to the large organic market so I could get everything I had become accustomed to eating. It was a large, bright place in a shopping mall for the affluent. I had been shopping there for years. I got my cart, pulled out my list, and started one of my favorite pastimes—shopping!

I was bagging onions when I glanced around and saw the broccoli. I saw the very fine mist spraying all over the broccoli. I dropped the onions and walked toward it. I just wanted to touch it. When I did, all hell broke loose! Every tear that I had swallowed or not allowed myself to cry spilled forward from the depths of my being. I began to wail—over the broccoli.

Every hurt, every insult, every disappointment came rushing into my mind. The memory of every loss, every poor choice, and stupid decision I had ever made in my entire life came back as clear as if it were happening right then.

By now, I was sprawled across the broccoli. The clerk had called the manager. Those two men were staring at me, and so was every shopper who could hear. "Did something happen?" "Madam, can we get you something?" "Is she alone?" "Does anybody know this lady?" I could hear them and I didn't care. Gemmia loved broccoli and I just needed to hold on to it. I needed to hold on to something, anything, that brought me closer to her. My heart was breaking, I could feel it. I could feel the depth of the pain of every loss I had ever experienced. I just kept pushing my face into the broccoli. I felt the broccoli spurs in my nose and eyes. One at a time, the heads of broccoli began to fall to the ground. I went along with them. Now security was involved.

"Somebody call an ambulance! Miss, can you tell me what happened? Are you hurt?"

Yes, damn it! I am hurt to the core of my being, and I am losing my mind, right here! Right now!

Thank goodness I could not speak. I cried until I had nothing left. When I looked up, there were 20 or 30 white people staring at me. There was broccoli everywhere. The produce clerk helped me to my feet. I thanked him, brushed the broccoli from my eyes, and left the store. No one tried to stop me and I never looked back.

I went home and got in my bed. I stayed there over a month. In the meantime, Lydia cared for Oluwa. She fed me. She washed and folded my laundry and took care of my dog and the cat. I slept and I read ten years' worth of Gemmia's journals.

In some journals, she kept a daily record of what she did and how she felt about everything. In others, she documented her spiritual studies and insight. I was amazed that she had kept a record of almost everything I had ever said, every lesson, every class. She also used her journals to write letters. When she had something to say that she didn't know how to say, she would write a letter. There were many, many letters to me that revealed her experience and thoughts about me. Some of them took me two or three days to read. I would take in a little bit then put the journal down, returning the next day for another dose. I was astonished. She loved me and she unequivocally hated me at the same time.

It was in her journals that I learned that Niamoja's father had hit her. Not once, but twice. The first time, she was young. She wrote that she didn't want me to know, because I would make her leave him. The second time, she must have been 22 or 23. This time she wrote that I could not know because I would kill him. She felt trapped because she did not want Niamoja to grow up without a father the way she had. She also felt trapped because she didn't believe that any other man would want her. Apparently, Jimmy had convinced her that she was ugly. It happened early in their relationship. It took her a while, but she eventually realized that it was how he controlled her and manipulated her into staying with him. Still, there was a part of her that believed him, and that believed that she would end up used and abused by men like her mother had been. She did not want that for Niamoja. Gemmia believed that if Niamoja had her father in her life, she would have a better chance of breaking the family pattern. Gemmia was very aware of the pattern and quite angry with me for not breaking it on her behalf.

It was the first time in my life that I had such an honest and intimate view of the way another person saw me. It was painful and it was enlightening. Sometimes, after reading a part of the journals, the only thing I could do was sleep. Sleeping seemed to be the only way I could reflect on and authentically receive what Gemmia had written.

Gemmia had also kept an up-to-the-minute account of her experience with cancer, from the day she was diagnosed until three days before she passed on. She wrote what the doctors said and what she felt about it. She wrote down everything she ate and how it made her feel. Some of what she wrote was so sad I wept for hours. Some of it was brilliant. The way she assessed herself and her behavior truly showed her metaphysical mastery. I could see her conflict, her confusion, and her resolve. Then there were parts where she had regressed and wrote with the heart and the mind of a 13-year-old. Those were the hardest parts for me to read. *What I had done to this woman? What I had done to my very own child?* All the days I left her alone to write a book that I never completed— those were days I could have spent with her, times that would have brought her joy. All the days I made her drink carrot juice when all she wanted was a piece of cake or a chicken wing.

If I could have admitted to myself that I *knew,* I would have allowed her to enjoy the last days of her life. All the things I didn't want to do, didn't know how to do, didn't take responsibility to learn how to do and pushed off on her; it was humiliating. She hated it and hated me for doing it. There was also a lot of joy in her journals. Things we did do together. Things we talked about. We really were good friends who had spent many good days together. I really missed her. And, even when she was alive, she missed me.

Some of the journals I read three or four times. Some I will never read ever again. By the time I read the last one, there were several things about which I was very clear. Gemmia was angry. She didn't show it. She didn't live her life that way, but she was sitting on years of fury. I was clear that those things, the things she stuffed down and held on to, the things that ate away at her, were the cause of the cancer. I also knew that she never believed that she would not be healed. She had literally fought for her life. She had the victory planned, and the victory song was written.

The most important thing I learned was that her death was actually an answer to her prayers. She had written many prayers in her journal. In most of them, she affirmed total surrender to God's will. She never considered that her death would be God's will, but according to her prayers, she would accept that if it were the case. One thing she wrote sent a chill up my spine. It helped to make sense of what I had heard in the car. Gemmia wrote: *Father, I know that you have great things ordained for me. I know you have ordained me to do great things. I even know that some of things you have planned for me, I will not be able to do in this body. This body is just physical. The greatness you have for me is of the spiritual nature, a nature I may never find in this body.*

I was thumbing through the journals, thinking and wondering who I would be on the other side of this experience. Based on what I had read, there were some things about me that had to change. They had to change not because Gemmia said so, but because I wasn't even aware that they existed. They had to change, or I would spend the rest of my life believing that I was responsible for my daughter having cancer. I had Oluwa and Niamoja to think about. I wanted to be a different kind of person and a better influence in their lives. I wanted to totally disintegrate our family patterns.

I was thumbing through one journal when I found a story that Gemmia had written. I read it several times. Each time my heart broke again. When I finished reading the story for the last time, I curled into a fetal position. I stayed in that position almost every day for the next five months.

Jenni and Her Mommy: The Birth of One Girl's Unworthiness

There once was a little girl—let's call her Jenni. Jenni was a sweet little girl who loved her mommy so much she would do anything to see her smile. Jenni liked it when her mommy smiled because that meant everyone, especially Mommy, was happy. Mommy being happy was a good thing. Mommy being happy meant a few extra cookies after school or that special chocolate cake with the orange icing that Mommy would make from scratch and put food coloring in. How else would it get to be orange? Jenni would love a piece of that cake right now. Jenni was a good girl. Did I say that already? She got the best grades in school. She always helped out around the house and did her best to stay out of trouble and not be a problem to Mommy. Mommy had other problems. She had Jenni's older brother and younger sister to take care of too. They picked on Jenni a lot. They said she was a crybaby and a tattletale. Mommy also had to work and take care of Daddy and Grandpa and Nana, so Jenni never got to spend a lot of time with Mommy. Jenni's brother and sister got more attention than Jenni. Not because they were better than her, but because they were always getting into something that required Mommy's attention. Mommy didn't seem to like this very much, and Jenni knew that this was no way to behave. Not that Jenni ever did anything bad, she just didn't get in enough trouble that Mommy would have to be called.

One day Jenni's mommy said she wanted to make life better for them. That the whole family would have to help out so that things could be better. We could not be one of those families like you see in the welfare office or living in the projects their whole lives. We lived there then, but we would not live there forever. It would just be a matter of time before everything was better for us. What this all came down to was that Mommy was going to go to college to get a degree. It also meant that she was going to be working and we wouldn't see her so much anymore.

Jenni missed her mom a lot. She wanted to have special times with her like the day Jenni came home from school and Mommy said I have a secret dragon do you want me to show him to you. Yes, Jenni said. Mommy sat down at the kitchen table next to Jenni and said don't be scared. Mommy took a puff of her cigarette and blew the smoke out her nose just like a dragon. Then she gave Jenni some cookies and milk. Those special moments didn't happen often anymore, because Mommy was making a better life for the family, and there just didn't seem to be time to do those silly things.

Jenni would have done anything to get Mommy's attention. Nothing seemed to work. When Mommy came to Jenni's school to teach dance, Jenni took dance class. Jenni wasn't the greatest dancer and Mommy certainly let her know it. But Jenni kept on dancing anyway, two left feet and all. It was fun and it was time spent with Mommy.

Jenni was about 8 or 9 when she got sick. She had tonsillitis and a stomach flu. This meant Mommy had to stay home and take care of Jenni. Finally Jenni was a cause worthy of Mommy's attention. Mommy stayed home with Jenni for what seemed like forever. Jenni liked it so much that when she started to get better and had to go back to school, she pretended to still be sick. Mommy took a few more days off and stayed home with Jenni, but then she put her foot down. "I can't do this anymore. I have to go to work, I have to go to school. I need you to act like a big girl and stop this." So Jenni stopped her faking and went to school the next day so that Mommy could go back to school and work. This went on for years and years. Mommy would work and Jenni would act like a big girl. Sometimes to the point that she was even playing Mommy to her brother and sister. Jenni just knew deep down that one day her Mommy would appreciate all that she was doing for her so that they could all live better, just like Mommy said.

Nana got sick and that really got Mommy's attention. It got Jenni's attention and everyone else's too. Nana stayed sick for years and Mommy did all that she could to accommodate and take care of Nana until she died years later. All the while, Jenni was determined to become worthy of her mommy's love and attention. She dedicated her life to her mommy. Jenni didn't do the things regular teenage girls did. Jenni always worked and she would give her money to make things better for the family. One summer Jenni worked a summer youth job and never got paid. It was Thanksgiving time and Mommy didn't have any money. Mommy was in law school now. Finally Jenni got her summer youth employment check in the mail. It was for $131. What did Jenni do, she took her check, cashed it and bought Thanksgiving dinner. Mommy was pleased. She smiled and Jenni was happy to see her smile.

Because Jenni spent so much time trying to be a big girl, she never really explored life. She didn't join teams and clubs at school. She went to school, kept her grades up, worked long hours. When Mommy started her own company, Jenni was there. When Mommy started speaking and writing books, Jenni did whatever she could to help out. Jenni enjoyed working with Mommy. Even when there was no money, she got to spend time with her mommy. And when there was money, they had even more fun together, even if they just went out for ice cream. It didn't matter to Jenni either way; as long as she could please her mommy she knew she was doing a good thing.

Years and years have passed now. Jenni still loves her mommy and does whatever she can to help out. Mommy is really famous now. She has written lots of books and traveled all around the world helping people. Jenni has gotten to go with Mommy to many of the places she's traveled to. It's been wonderful. Mommy did exactly what she said she was going to do. She made a better life for the family. Jenni is proud of Mommy and all that she's done to help Mommy out over the years. There's just one thing: in living her life for Mommy, Jenni never really lived a life of her own. Now Jenni is all grown up, with a daughter of her own who she always tries to share special moments with, yet she is still longing for some sense of worthiness. Jenni never realized that her worthiness would not come from her mother's approval of her. Her worthiness would have to come from her doing something with her own life. Sure, Jenni has dreams and goals of her own, she just seems to have a hard time following them. She feels guilty if everything is not perfect for Mommy and she can't do anything about it. She feels bad when things don't go well for Mommy. She feels resentful when she does all she can for Mommy and someone else gets the credit. Jenni was just trying to be a big girl, and now that she is, she realizes she doesn't even know what that means.

Jenni is sick again. This time she's not faking it to get Mommy's attention. Jenni knows that the last thing Mommy wants is for her to be sick. But over the years Jenni has developed a belief in suffering and unworthiness. Jenni, over the years, has come to believe that only those who suffer and struggle long and hard like Mommy did will become worthy of fame, fortune and attention. Jenni doesn't believe that she has suffered enough to be worthy yet. Jenni has cancer. She doesn't want to be sick and it frightens her, but she hasn't yet learned what it is she needs to learn to overcome this belief in unworthiness and suffering. What is the lesson?

✠✠✠

When you become committed to knowing what you need to know and to seeing what you need to see in order to heal, you will know and you will heal. When life forces you to sit down, get still, and get clear about what it is that is hurting you, you will sit down and you will get clear. You will get clear about how you have hurt yourself and others, about how you continue to do it, and about the payoff you receive for staying in pain. When you bring a child into the world and find yourself with the task of placing one last kiss on the face that you have washed and kissed and nuzzled just before you close the lid of that child's casket, you know something that you wish that you did not. You see things that you would rather not. And you become clear about one thing: If you can live through burying your child, you can live through anything.

When I got still, I recognized my addiction to suffering. My habitual search for pain. I also realized that it had nothing to do with anyone or anything outside of myself. Sure, I had been taught and experienced some things as a child, but I had grown enough, learned enough, and healed enough to know better. I knew better! And if I didn't know before, I knew after reading Gemmia's journals. However, because no one had ever validated my learning, growing, or healing, I invalidated what I knew and saw and felt. The worst part of it for me was that I had taught Gemmia to do the same thing. To deny herself. To discount herself. She had watched me so closely. She had learned so much about me. And she had taught me a great deal.

The most important thing I learned from Gemmia, and the thing she recognized about me that I had discounted, was my capacity to love. Despite all of my issues, she was clear that from the inside out, I had a loving soul. Her words echoed those of Ms.

O. Gemmia saw me as a very, very big person. She also saw that my bigness was not attached to ego or pride. It was attached to the depth of my love.

I didn't understand any of this throughout my life or my marriage. I became confused by people's response to me. I was very confused by my husband's response to me and my loving. It took me five months in bed, reading and rereading those ten years' worth of journals to come to the realization that in the face of my bigness—the grace and favor of God in my life—most people, including my daughter, felt that they did not measure up. In the case of my husband, because he did not believe he could measure up, he had to attempt to tear me down. As for me, I didn't accept my own love and depth of my humanity. Instead, I attracted and invited people into my life to prove that my personal lie was true—that I was bad, wrong and unlovable. It was the pathology I inherited. It was the story running through my DNA. It was a down right filthy lie and, I was going to put an end to it. I had no clue that Gemmia had already done it.

Your mail really piles up when you don't read it for five months. One of the first things I did when I got out of bed was go through my mail. I had missed all of the spring sales and most of my coupons were expired. Two of my magazine subscriptions had expired. There were literally hundreds of cards and equally as many demands for payment. There were several notices indicating that something was going on with the mortgage on my house. This, I assumed, was the reason there were three notices for certified mail.

One certified letter came from Florida. I didn't recognize the name or the address on the envelope. I put it in the pile with the magazines and catalogs I wanted to keep. I took the pile into my garden, by the waterfall where the frogs were doing their spring mating calls. There was one bullfrog whose mating call was so loud, I considered buying him a female frog just to shut him up. Instead, I opened the mail. The letter from Florida was a petition for an uncontested divorce.

When did I get lost?
How did I get lost?
How long have I been lost?
Was I ever found?

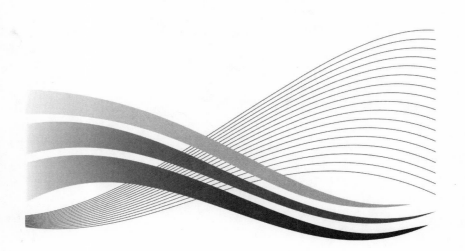

CHAPTER 19

STARTING OVER

I have discovered that life doesn't actually knock you down. It does, however, provide you with many opportunities to evaluate your standing in life: what you stand on, what you stand for, how you stand within yourself and for yourself. When your standing is weak, you don't get knocked down. You fall down. You trip over the fallacies and fantasies that you have created or inherited. You slip on your dysfunctional puzzle pieces and your distorted sense of self. Sometimes, if you are lucky, you fall when no one is looking, so you can limp away and lick your wounds privately. More often than not, though, you fall in front of other people, and your dress flies up over your head, exposing your ripped panties to the spectators who are doing their best not to laugh at you. Those who do not laugh, but rush to help you up, often have no idea that your ego is more bruised than your knees.

As the result of my public fall from television, I discovered that what I was standing on was quicksand. Thank goodness there were two things I could grab on to and pull myself out of the pit. The first thing I grabbed on to was my unequivocal desire to serve God. The second thing was the love and support of the women in the community in which and through which I served God.

Lydia ran my household. Almasi, Helen, and Deanna kept my business and ministry afloat. Yawfah, Rene, and Vivian kept reminding me that Gemmia's transition, the dissolution of my marriage, and the shift in my career were not my fault. Shaheerah and Raina told me over and over again that there was something extraordinary that I was being prepared for, and the only thing required of me was to keep my heart open and my mind at peace. All I was experiencing was teaching me to become fully reliant on my inner authority, the power of God within me.

It was a hard pill to swallow. Did my daughter need to die in order for me to become a better person? Did my husband need to reject me and dishonor our commitment so that I could have a greater purpose in life? *Wrong questions!* The greater, grander, deeper inquires I needed to make of myself were: *What am I being asked to practice? What character values am I being asked to embody? What service can I offer the world as a result of the lessons I am learning?* The answers to these questions and many more came in the form of a telephone call from the executive producer of a television program called *Starting Over.*

The year before she made her transition, Gemmia had insisted that I throw my hat into the ring to be considered as one of the life coaches on *Starting Over.* I wasn't interested. I had already been burned. And there were still remnants of shame from my *Oprah* experience lingering around the edges of my ego. Gemmia would not take no for an answer. When the producers called me, I was shocked. They were interested. I was ambivalent. I made my decision when they asked that I come live in Chicago that winter in order to shoot the first season of the show. I don't do cold! Not the Chicago kind of cold. Besides that, my husband had moved out, and I had Oluwa to consider. By the time the second season rolled around, the show was moving to Los Angeles. They still had my application from the first season. Was I interested?

Not really. I had buried my daughter six months earlier. I had a 12-year-old grandson to raise. I was the closest thing that my granddaughter had to her mother. Even if I could work out all of the other loose ends, I could not leave Niamoja.

A lot had happened since her mother's death. Nisa had moved into Gemmia's house and was caring for Niamoja after school. Her father was on his way to getting married. He and his girlfriend were busy making plans for their future. He felt that I was forcing Niamoja to "hold on" to her mother. He said that I made everything about Gemmia. When I asked him if Niamoja could spend her first Mother's Day without her mother with me, her grandmother, he told me that they had other plans. They were going to spend the day with his future in-laws, in another state. When I asked him if he had noticed how withdrawn and lethargic Niamoja had become, he said she was only like that around me.

I could sense and feel that my granddaughter was in trouble, emotional and spiritual trouble. I was also aware of a pattern that could have a devastating effect if it were not handled cautiously and consciously. My mother had died when I was young. I was raised by my grandmother. Niamoja's grandmother, Jimmy's mother, had died when he was young. He was raised by his grandmother. Now here I was, faced with the possibility of being the caregiver for a grandchild. I wanted to be aware, awake, and available, to be there for her in a loving, positive, and powerful way. But it was quite difficult. When I called Niamoja, it was rare that anyone answered the telephone. I often left messages that were not returned for weeks. When she did call, she was sullen and withdrawn. When I went to see her after school at Gemmia's house, she seemed almost catatonic. I asked her father if he had considered putting her in therapy. He informed me that the school psychologist had told him it wasn't necessary; she thought that Niamoja was adjusting very well. I suggested that the psychologist be horsewhipped!

Maybe my control issues were raging. Maybe I was holding on to Gemmia's memory in an unhealthy way. Maybe I really was the crazy b—— he thought I was, trying to usurp his power as a parent. I didn't know for sure and I really didn't care. One thing I had learned from my own childhood experiences and the mistakes I made raising my own children was to put the needs of the children first and foremost. Jimmy did not agree. She was living under his roof, and I needed to keep my opinions to myself. It was that man thing again! Here was another man in my life attempting to dismiss, deny, and dishonor me. Here, again, I had a man in my life whom I had trained to treat me poorly, and I accepted it because I thought he had something that I needed and wanted. *Damn! How are you going to handle it this time, Ms. Iyanla?*

I decided that I wasn't going to make this about him and me. I was going to remain focused on the child. I wasn't going to shrink back in fear of upsetting him. I was going to stand up for her and myself in a way I had failed to do many times before. I was going to ask for what I wanted, even if I was denied. More important, I was not going to judge my sense of what Niamoja needed in order to heal based on his often very nasty, very hurtful, and very selfish responses. Jimmy did his best to make it all about me: my attitude, my control, my insane devotion to my dead child. I decided that he was crazy. And I would treat him as such.

Many men believe it is their right to step in to tell you what to do. I saw another pattern in action. When I was graduating from junior high and headed to high school, I wanted to be a nurse. At that time, that pursuit meant that I should attend a vocational high school. My father, who had completely absented himself from my education, swept in and declared that I would go to an academic high school.

Niamoja's circumstances brought me face to face with the lineage of men in our lives who decided it was their right to dishonor our desires and dictate our destinies.

Niamoja was not my only concern. There was also Oluwa, now 13, who had just had his closest encounter with death. He had lost the woman he knew as his mother. He had also lost his grandfather and my ex-husband, the primary male figure in his life. I saw signs of some serious problems creeping into Oluwa's behavior—and no surprise. His entire life had been turned upside down. His hormones were raging. I was emotionally drained, unable to give him the support or the discipline he needed. He began running away at least once a week. His grades were a disaster. In our affluent, undiversified Maryland suburb, the school he attended was struggling with resistance to integration in the 21st century. There were fights, name calling, bus suspensions, and threats of expulsion. And it wasn't just the children. The adults had some issues of their own with young African American males who had voices and opinions.

I was too awake to pretend that I was asleep. I would either have to beat him down grandma-style or ignore and enable him, as Nett and Aunt Nancy had done. I would not arrest the development of one more black man in my lineage. I had coddled and enabled bad behavior in my family long enough. I seized the opportunity to end the pattern. From where I sat, I had my clothes on and my shoes tied. I couldn't get back into bed and pull up the covers over my head.

One afternoon, I got a call from the school saying that Oluwa had been suspended. When I asked why, I was told that I needed to speak to the principal. I tried for three days before I got a letter indicating that Oluwa had been involved in an incident that was under investigation. His version of the story was that a girl on the bus was being pummeled with candy and Oluwa went to her aid. She attacked him, probably in fear. The other kids told him it was against the law for a nigger to touch a white woman. Oluwa had a few choice words in response, and they were the only thing the bus driver heard.

The girl wrote a statement indicating that Oluwa had tried to help her. The principal held the "investigation" open pending the discovery of additional facts. As a trained attorney, I explained to him that the facts were clear. I reported the incident to the NAACP, which had a series of complaints against the school dating back three years. I never heard from them again. I withdrew Oluwa from the school, home-schooled him for a few months, then decided that the kind of structure and discipline he needed could best be found in a Virginia military school.

With Oluwa away at school and Niamoja's father standing between her and me, there was nothing stopping me from accepting the *Starting Over* offer. Nothing, that is, except fear and shame and guilt. The old Iyanla who played small and believed she was unworthy was on her way out. Unfortunately, the new, loving, wise, brilliant Iyanla had not quite found her footing. She was still working through the old Iyanla's shame about having her name removed from the wall of her television studio. She was still grappling with the old Iyanla's guilt about not doing everything in her power to save Gemmia's life. How could she help people all over the world and not save her own child? How could she speak to the masses about the power of love and the beauty of relationships and fail so miserably in her own? The new Iyanla, the faith-filled, self-assured, self-loving Iyanla was not quite sure that she had enough experience or strength to return to national television. She had never done anything of this magnitude without her best friend, Gemmia. Sure, she had some new awareness and bit more understanding, but was she *really ready?*

According to the community, she was more than ready. She was born to do this. It was a new beginning. An opportunity to *start over* in a very real sense. It was, they said, what Gemmia would have wanted for her. It was, they said, an answer to their prayers. The new, improved, although slightly wobbly Iyanla needed to pack her belongings and go to Los Angeles without a second thought. So she did. I mean, I did.

Starting Over was network television's first daytime reality drama. It placed six women of different ages and backgrounds in a house and offered them support for addressing one major challenge in their lives. Each woman was assigned a life coach. The coach, with the support of a therapist, engaged the woman in a series of coaching exercises and soul-stirring conversations as the catalyst for change. As the woman moved through the various challenges, she became more self-aware, self-assured, and self-actualized. After six to eight weeks in the house, she received a makeover to celebrate her new lease on life and then graduated, to be replaced by another woman who would walk through the process. As a life coach on *Starting Over*, I encountered every one of my issues with a different name and a different face, clothed in a different set of circumstances. I encountered my daddy issues, my mommy issues, the issue of diminished self-worth and self-value. I saw how I had denied myself, abused myself, and punished myself. The good news was, I was able to recognize my issues and address them with the women head-on and authentically. The adage "we teach what we need to learn" came alive in a very clear way for me.

The not-so-good news was that I was doing this work on national television, before hundreds of thousands of people, when I hadn't quite sharpened my skills. This meant that I had to carefully navigate and sometimes challenge the line between entertaining the audience and supporting the women. I didn't always show up in the most loving way. At least that was the way it felt to me.

Many nights that first season, I would return late to my tiny apartment and cry myself to sleep. Had I done the right thing? Had I used the right words? Did I look fat on camera? I was getting rave reviews from back home, and the women in the house seemed to be faring quite well, but remnants of the old, self-doubting Iyanla were creeping back into my consciousness. This nagging sense of inadequacy, not being to contact Niamoja, and Oluwa's difficulty adjusting to military school all threatened to make my first season on *Starting Over* a wretched beginning.

Back when I first started my spiritual journey, I recall one of my teachers telling me that prayer and meditation would heal the soul of almost any affliction. The only things, he said, that could not be cured by a daily spiritual practice was failure to have a daily spiritual practice. I have heard the same theory from many modern day spiritual teachers. I had a practice but it was not sustaining me. I needed to go deeper, but I didn't have the time. I was working 10 to 12 hours, often longer, each day. I missed home, and to cover the pain, I would veg out in front of the television. Then I went home for the Christmas break and everything shifted—forever.

This was my first Christmas without Gemmia and the one-year anniversary of her transition. In my mind, Niamoja needed to be with me and her mother's side of the family. Of course, her father did not agree. We went back and forth, arguing with sweetness but both, I am sure, calling each other names beneath our breath. He finally gave in and agreed she could spend the holiday with me. She, Oluwa, and I decided we would not stay home that Christmas. We would go skiing and spend the holiday doing something fun. Off we went to Pennsylvania, to a sweet little hotel. We had a lovely time, but it was very clear that we would rather have been home doing what we would have done had Gemmia been alive.

It was almost New Year's when the telephone rang. I didn't recognize the number and I did not answer. Within seconds, the telephone rang again. The third time, I answered. It was him. My undivorced husband. Just checking in. Couldn't reach me on Christmas. How were the kids?

"I see you have a new telephone number," I said.

"Yes, I changed carriers."

"Whose name is that? I know that name."

"Just a friend."

Something didn't feel right. I made a few calls of my own until I tracked down the name. It was the widow of his good friend who had died a year earlier, just before Gemmia. I knew her, not well, but I knew her. When her husband was ill, my husband encouraged me to pray with her for him. I did. When we had prayer and healing ceremonies for Gemmia, I invited her. She came. *Hey, wait a minute! Are these two together? Was this going on right under my nose? He never had any intention of finding a vision and coming back!*

With a few more calls, I discovered that not only were they together, they were open about it with people whom I considered close friends. They attended a spiritual class taught by one of my students, a student who knew that this was my husband sitting in front of her with his girlfriend. And no one, not one single person who prayed with me to save my marriage, not one person who knew how torn up I was about it, ever said a word to me— that is, until I started asking questions. At first I felt betrayed. Then, I was *livid!*

When you are starting your life over, with a new sense of self, who you once were is going to challenge you. Who you once were is going to dangle old carrots, old wounds and issues, in front of your face. When that happens, you will be tempted to revert to old feelings, old patterns of thought, and old patterns of behavior. When, however, you have made up your mind that the old you is dead and buried, when you have embraced a certain level of clarity about who you are and are not, as well as who you are choosing to be, you have a different response. You recognize that the new you has a different character, a different posture, a different presence than the old you had. You realize that you must regain possession of your mental and emotional faculties, rather than allow them to run amuck with thoughts of right, wrong, fair, and unfair. The old you went first to doubt and then to helplessness. The new you is willing to get up, stand up, and step up for your honor and dignity. The old you may have behaved like a handmaiden, waiting to be told what to do and how to do it. The new you is the queen, ready and willing to take the throne of your life and rule your inner and outer kingdom with dominion, power, and authority. The queen wants to know what is best for the good of the kingdom. She knows that the minds and hearts of the people are at stake. The queen must possess a gracious personality and not bear a grudge against anyone. For if she does, people—perhaps the wrong people—could be beheaded!

I knew where my husband was going to be and when, so I went there too. I talked to her. I talked to him. I talked to the friends who had entertained them together and never thought to mention it to me. On the drive home, I was tempted to stew in anger, true to my old pattern. But I was pleasantly surprised to find that I did not really feel hurt. Stewing would cause me more harm than I was willing to take. Finally, I asked myself: What would Gemmia say if she were here? Her words flooded my mind and heart—*Save yourself and leave those people alone!*

After transferring Oluwa to another school, a boarding school, I went back to *Starting Over* with a new sense of self. Sure, there were some lingering memories and a few pangs of sorrow, but for the most part, I felt complete. I recognized this as another pattern of my life coming to a close. I had lived through Aunt Nancy's physical fight to make her husband honor her. I had watched Nett, my stepmother, shrink in life at the realization that her husband had another family on the other side of town. I had seen good friends move through varying degrees of self-inflicted torture after discovering that they were sharing their bed with more than one person. I had read about Gemmia's experiences with Jimmy in her journals. I realized that family patterns live on not just in behaviors. They live on in patterns of thought. They live through a certain acquiescence, a belief that things will never change so you must go along in order to get along.

I was not willing to tolerate the pattern of self-denial any longer. I was choosing another way for myself. I was going to take the throne in my life, knowing that I had an opportunity to do for Niamoja what I had not done for Gemmia and Nisa: Teach her how to say no, without an explanation. I was protecting the boundaries of my kingdom. The blessing was that I had the opportunity to share on national television what I was learning as I was learning it.

One day I sat down and had a conversation with my brother-friend Rev. Michael Beckwith. After I shared my story with him and asked him if I was moving in the right direction, he not only supported me, he encouraged me to do it all in the name of Gemmia. He said, follow the Buddhist tradition of taking your sorrow and sadness and doing something positive with it in the name of someone you love. That is exactly what I did for two seasons on *Starting Over*. Those were the two most productive and healing years of my life. Even so, they were just preparation for what was to come next.

In the morning, when I rise,
I want to rise Holy when I rise.

— Negro Spiritual

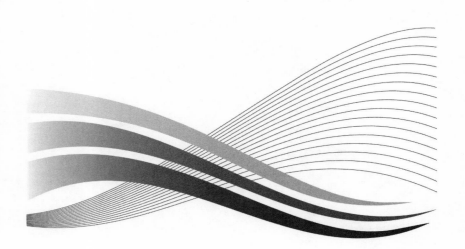

CHAPTER 20

STANDING IN GRACE

When have you been through enough? When does who you are, what you have learned, and how you have grown become enough to sustain you? These were the questions on my heart when I returned home to Maryland following my two seasons on *Starting Over*. I had given all that I knew and all that I had to give. I had learned a lot in the process. Now I just wanted to be left alone to feel what was going on inside of me. I was aching somewhere deep in my bones. It was the ache of being back in my home without my husband or Oluwa. It was the ache of being back in my life without Gemmia. It was the ache of being denied access to my granddaughter. It was the ache of not knowing what to do next in my life. I spent days in my backyard, listening to the birds chirp and the stream flow, and allowed my heart to weep. The tears in my eyes had dried up a long time ago.

Going through the mail, I discovered a series of letters from my mortgage company. I opened the oldest one first. From the date on the letter, which was 22 days ago, I had 48 days to pay off my mortgage — $378,000. I called my accountant. He explained to me that I had a balloon payment on my mortgage. It was something he and Gemmia had worked out with the intention that I would buy my house outright. It was also the only way I could get a mortgage at the time. I vaguely remembered Gemmia talking about it, but she had handled all the business matters. Buying my house was something we planned to do with my salary from the *Iyanla* show before its untimely demise. According to my accountant, no one would refinance a mortgage with a balloon payment, which meant I now I had to produce the money or they would foreclose on my home.

Then there was the tax issue. Although I had been given a year of grace, I needed to resume the payments of $30,000 or file for bankruptcy. Bankruptcy! No way! I owed the money and I would pay it! This was my family's home! I was a first-generation homeowner. My children and grandchildren knew this to be the place we gathered. But Gemmia's care had depleted my savings. Oluwa's tuition and my living expenses took me right to the edge each month. I had no family to ask for help, and most of my friends asked *me* when they were in trouble. My daughter, my marriage, and now my home. When is enough enough?

Filing bankruptcy would help me with the back taxes, but it also meant I would need to sell my house. It was unfathomable. It was devastating. It was embarrassing. I had a law degree, a Master's degree, and six credits toward my Ph.D. Maybe I could get a job, perhaps go back to practicing law. Maybe I could borrow the money or get someone to buy my house and rent it back to me. I didn't have time for any of that. It wasn't fair! It just wasn't! Then the pathology of guilt surged up from my DNA. *Why didn't I . . . How come I . . . I am being punished for . . .* Guilt's first cousin, shame, followed closely behind. *Look what you did now! Everyone is going to know. How can you call yourself a spiritual anything?* The internal battle went on for days as I tried everything I knew to stave off the unthinkable. Then it happened.

On a bright and sunny Tuesday afternoon, the bankruptcy trustee, a real estate agent, and an estate appraiser rang my doorbell. They were there to assess my assets. The appraiser put on rubber gloves and methodically went through every room in my home, every closet and dresser drawer. He counted my silverware, my china, my stemware.

"Where's your jewelry?"

I opened the drawer.

"Do you have a safe?"

"No."

"Where do you keep your diamonds?"

"I don't have any."

"What about your furs?"

"I don't have any of them either."

Then he turned to the art hanging on the walls.

"Is Bibbs a friend of yours?"

"No. He is an artist. A black artist."

Speaking to the realtor as if I wasn't there, he said, "Interesting. I've never heard of him."

"And who is Fennell?"

"Another black artist."

"Nice. I'm not sure what they are worth, but they are decorative."

I followed the appraiser from room to room as he peered and counted. When he reached the front door, he turned to me.

"I am really sorry about this. You have a really beautiful home."

With that, my house went on the market for sale.

On August 15, I was informed that I had until October 1 to leave my home. In the meantime, the realtor needed permission to show the house to prospective buyers. This was an indignity I could not and would not endure and stay sane. With the bankruptcy, my credit was shot. I was not allowed to have any savings and file bankruptcy. The remaining remnants of my life were unraveling. I felt lost, alone, and terrified.

My community family was watching me and praying for me. Some of them just shook their heads, like me, saying, "Enough already!" Others encouraged me, saying, "You know what to do." And I did. I knew what to do. I was too weary to do it, but too afraid not to do it. So I prayed and praised. I cried out with my whole heart. I was glued to my prayer partners, Shaheerah and Raina. I held onto my right hand, Almasi, and my left hand, Lydia. I learned quickly to let people help me. I learned how to ask for help. I had 45 days to leave my home. I needed to pack. Two of my students, Deborah and Laura, helped me do that. But where the heck was I going?

One morning it all came together. I went into my prayer room to meditate. After lighting my favorite incense, I sat in my favorite chair and read my favorite Psalm, Gemmia's favorite too. Psalm 27 begins, "The Lord is my light and my salvation." I had read it over several times when I started to feel the cool breeze. I closed my eyes and surrendered to it. I could smell her. I could feel her. Gemmia's presence was in the room. I felt the warmth of my tears falling across my cheeks. "Whom shall I fear?" I could hear my heart beating, and my entire body began to pulse. "For in the day of trouble he will keep me safe in his dwelling." I wanted to open my eyes to see if I could see her, but they would not, could not open. "Hear my voice when I call, O LORD; be merciful to me and answer me."

All I could feel in that moment was love. I wasn't sure if it was Gemmia's love or God's love, or maybe they were one and the same. I wondered if I were imagining the experience or totally losing my mind. But I had felt like this before, and, no matter what anyone else thought, it was real for me.

I remembered the times Grandma told me that I was a heathen. Maybe I was. I remembered all of the times my deeply Christian friends had warned me that dabbling in the spirit world was dangerous. Maybe it was. On this day, however, I was in my home, in my prayer sanctuary, where the energy was clean and the intention was clear. I needed guidance. If it had to come from the other side of life, so be it. "Do not turn your servant away in anger; you have been my helper."

Then I heard a woman's voice. I listened with every fiber of my being.

"You haven't done anything wrong."

My body crumpled forward and I wept as I heard it again.

"You haven't done anything wrong."

I wanted to believe that so much. I needed to know that I was not the reason Gemmia died; that I was not the reason my marriage failed. I needed to know that I hadn't messed up my life or my children's lives and that I was not losing my home as some sort of divine punishment. I needed somebody, anybody, living or dead, to let me know that the deepest desires of my heart were not fraudulent. Then I got the message that I believe will govern the remainder of my life.

"You are a bridge. A bridge between lands, times, cultures, and people. Your life is an anointed one. You have work to do and gifts to give. Your daughter was born to assist you. She was a short-timer. She came with one mission—to take away 17 generations of anger over women being abused by men. She took it on so that you would not have to, so that you could complete your work. She gave her life so that yours would be spared. It was her agreement."

Then I heard the names of the 17 generations. Sahara, my mother; Elizabeth, her mother; Rachel, Ruby, Celia, Pheobe, Annice, Zola, Fanta; and then names I could not make out. They sounded like Lebedi, Okani, Yapanni, Ecruda, Ela, and Yohuri. At some point I picked up my journal and began to write what I was hearing.

The tears had stopped and so had the voice. I closed my eyes again. "Teach me your way, O LORD; lead me in a straight path because of my oppressors."

Then I heard, "Some of these women were beaten. Most of them were raped. Men they loved betrayed them. Men they did not know violated them. They carried sickness in their bodies. They carried sickness in their hearts. That sickness was due to be passed on to you. Your daughter has lifted the line and healed all generations. The purity of her heart has cleared all the women for 17 generations. You are opening the way for the next 17."

In that moment I remembered something that I said when I learned that my mother had died of cancer: I'm not going out like that. I am not going to die of cancer! Just not! I also remembered that I forgot to include my children in my proclamation.

"You haven't done anything wrong." It was as if someone was reading my mind. "All things are as they need to be."

I sat for a while longer, at peace with myself and everything else. "Though my father and mother forsake me, the LORD will receive me."

✣✣✣

A sister-friend who knew of my situation called to tell me she had just seen a house for rent. Could I be there in 40 minutes to meet the owner?

I decided to take the back roads to see a house that was located about ten minutes from where I lived. I love those back country roads. As I was driving, an ocean full of tears welled up inside of me. Doing 25 miles an hour, I decided to let them fall; goodness knows, I had enough to cry about. I was determined not to be defeated, but the depletion of my heart and mind could not, would not be denied. My silent tears quickly erupted into a noisy ugly cry which, within seconds, became an all-out weeping fest. But something was different. I suddenly felt my heart opening and expanding. I had slowed down to about ten miles an hour before I realized I needed to pull over or run into one of the beautiful trees that lined the road.

I sat for a moment wiping my nose with the hem of my skirt before I recognized what I was feeling. It was sheer joy! The joy of freedom? The joy of knowing I would have a place to live? I wasn't sure, so I did my best to get still and listen to Spirit.

What you are feeling is joy.

Joy! What do I have to be joyful about?

You're in love!

In love! In love with who?

With her?

Her? Her who? Have I switched sides? The words welled up inside of me like a well-scripted movie scene.

You love her because she makes him happy. Oh my God! This was deep, so I continued to listen.

You love him and you will always love him, but you could not make him happy. She does, so, you love her for that. You love her because she was there for him in a way that you could not be, did not want to be. You love her because she can hear him and listen to him in a way that you did not, and it has restored him to his sense of self. You have always wanted him to be happy. You have always wanted him to know love. She has given him what you could not. She is your sister and you love her for what she has given your Beloved.

The next thing I heard was not so spiritual: *Iyanla, you have lost your mind!* I knew it was true. I did want him to be happy because I really did love him. I didn't want him to hurt or be alone or be miserable. My pride and ego were totally deflated that I could not be who he needed and wanted, but there was a part of me that was happy for him and happy for me. This meant that my endless search for daddy was complete. I was all grown up now. This meant that I, Iyanla, was finally ready to have a real relationship with myself, where I could stand on my own two feet without and hidden agendas or needs that I did not put on the table. This meant that in my new home, I could be happy. I could be at peace.

I sat on the side of the road without any thought of what time it was or where I needed to go. The awarenesses were pouring forth, and I needed to hear them and know them. I remembered Gemmia's words, *"Release the physicality."*

It applied to more than my lifelong relationship with Eden. It also applied to my house. That house represented my fantasy of having a healthy family and a home where we all could feel safe and loved and protected. It represented the guilt I felt about achieving a level of success that no one else in my family had ever known. I had purchased that house with guilt money, and I now realized I could let it go. In that house, I felt responsible to take care of everybody and to make everything alright for everyone. Gemmia, my husband, my grandson, my granddaughter, and my staff. I had spent hundreds of thousands of dollars providing everything for everyone and working myself to death to do it. My house had been a status symbol of what I could do, of how I provided a shelter for everyone except myself. I had internalized the pathology of my childhood memories of home—the place where I was dishonored, disrespected, and violated. Huge pieces of the puzzle began to fall into place. I could see them, and more importantly, I could feel the shift taking place in my body. Leaving that house was not just about my inability to pay the mortgage. It was about leaving the past behind and creating a new future for myself. A future that did not include people-pleasing and catering to the hidden command to always put myself last on my to-do list. I wish I could explain all of the things that became crystal clear to me that day, on the side of the road, but there are simply not enough words.

What I do want you to know is that the person who stopped on the side of the road between the house she was losing and the house she was about to rent was not the same woman.

Thank you God!

Life for me ain't been no crystal stair . . .
And still I climb.

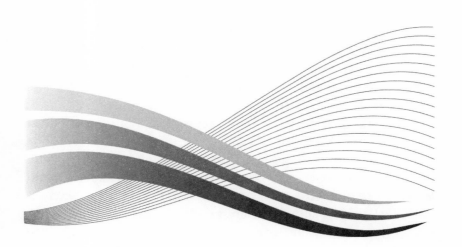

EPILOGUE

I watched Niamoja walk deliberately up the crumbling brick steps to the house where her father lived. Even though she was only 14, she had the walk, the essence, of a woman twice her age. She was focused. She was clear. And she was pissed.

We had prayed before she got out of my car. She said she was nervous. It felt more like she was terrified, and rightly so. She hadn't seen or spoken to her father in eight weeks, and their last meeting was anything but warm and fuzzy. Now here she was on a rainy afternoon in August, prepared to ask for—no, demand— something she needed and wanted from him.

Watching my granddaughter mount those stairs brought up all kinds of feelings for me. The first was pride. I was proud of her courage. She was about to do something that I would have never done, did not know how to do, at her age. My granddaughter was going to ask a man for something she needed. It didn't matter that he was her father. He was a man.

I was also scared to death. I was afraid he would disappoint her. I was afraid he would reject her. I worried that her budding courage would be smashed into little pieces that would take years to put back together, and that she would feel it in every part of her life where courage was required. I also felt a strange sense of excitement. I was thrilled to be a part of the birthing of a young woman.

I knew I had prepared her for this labor of self-determination and self-realization. I had taught her how to breathe and how to push without bearing down too hard. I had told her the truth— that she had a right to ask for what she wanted, and that no matter what the response was, she could be proud of her willingness to stand up for herself. That truth alone was more than anyone had ever told me when I was her age. I had also rubbed her hands and feet with lavender oil. It would help her stay calm. We had had no fewer than ten conversations about what she was going to do, why she was doing it, how she felt about doing it, and what she expected to receive in return.

She was ready. I was not.

It seemed as if she knocked for ten minutes before the door finally opened. I watched her disappear into the house. It was then that my stomach somersaulted and my mouth got sour. I propped my head on my hands still gripping the steering wheel, and I prayed: *Dear God. Make him civil. Don't let him hurt her. I don't want to go to jail today. Thank you! Please!*

I had brought my granddaughter to see her father because we needed him to sign off on the financial disclosure statement for a private, all-girls high school. It was something that she really wanted. It was something that I wanted for her. It was the very thing that Gemmia had talked about since the day she gave birth to her only child. It seemed like a simple request. In fact, it was. What made it difficult for me was the adversarial relationship that had developed between me and the man I once knew and loved like a son.

What made it so difficult for Niamoja was the fact that he had dropped her off at my home eight weeks earlier and never once called or come by to check on her. When he did call, he thought they would pick up where they left off. She had another idea. She missed her mother desperately and did not feel comfortable around him, his new wife, and their two children. She missed me and her mother's side of the family. We were what she had known all of her life. We were her community, her biological and spiritual blood. We were in her genes.

After their separation, Jimmy was a weekend dad who, toward the end, had a strained relationship with my daughter, and who was locked into a permanent power struggle with me. Perhaps if I had not been grief-stricken to the point of insanity after Gemmia died, I would not have allowed Niamoja to go and live with him. Perhaps if Gemmia had not believed so desperately that she was going to live, she would have left specific instructions about her desires. In the four years since Gemmia's death, my granddaughter was the carrot that Jimmy dangled to keep me in line. He made sure that I saw her only when it suited his needs, his timetable, and his feelings about me in the moment. Her needs were secondary.

But I had a relationship with Niamoja that was separate from his relationship with her. Leaving his child at my home for eight weeks without calling sent her a very strong message: As long as she was with me, he wanted nothing to do with her. In her mind, that meant that she had to make a choice. I'm not really sure that she was choosing me over him. I am sure that she was choosing what was familiar, what felt right for her, and what kept her closest to her mother.

Jimmy might not have abandoned his daughter literally, but through his unconscious and angry behavior, he had abandoned her emotionally. It was the same thing that my father had done to me, which was the same thing that Gemmia's father had done to her, which was the same thing that Jimmy's father had done to him. I was sitting in the middle of a multigenerational family puzzle, trying to figure out what piece went where, because I was determined to cure the pathology, to end the karma and the drama once and for all.

In Niamoja's circumstances, I was revisiting an earlier incarnation of myself. There she was, feeling abandoned not only by her father, but also by her mother's death. Just like me. She was a young woman trying to get comfortable in her blossoming and ever-changing body. Just like me. She was a child trying to navigate the maze of dysfunction and disorder brought about by the big people, the adults in her life. It was everything—almost everything—that I had lived through at her age. The difference was that she had me, a wildly conscious, boldly brazen grandmother who was willing to take down the biggest and the baddest to protect her. I prayed that she knew that no matter what, I would not leave her alone to fend for herself, and anyone coming after her would have to get past me first. I was that someone I did not have at her age.

I lifted my head from the steering wheel just in time to see Niamoja come out of the door. She started down the steps with the same deliberation and focus that had propelled her up them.

I was desperate to know what her father had said, but at the same time I understood it really didn't matter. This was about so much more than a little girl who needed her father's permission or his financial help or his blessing to go to the private school of her choice. This was the transmutation of patterns woven deep into our family's DNA—a final karmic reckoning. We would no longer settle for pieces. We claimed the right to our wholeness. Gemmia's death was the way the universe supported us in our healing.

Years ago, when my career was at its height and I was speaking all over the world, an interviewer asked me a simple question. "Who is Iyanla Vanzant?" It was an innocent question, with no hidden agenda, asked by someone who genuinely wanted to know. To my horror, I found that I had no answer. Now, I do.

I, Iyanla Vanzant, am a woman, a teacher, an artist, and a willing servant of God. I am Damon and Nisa's Mumzie. I am a grandmother who gives to her loved ones from a bottomless well of love. I, Iyanla Vanzant, am a human being with flaws and weaknesses, strengths and gifts, and a vision that sees beyond who and what I am not. I am Sahara and Horace's daughter. I am Ray's baby sister. I am whole and complete, with a few cracks, dents, and scratches—nothing a little prayer and faith won't fix. I am willing. I am open. I am at peace knowing that Gemmia is very proud of the ways I have made our broken pieces whole.

I am ready for the next leg of the journey.

ACKNOWLEDGMENTS

Where would I be if not for His grace?

God's grace has manifested in my life as the loving support of many people who have stood for me as demonstrations of unconditional love. With humble and reverent gratitude my spirit bows to my parents Horace Lester Harris and Sahara Elizabeth Jefferson. It has taken me more than 50 years to realize and acknowledge the gifts you have given me. My offspring Damon Keith and Nisa Camille for being captive participants in my journey toward a place of healing and peace. I am honored you chose me.

Although they are mentioned in this work, I must praise God and His grace for showing up in my life as my brother and friend Tavis Smiley for insisting I produce this work. He along with Akmal Muuwakkil, Almasi Wilcots, Carl Big Heart, Carol Small, Dr. Caryl Mussenden, Jeff Chandler, Ken Kizer, Renee Kizer, Laura Rawlings, Lydia Ayo Mu'Ase Ruiz, Marcy Francis, Muhsinah Berry Dawan, Raina Bundy, Rev. Carmen Gonzalez, Minister Louis Farrakhan, Rev and Mrs. Willie Williams, Rev. Michael Bernard Beckwith, Rev. Nancy Yeates, Rev. Shaheerah Stephens, Rev. AdaRA Walton, Rev. John Mann, Rev. Irene Robinson, Rev. Elease Welch, Rev. Deborah Chinaza Lee, Rev. Candas Ifama Barnes, Rev. Deanna Mathias, Rev. Helen Jones, Rickie Byars Beckwith, Steve Hardison, Susan L. Taylor, Suze Orman, Tamara Simmons-Wilson, Vivian Berryhill, Yahfaw Shakor, Danni Stillwell, Reid Tracy, the late Master Coach Ron Davis, and the entire faculty and student body of the Inner

Visions Institute For Spiritual Development who have been my bridges over many troubled waters.

My EFT coaches Lindsay Kenny and Dr. Helen Guttman. My Matrix Re-Patterning Instructor Karin Davidson. Thank you for giving me the tools I needed to re-frame the pathology of my gene pool. I would also like to thank Gary Craig for his work in presenting EFT to the world and Karl Dawson for uncovering and sharing the power of Matrix Re-Imprinting.

The SmileyBooks team members who helped me cross the finish line: Anne Barthel, John McWilliams, Kirsten Melvey, Alexandria Malone, and Nick Welch. You have my eternal gratitude.

And finally Ms. Cheryl Woodruff, my mid-wife, cleverly disguised as an editor. Your patience, insight, gentle manner and commitment to my vision gave me the strength and courage to pull all of my pieces together. Thank you is so inadequate for all you have given and put up with from me. But for now, it is the best I can offer in addition to my love.

ABOUT THE AUTHOR

Iyanla Vanzant is the founder and executive director of Inner Visions International and the Inner Visions Institute for Spiritual Development. The author of 13 titles—including five *New York Times* bestsellers and the Inner Visions CD Series—she is the former host of the television series *Iyanla,* and former co-host of the NBC daytime reality show *Starting Over.* The proud grandmother of eight currently resides in Maryland where she spends many quiet days making scrapbooks and homemade herbal soap.

NOTES

NOTES

NOTES

We hoped you enjoyed this SmileyBooks publication.
If you would like to receive additional information, please contact:

SMILEYBOOKS
Distributed by:

Hay House, Inc.
P.O. Box 5100
Carlsbad, CA 92018-5100

(760) 431-7695 or (800) 654-5126
(760) 431-6948 (fax) or (800) 650-5115 (fax)
www.hayhouse.com® • www.hayfoundation.org

Published and distributed in Australia by: Hay House Australia Pty. Ltd.
18/36 Ralph St. • Alexandria NSW 2015 • Phone: 612-9669-4299
Fax: 612-9669-4144 • www.hayhouse.com.au

Published and distributed in the United Kingdom by: Hay House UK, Ltd.
292B Kensal Rd., London W10 5BE • Phone: 44-20-8962-1230
Fax: 44-20-8962-1239 • www.hayhouse.co.uk

Published and distributed in the Republic of South Africa by: Hay House SA
(Pty), Ltd., P.O. Box 990, Witkoppen 2068 • Phone/Fax: 27-11-467-8904
info@hayhouse.co.za • www.hayhouse.co.za

Published and Distributed in India by: Hay House Publishers India, Muskaan
Complex, Plot No. 3, B-2, Vasant Kunj, New Delhi 110 070 • Phone: 91-11-4176-
1620 • Fax: 91-11-4176-1630 • www.hayhouse.co.in

Distributed in Canada by: Raincoast • 9050 Shaughnessy St., Vancouver, B.C.
V6P 6E5 • Phone: (604) 323-7100 • Fax: (604) 323-2600